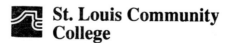

A BEHIND-
THE-SCENES
LOOK AT A
YEAR WITH
BILL BLASS,
LIZ CLAIBORNE,
DONNA KARAN,
ARNOLD SCAASI,
AND
ADRIENNE
VITTADINI

IRENE DARIA

SIMON AND SCHUSTER

*New York   London   Toronto
Sydney   Tokyo   Singapore*

THE

FASHION

CYCLE

SIMON AND SCHUSTER

Simon & Schuster Building

Rockefeller Center

1230 Avenue of the Americas

New York, New York 10020

Copyright © 1990 by Irene Daria

Photographs of Adrienne Vittadini © 1990 by Roxanne Lowit.

All other photographs © 1990 by Irene Daria.

Designed by Bonni Leon

Manufactured in the United States of America

10 9 8 7 6 5 4 3 2 1

Library of Congress Cataloging in Publication Data

Darla, Irene.

   The fashion cycle : a behind the scenes look at a year with Bill Blass, Liz Claiborne, Donna Karan, Arnold Scaasi, and Adrienne Vittadini.

   p.   cm.

   1. Costume design–United States.   2. Costume designers–United States.   I. Title.

TT507.D345   1990   *90-9968*

746.9'2'092273–dc20   *CIP*

ISBN 0-671-66729-7

Grateful acknowledgment is given to Bill Blass, Liz Claiborne, Donna Karan, Arnold Scaasi, and Adrienne Vittadini for use of their original sketches.

Introduction

Fashion designers. Their names and faces are as familiar to us as those of movie stars, but until now we haven't known much about how they work. Where do their ideas come from? How are those ideas executed? In short, how do their minds and their businesses work? *The Fashion Cycle* answers these questions and more.

For one year, from March 1988 to March 1989, five of America's top fashion designers opened the doors of their studios to me. I saw firsthand how Bill Blass, Liz Claiborne, Donna Karan, Arnold Scaasi, and Adrienne Vittadini created their spring 1989 collections.

This book follows the conception of one collection, but the creative and business steps that I observed are repeated season after season. Although the type of merchandise produced changes every year, the creative process I witnessed is timeless.

The American women's fashion industry, which accounts for $54 billion in sales per year, has two main selling seasons—fall and spring—and the conception of one overlaps with the completion of the other. Every year American designers present their fall collections in April but must start reviewing spring fabrics for their next collection in March, before they've even finished creating fall. Similarly, they show their spring collections in November but must look at fall fabrics in October.

The timing of the rest of the steps (sketching, draping, scouting production locations, sample-making, designing coordinating accessories, approving licensed products, planning advertising campaigns and runway shows, selling the clothes) varies from company to company. Large firms like Liz Claiborne and Adrienne Vittadini, which produce huge quantities overseas, work well in advance of the season, while the designers of higher-priced, much smaller collections have sample-making rooms right next door to their studios and often wait until the final moments before their fashion shows to finish their collections. This fact is reflected in the structure of *The Fashion Cycle:* we meet the designers at Liz Claiborne in March, while Donna Karan does not appear until much later. Although other designers participated in the research of this book (I would particularly like to thank Carolyne Roehm and Louis dell'Olio at Anne Klein for the time they spent with me), I chose to write about the five designers featured here because they each represent a different aspect of the fashion industry. Liz Claiborne showcases the difficulty of designing for a colossal, publicly held, empire; Arnold Scaasi, the social aspect of designing made-to-order; Bill Blass, the necessity of self-promotion to uphold the name recognition so necessary for a profitable licensing program; Adrienne Vittadini, the difficulty of designing knitwear overseas where she cannot see the products until it is almost too late to change them; and Donna Karan, the overwhelming stress that accompanies the astonishingly rapid success of a new business. Certainly there are other designers who are equally famous and established but, in conducting my research, I found that, in time, the design cycles became repetitive and that, in watching these five designers work, you will have a great sense of what all designers, the world over, do each season.

Since fashion reflects the time during which it was created, no discussion of a season would be complete without a look at the economic, social, and fashion trends that immediately preceded it. For all practical purposes, the gilded eighties, the party-till-you-drop decade, ended when the stock market crashed on October 19, 1987.

Immediately before the crash, the couturier of choice was Christian Lacroix, whose clothes were perfect for the big-money, big-spending mood of early 1987. Like a mirror, Lacroix captured society's conspicuous consumption, piling pattern upon pattern, color upon color, fabric upon fabric. Society women scooped up his $15,000 creations like favors at a dinner party. Other designers promptly set about imitating Lacroix's work.

In early 1988, however, other American women began publicly questioning the absurd appearance of Lacroix's clothes, as well as their high prices. In an April issue of *The New Yorker*, for instance, Holly Brubach wrote, "Like many . . . people I can't help wondering what all this says about these delirious times and the febrile state of our society, when women are dressing up like dolls, and I often find that the Lacroix dress that looked so fetching in the abstract, on the runway, looks a bit ridiculous plunked down in the middle of real life."

That same month, a column in *The New York Times Magazine* asked, "What would you rather have? A Christian Lacroix pouf or the down payment on a one-bedroom apartment in Tudor City?"

Manhattan, inc., meanwhile, ran a story headlined "The Thrill Is Gone." "It's clear that society's champagne days have gone flat," said the magazine.

No one read these articles more closely than fashion designers, and by the time they showed their fall collections in April 1988, they too agreed that ostentation was passé. The pouf poufed and *Women's Wear Daily* declared fall the season of "Quiet Chic."

In May, *New York* magazine called fashion's "new restraint . . . refreshing and reassuring," and said that "while the giddiness [of past seasons] was appealing, it barely excused the effrontery of flaunting wealth while the homeless sleep on the sidewalks." By June, Ivana Trump, who in March had bought a $25,000 Christian Lacroix suit, announced that Parisian clothes were just too expensive, and from now on she was buying from the significantly cheaper American knockoff artist Victor Costa.

By the end of the spring 1988 retail selling season, American women, once dictated to by the fashion establishment, showed that they would no longer blindly accept edicts issued by designers. That spring many stores and magazines, always looking for new products to sell and publicize, pushed short skirts. The fury unleashed by these skirts was astonishing. *The New York Times* covered this rage in a front page story headlined "Women Balk and Minis Fade" and ran an editorial titled "Miniskirt, Maxi Blunder" on its Op Ed page. Written by a female reporter at National Public Radio, the editorial called minis "a stupid and sexist idea," asked if Lee Iacocca could have bailed out Chrysler wearing short pants, and urged women to "Hold the line. Don't buy. And the mini will die."

They did, and while the short skirt didn't die, it faltered. During the April presentations of the fall collections designers hedged the hemline issue by declaring that pants were back and offering a wide range of skirt lengths. Giving women a variety of choices, they believed, might be the way to reverse a precipitous decline in sales that began during the summer of 1987, even before the stock market crash.

Black Monday received much of the blame for the more than year-long slump of apparel sales, but Goldman Sachs, the investment bank, released a research report that summed up other, more telling, factors. Basically, the report said, fashion designers had not noticed that the bulk of the American population was in its thirties or early forties. Women were now spending more time at work and at home (rather than at parties) and, with mortgage payments to think about, were spending less on clothing. They wanted sensible clothes that could be worn for years. And what had designers given them? Short skirts and frivolous poufs. It's no wonder that many women stopped buying clothes.

It was in this environment that designers began creating their spring 1989 collections, collections that many of them viewed as pivotal, both for their own businesses and for the fashion industry in general. All of them knew that most

American women had well-stocked closets and could get by without buying apparel for another season or two. This meant the designers had to create something so spectacular that when a woman looked at their collections she would say to herself, "I have to have those clothes."

Designers' workdays encompass much more than the creation of garments. In *The Fashion Cycle*, we will follow the designers as they perform other seemingly more glamorous tasks: we will work in Hong Kong with Adrienne Vittadini; attend charity events with Bill Blass and Arnold Scaasi; watch Donna Karan be photographed for a story in *Self;* listen as Liz Claiborne addresses stockholders; and stand next to many of them as they make personal appearances.

As I learned, a designer's life is not as grand as it seems. Without exception, each and every designer works extremely hard and is under great pressure each season to come up with clothes that are new and creative enough to be heralded by the press, yet mainstream and practical enough to be bought by the consumers. For all of them, the most important part of their jobs is the clothing they create. Their understanding of what their customers want to wear, more than anything else, explains why the designers featured in this book have reached for, and attained, the pinnacle of success. Anyone who becomes a fashion designer because of the parties, the magazine, newspaper, and television interviews, the lavish business lunches and dinners, and the trips around the world—and not out of a true desire, first and foremost, to create exquisitely crafted apparel—may as well take the $1 million minimum required to properly start a design business and kiss it goodbye.

Because of the anxiety arising from needing to create anew each season, as well as perpetual uncertainty—will the clothes look the way I thought? Will the shoes arrive in time for my show? Will the press like what I've done? Will the consumer?—stress is a constant presence in their lives. "Now you can see why I'm always on the verge of a nervous breakdown," Bill Blass said to me toward the end of our time together.

"How do I handle it?" Donna Karan said. "Do I look like I'm handling it?" By early 1989, after Donna launched her ancillary lower-priced division, stress had, literally, crippled her. It activated an old back problem and Donna was bedecked in a neck brace and had to place a ball behind her back for support whenever she sat down. Because of her new business, Donna received more publicity than her colleagues did during the same period. On the outside, for all those magazine pictures, Donna was smiling, but inside she was cringing.

Why does she do it? Why design if the process, as she gamely puts it, is literally "a pain in the neck"? She says she is undergoing psychotherapy to discover that answer. What drives these people to push themselves so hard? How do they sustain their creativity, season after season after season? Read on and discover. . . .

Liz Claiborne *March 31*

"OK, so what do we want to wear next spring?" says Jay Margolis, the tall, boyish thirty-nine-year-old president of women's sportswear at Liz Claiborne, Inc. He is addressing ten people sitting around a huge white table in a frigidly air-conditioned, fluorescent-lighted conference room on the twelfth floor of 1441 Broadway, a building occupied exclusively by women's-apparel firms. Among the people he addresses is Liz Claiborne, chairwoman and chief executive officer of the company that bears her name.

All of those present are involved with the design of garments or fabrics for the Liz Claiborne Collection, the largest and dressiest of the three sportswear lines the company produces. (The other two are Lizsport, which, as its name implies, is sportier than the Collection, and Lizwear, which is the most casual and includes jeans.) In total, sportswear accounts for more than half of the NASDAQ-listed firm's $1 billion-plus sales volume. Other divisions that constitute the company are: dress, petite, menswear, large-size, knitwear, a number of licensees, as well as retail stores.

The meteoric growth experienced by this company has been unprecedented in the apparel industry. It astounded Wall Street analysts, earned its principles standing ovations at annual stockholders' meetings and caused the chairman of Macy's to call Liz Claiborne, Inc., "the most outstanding apparel company in the world." In any one season the company has over 5,500,000 pieces of apparel in stores throughout the country; in one year it ships 35 million garments and accessories.

In January 1988, *The New Yorker* ran an article on Liz Claiborne, Inc., calling it "the hottest company in the business." But just as those issues of *The New Yorker* hit the newsstands, Liz Claiborne's first delivery of spring clothes entered the stores and, unfortunately, many of those clothes never left. This began a first-time ever downward sales spiral as customers rejected a large part of what Liz Claiborne was shipping.

Considering the fact that, unlike many fashion companies, Liz Claiborne will not take back clothing that doesn't sell, and will not provide any extra money to cover a store's losses when it has to put merchandise on sale, retailers were justifiably unhappy. (As one Liz Claiborne executive put it, "We are the backbone resource in our departments. Stores put us in all their branches. We account for a good thirty-five percent of a whole division's business so a bleep from us is a major bleep.") The press, however, was kind. Most articles blamed Liz Claiborne's poor performance on a generally sluggish economy. After all, retail clothing sales were the worst they'd been since the 1982 recession, so it couldn't *all* be Liz Claiborne's fault.

The executives at Liz Claiborne, however, were placing the blame squarely on their own shoulders. They knew something that the press and retailers did not—Liz and her husband, Arthur Ortenberg, with whom she founded the company, were planning to retire soon, and in trying to wean themselves away from the company had in January 1987 begun a work schedule that had them working every other month. It was during their absence that the company ran into trouble. After the stock market crashed the following October, Liz and Art decided to postpone their retirement and once again take full part in the direction of the company, trying to shape and mold their successors, to fix what went wrong, and to make sure it would never happen again. This was especially important at Liz Claiborne since it is a public company and, as such, needed to rebuild stockholder confidence. (Before Black Monday, October 19, 1987, Liz Claiborne stock had been trading at 29½. Today it stands at 16.)

Liz's design sense (a talent she developed as a teenager who, along with the rest of her family, followed her army-enlisted father around Europe) was what these stockholders had bet their money on. This talent was first recognized when she was nineteen and spending a summer in New Orleans with her mother. While there, Liz entered a *Harper's Bazaar* design competition and won. "The prize was a trip to Paris, but since we were going back to France anyway, that really wasn't such a big deal," she says.

When Liz was twenty-one, her father decided to retire from the army and go fishing on the Gulf Coast. The family came back to the States, and as they drove through Manhattan, Liz said, "I'm staying."

Her father pulled the car over, got out, opened the trunk, took out Liz's bag, handed it to her along with fifty dollars, and said, "Good luck."

"It wasn't as bad as it sounds," Liz said. "My grandmother was spending the month in New York and I stayed with her until I found a job and my own digs.

"I went to all the department stores looking for a job as a salesgirl," she continued. "Then I went to *Harper's Bazaar* figuring that, after all, I'd won their prize so maybe they could help me find work. They thought and scratched their heads and said, 'Well, how about Tina Leser? She always needs sketchers.'"

Liz applied for a job with this designer of Hawaiian-inspired casual clothes. "Thinking I was a sewing-machine operator they sat me down at a machine and gave me a bundle with no instruction," Liz said. "I knew how to sew but I certainly didn't know how to sew just by matching notches, which they soon discovered and took me to the sample room.

"Then one day the showroom model was out sick and Tina Leser said, 'You! Out here.' And that was how I became her showroom model.

"I had long hair," she said. "My father had always refused to let me cut my hair, and as soon as I could save up enough money I went to the chicest hairdresser and had him cut it shorter than it is now. I went back to work and Tina said, 'What have you done? One of the reasons I hired you was your long hair.' She made me wear a fake bun."

Liz worked at Tina Leser for one year and then had a few other jobs before settling at Jonathan Logan for sixteen years. She designed dresses for Jonathan Logan's Youthguild division, and when that division folded in February 1976, she and Art established Liz Claiborne, Inc. Art, who had twenty-five years of experience in the apparel industry, phased out his consulting business and became the firm's administrator and financial manager. On the day of this meeting he is co-vice-chairman.

The couple had two founding partners—Jerome Chazen, who was Art's roommate at Wisconsin College, and is now the other co-vice-chairman, and Leonard Boxer (now retired), who became production director after answering a classified ad for the position.

These latter two partners brought their own brand of very necessary skills to the firm. As a former retailer, Jerry knew how to handle the stores, while Leonard thought nothing of rolling up his sleeves in a dingy Asian factory, sitting down behind a sewing machine and showing the workers exactly how a garment should be made. The factories did their best work for him, and Liz Claiborne soon became known as a company that offered tremendous levels of quality for relatively low prices.

The four original partners put up $25,000 each and raised the rest of the $250,000 start-up capital from a number of friends. In the beginning, Liz, Art, Leonard, a showroom model who doubled as a receptionist, a pattern maker, and Leonard's wife, who worked for free as the bookkeeper, were based in Art's former office—a 1,200 square foot space on West Fortieth Street across from

Bryant Park. "We used to look out the windows and watch all the drug arrests," Liz says.

In the beginning, Liz and Art worked on the line together. She would design it, and he, whose background is in textile design, would merchandise and edit it. (As with literature, editing a group of clothing means deciding what, if anything, should be deleted and correcting what remains.) Liz would chat with the store buyers in the showroom and Art would wipe fingerprints off the elevator doors.

Jerry, who was an initial investor, "could not afford to" leave his post as head of sales at another sportswear company until 1977, when, as he puts it, the "handwriting" spelling the success of Liz Claiborne "was on the wall."

The company was launched at the tail end of the women's liberation movement, when women were just beginning to enter the work force in huge numbers and desperately needed office attire. Liz Claiborne realized that not every woman worked in a law office or a bank, and therefore not every woman needed a closetful of uptight navy blue or gray suits. The company provided them with relaxed but well-styled jackets, skirts, pants, and blouses and then happily listened as retailers told them stories of women buying their clothes in as many as six different colors. Liz Claiborne had tapped a real need in the market and was filling it as no other apparel company had ever been able to do.

Within six months the company was doing an annual volume of $2,500,000. By 1980 sales were $80 million. The firm went public in June 1981, with stock selling for $19 a share. Each of the four original owners sold 153,689 shares, for which they received slightly more than $2.7 million. Sales continued to grow, and in 1986 the company entered the Fortune 500.

As the company's profits increased, so did that of its principals. Liz and Art's combined net worth has been estimated at more than $200 million. But even though they are now wealthy, the two remain surprisingly down-to-earth. They shun the social limelight and often wear jeans to work. As Art puts it, "We are just like ordinary people, only richer."

Indeed, the fact that Liz knew what "ordinary" women around the country like to wear is the prime reason for the company's success. For the most part, American women favor the same clean, simple designs that Liz would put on her own back. When the company was first established, Liz did all of the designing but, as it grew at breakneck speed, and as new product categories were added, she was forced to delegate more and more of her design responsibilities. Although women's sportswear remains the bulk of the company's business, and is the area in which Liz works most closely, she also approves products for the dress, petite (sportswear and dresses), accessory, fragrance, and menswear divisions. Additionally, she gives final approval of the goods produced by the shoe, hosiery, and eyewear licensees, as well as of the company's Dana Buchman higher-priced sportswear division and the firm's chain of retail stores, called First Issue. (Both First Issue and Dana Buchman do not bear the Liz Claiborne name because the firm did not want to oversaturate the marketplace with its brand.) Liz is also involved with conceptualizing the company's launch of other stores, as well as a line of clothes for large-size women (which will be labeled Elisabeth), a knitwear division to be called Liz & Co., and a possible lingerie line.

Today, she does no designing herself. Instead, she serves as teacher and editor, saying yes or no to concepts conceived by her design staff. Each clothing division in the company has a division head and two designers, one of whom creates woven clothes and one whom creates knits.

After the designers have presented their concepts to their division heads, they, as a team, present those concepts to Liz who, more often than not, says no to many of them. Not that there is anything necessarily wrong with those ideas. It's just that, as Liz says, "American women are not the chicest things in the world. They want clothes that are comfortable, young, and snappy. Given the chance, many of the designers who work here will design clothes that are too sophisticated for our customers."

In 1987, as Liz and Art tried to phase themselves out of the company, Liz decided to let the designers run relatively free. She thought maybe they were right, maybe the company needed what she calls "a fresh look, with things that were a little funkier, a little more advanced." Starting with the clothes that would be in the stores for spring 1988, she let them design clothing that she herself would not wear. Additionally, the designers, misunderstanding some of Liz's gently given criticism, went ahead and, during her absence, put into work some of the clothes she thought she had clearly vetoed. It was once these clothes hit the retail floors that sales declined.

These declining sales figures were brought home to the company's designers via weekly confidential in-house sales reports the firm calls SURF, short for Systematically Updated Retail Feedback. Prepared by the corporate marketing division, SURF tracks the selling of Liz Claiborne merchandise in a variety of stores, as well as the sales of its competitors' goods. (If a competing firm has designed a best-selling look, Liz Claiborne, like other companies, will often "reinterpret" the style into its own line.)

According to the SURF reports, career clothing was what women were interested in buying, and the sales and marketing division quickly instructed the

Collection designers to gear 75 percent of their new spring line toward career women. They also told them what else had been wrong with the previous season's merchandise.

This division's January/February 1988 delivery of spring merchandise had consisted solely of a disastrously selling group of pale separates called "Seashore." The company's other two women's sportswear divisions delivered sandy colors at the same time, and, since most stores hang all three divisions in one department, this uniformity of color resulted in a boring presentation on the retail floor, with no bright, unique colors to catch the consumer's eye.

Besides this, Liz Claiborne, Inc., had misjudged the type of merchandise women would want to buy. A year ago, in 1987, casual clothes were hot in its area of the market and, in designing its spring delivery for 1988, the company took its cue from this fact. This January, however, career clothing turned out to be in demand. Since Liz Claiborne manufactures such huge quantities (anywhere from 1,000 to 150,000 pieces per style made in 26 different countries) and needs to get everything back to the United States and into the stores at the proper time, the company works almost a year in advance. Liz Claiborne, a lumbering giant, delivered millions of unwanted, unneeded casual items.

Plus, in a phenomenon that took the entire fashion industry by surprise, the female American population seemed to mature overnight. As Liz Claiborne began manufacturing its spring 1988 clothes, short skirts were being hyped as all the rage. Liz Claiborne fell for this hype and actually spent hundreds of thousands of dollars shortening skirts to conform to this new trend. En masse, however, women rejected the mini.

Liz began receiving letters from consumers saying, "What has happened to you? You've fallen down on the job. I used to be able to count on you for my entire wardrobe. Lately, I haven't bought a thing that you've designed." Neither did Liz. She was buying things from the Gap and from other designers.

As part of the solution to their problems, three months ago the company decided to make Jay, who had been head of the company's menswear division, president of women's sportswear. Formerly the president of the menswear firm Ron Chereskin, Jay had come to Liz Claiborne in 1984 to oversee the development of the men's clothing business. Launched in 1986, this business was doing a volume of $75 million within two years. At the men's division Jay worked closely with Liz and developed a clear knowledge of her design preferences. He learned, for instance, that Liz likes simple, clean looks, hates most patterns, and despises all shiny, slick fabrics. Among other things, she also hates purple, peplums, and vests.

More importantly, he developed an uncanny ability to read the hidden messages behind whatever she says. "Until recently Liz would never tell you she hated something or give you a flat 'No,'" Jay had told me earlier. "She's getting better but usually she says she loves something else. Or she'll say, 'Do you really need it?' 'I don't understand it,' or 'Explain it to me.' That means she doesn't want to see it on the line but her way of telling you is so subtle that a lot of the designers were missing what she meant. My role here is to make sure we do what Liz wants done."

Believing that Jay's understanding of Liz was what was needed in the women's area, the company put him in charge of all three women's sportswear divisions, with both the design and sales executives reporting to him. Now, when Jay, who is also a senior vice-president of the corporation, says, "OK, so what do we want to wear this spring?" everyone in this conference room knows he means business. Big, big business. They also know he is really asking, "What would Liz want to wear?" They can't help noticing that today Liz is not wearing anything that has her name on the label. She is dressed in a chartreuse T-shirt and a short orange jacket by Dana Buchman, the higher-priced division of the company.

Normally, fifty-nine-year-old Liz, a tall, thin woman with close-cropped hair, impeccably manicured fingernails, and a perpetual tan, would run this meeting but she has a cold and her voice, usually deep and regal, with southern overtones, is extremely hoarse. Since Liz can barely speak, Jay asks the questions, but it is Liz, sitting here with a box of cherry-flavored Luden's cough drops in front of her, who will approve or disapprove of the answers about to be given.

As is her wont, Liz is sitting in the chair closest to the door of this conference room, with the strap of her small pocketbook slung across her chest. She spends her days going to meeting after meeting of the firm's many divisions, and the fact that she doesn't even put down her pocketbook indicates how little time she has to spend with each of them.

Dennis Gay, a thin blond, who is senior vice-president and division head of Liz Claiborne Collection, is the one who will answer Jay's question. Like the other division heads, Dennis oversees a huge, complicated business whose products are manufactured all over the world. Pants and a jacket that are to be exactly the same color may be made at opposite ends of the world, while the matching shirts are made somewhere else. Everything has to be manufactured on time and then shipped to one of Liz Claiborne's eight warehouses, where it will then be repacked with its coordinating pieces and sent to the stores. If even one item falls behind schedule it may throw off the shipment of an entire group.

All the division heads oversee the progress of five seasons at once. Right now their Fall collections, are being sold to the stores in the showroom; Holiday is being shipped to the warehouse; they are just finishing Pre-Spring designs and colors; Spring I is in its conceptual phase, and they are gathering market information to help them begin their imminent conceptualization of Spring II. Only the Summer collections are dormant, sitting in the warehouse waiting to be shipped.

Meeting deadlines is a religion in this company. This is one place where you will never hear designers say they weren't ready to make a presentation because inspiration hadn't struck. Here inspiration strikes like clockwork and it's easily understandable why Liz sets her watch five minutes fast to insure that she is never late.

Dennis, a former merchandising vice-president at Bergdorf Goodman, seems like an unlikely person to be heading up Liz Claiborne Collection. Seemingly referring to himself, he recently told me about "a friend" who dreams of opening a store selling only black and white clothes, and he speaks sarcastically of the types of things he and his staff are instructed to design. Earlier he had described these clothes by pointing to a yellow scrap of paper that was taped to his office wall and was serving as inspiration for the development of the new line. This paper had the words "young, jaunty, and colorful" handwritten on it in pencil. "Those are words Art uses," Dennis said. "I'm not sure I know what jaunty means but I think it means spirited.

"If you work here you can't have an ego," he said. "Your original ideas never go through unchanged. Everything is done by committee. It's a challenge daily to depersonalize yourself from the product and take a hard look at it and think, 'Does this represent what women in America want to buy?' and 'Does it personify the Liz Claiborne point of view?'

"It sounds easy," he said, "but it's the hardest thing you can imagine. When Donna [Karan] or Calvin [Klein] come up with a line it's a personal statement for them. Their clothes don't have to sell to God knows how many people. My division alone does $285 million between petite and missy sizes. [Missy is the industry term for standard women's sizes.] We have to constantly ask ourselves, 'Is this the right look, is this the right detail to sell to millions of women in America?'"

Now Dennis blushes as he passes out a line plan to the people in the room. This line plan shows how Dennis plans to allocate his division's $45.2 million budget. (Before assigning each division a budget, the company will call its retail clients and ask them how much money they plan to commit to Liz Claiborne for the following season. The budget is then allocated according to the total upcoming commitment.) The line plan features a sketchy description of the seven groups Dennis and his two designers have planned for spring. (A fashion line is always divided into groups, composed of items which are related to one another by color and style.)

Dennis is sitting at the head of the table. On his left is Judith Leech, a British girl with close-cropped, almost punky, brown hair who designs Collection's woven clothes. On her left is Katy Allgeyer, who is responsible for knitwear.

Following the marketing department's instructions, Dennis and the designers have come up with concepts geared at working women, and, also because of marketing, they have designed more groups than usual to insure that the large amount of business lost this spring, when a huge group bombed, wouldn't be lost again.

As everyone scans the first page of the plan, on which Dennis has handwritten the names of the seven groups, their proposed colors, the percentage of the line each group comprises, and the millions of dollars each accounts for, Dennis says, "Italian Linen is the only group we have to have, because we have that linen left over from last spring. Everything else can drop out."

Each of the following seven pages is devoted to a single group, describing the silhouettes to be included, as well as the number of stores and their branches that will receive these goods. The groups are presented in the order of their deliveries. Dennis turns to the next page of the line plan, which describes Silk Stones, a lightweight knit group that is a continuation of a similar, very successful group called Naturally Neutral which they shipped last year. On Dennis's plan this accounts for 8 percent of the line.

"This is the first group of Spring I to hit the stores," says Dennis, meaning that it will be delivered next January. He passes around a pair of lightweight knit beige pants that were a part of the earlier group so that everyone can see what the fabric looks like. Looking at the Macy's price tag attached to the pants, Jay jokingly says, "What? We had to go to Macy's to buy our own goods? That is sacrilege."

In the meantime Liz is looking at the sketches Judith has placed before her. "These sketches are too young in feeling," says Liz. "I have seen women in New Jersey wearing Naturally Neutral. Judith doesn't get to New Jersey, so she doesn't know what I mean. These sketches are not the Liz customer."

Liz considers New Jersey "real middle America." The fact that something sells well in New Jersey, as the earlier version of this group did, is a good thing for Liz Claiborne because it means it will be accepted well in the rest of the country.

"Burdine's would love this in December in their southern stores," says Ellen

Daniel, senior vice-president of corporate design. She is a perky woman with short red hair who calls herself "Liz's right arm," and has a hand in directing all sportswear, including petites and Dana Buchman.

Like most Liz Claiborne executives, Ellen began her career in retailing. She was instrumental in the very first Liz Claiborne launch (at Saks Fifth Avenue in 1976), and, later, bought the Liz Claiborne line for Federated Department Stores' corporate division. She joined Liz Claiborne in 1982.

Ellen spends 25 to 30 percent of her time on the road. Her main role is to follow firsthand how Liz Claiborne merchandise is selling and investigate what its competitors are doing. As much as anyone else she knows exactly what the stores are looking for.

Judith's sketches are put back in a manila folder with the understanding that the fabric has been approved but the styling has to be changed.

The next group, made of the leftover linen, is Linen Classics, and it accounts for 25 percent of the line. As everyone turns to the next page of their line plan, Dennis holds up a sheet of typing paper covered with small swatches of black, cream, taupe, and gray linen. "This is currently in the stores and it's doing well," he says. "We have four colors but in different quantities. We can always recolor some of it." Then he spreads out papers covered with swatches of beige-tone plaid and striped suit fabrics that will be a part of this group.

"This follows the same formula as Class Appeal," says Judith, referring to a group in their Spring I 1988 line. She shows Liz eight 8-by-10 color photos. Liz points to one of the photos and says, "What is this? I don't understand this."

Judith blushes. "It's a novelty jacket."

"Take it away," says Liz. "It diffuses the message." Jay gives me a significant look and I understand that he is proud of Liz's newfound ability to dish out criticism.

"I don't understand having two novelty jackets in the same group," Liz continues, looking at the photos. "And I get terrified of everything looking the same. So far it's all beige, white, and brown. We start to look mushy again. It's the same problem as Seashore."

As they speak, Liz's husband, Art, who had been down the hall at a meeting, walks in. He is a tall, slim man with gray hair and striking, sky-blue eyes who (as usual) is casually dressed in khakis and a blue oxford shirt. He listens for a minute and then, speaking in his controlled, precise manner says, "I've only been here for a few minutes and I'm terrified of what I'm hearing. The paucity of career clothes. We need good-looking, young, jaunty go-to-work clothes. Something young-looking and with color. Not serious."

"Do we need an accent color?" says Judith to Liz.

"Yes," says Liz.

As the designers present more color, silhouette, and fabric concepts for this group, they say they "could" do this or that. Of prime concern to everyone is how the clothes will look on the retail floor. As she approves bright coral and wintergreen fabrics, Liz says, "This will make the floor pop a little." Satisfied with what he is seeing, Art leaves.

Judith shows Liz a sketch for a possible suit and, in a *yech* type of voice Liz says, "The skirt is going to be long?" As Dennis flushes, Liz, not looking at him, says, "I have a terrible time with long skirts with suits."

Pointing to a swatch of large plaid fabric, Ellen says, "The conservative woman can't wear that to work. Maggie wouldn't wear that." She is referring to Maggie Gillian, a financial analyst at First Boston who follows Liz Claiborne Inc.'s performance.

"Yes she would," says Liz. "But, maybe make the plaid smaller to tone it down."

Liz looks at the very first sheet of paper Dennis showed, the one with the black, cream, white, and gray swatches on it. "Gray screws us up," she says. "Try to refinish and redye it. If that doesn't work, then throw the gray into another group rather than messing up a group that looks like a winner."

"Gray is not young," says Ellen.

"It's death," says Dennis, and with that they move on to the third group, Animal Prints. It's composed of large and small giraffe and zebra prints and accounts for 12 percent of the line. Dennis displays swatches of black-and-cream print fabrics. "I like the black-and-cream because it's animal prints without being Norma Kamali feeling. It's not as advanced," says Dennis.

"I don't think Maggie is going to wear this to the office," says Liz.

"It's a special group," says Ellen. "It's restaurant dressing for after work."

"I want beefier fabrics," says Liz, feeling the swatches. "If it's a simple style we can afford a better fabric." As a rule, simpler styles are easier to make and therefore are less expensive. Since production costs will be lower, they can afford to upgrade the fabric.

"It's planned for eighteen hundred doors," says Dennis. "Doors" is an industry term that refers to the total number of stores that will sell the merchandise. For example, if the line is sold to one store and this store puts it in twenty-three branches, then the merchandise will be carried in twenty-three doors.

"I think that's very high," says Jay.

"I have never known animal prints to bomb," says Dennis.

"What about Animal Magnetism?" says Jay, referring to a group they offered two years ago that did not sell well.

"The problem with Animal Magnetism was that we gave them animal prints with not enough solid colors to wear with those patterns," says Liz.

"Now we're going to give them black," says Dennis.

"The trick for this group," says Ellen, "is to give the customer a blouse that works with both the pant and the jacket so that she can understand it without having a salesperson or a display explain it to her." Along with most companies, Liz Claiborne's major beef about stores is that they do not properly display clothing. Instead, they often intermingle pieces of various groups together so that the customer is not sure of what should go with what. Another major complaint is that stores don't have enough trained salespeople to show the customer the different ways a look can be put together, thereby generating multiple sales. Therefore, when creating a line, many designers try to make it as simple as possible so that the customer can understand the look on her own.

The fourth group is Small Linen Suits/Office. Its colors are rose, orange, apricot, navy—and, according to the line plan, it accounts for 7 percent of the line.

"This is based on Armani," says Judith. "It's pretty, rosy, and relaxed."

"This could be our answer to the softer, Carole Little feeling," says Ellen. "It could be a restaurant-dressing group."

Liz, however, dismisses the group, saying, "It's too sophisticated. Our customer would not mix these colors herself."

The fifth group is Suits with Special Linings. This consists of three black suits in classic fabrics, with lime green or red linings printed with large white polka dots or stripes. Including its coordinating blouses, the group will account for 15 percent of the line.

"This started from us seeing so many great blouses in Europe," says Judith, who, along with all the other designers in the company went to the European fabric fairs earlier this month. While in Europe they all visited stores looking for styling trends. Among the main ones they spotted were menswear-patterned suits and blouses, as well as animal and ethnic prints. "It's a way to maximize the blouse business," she says, referring to the coordinating blouses and linings.

"Details being very important," says Dennis. "We see a red lining or a striped lining in the jackets. This is power, Wall Street."

"Maggie," says Ellen, meaning that she could see Maggie Gillian wearing it. Liz gives her approval.

The sixth group is Red Hot & Coco, consisting of red-and-white checked suits with gold buttons. The line plan has it down for 10 percent of the line. "I love it," says Liz, "but red doesn't do what navy does. Hot colors don't sell as well as cool colors." She looks at the magazine photo of a red-and-white checked Chanel suit with gold buttons that Judith has placed before her and says, "Would Maggie wear it?"

"Brenda Gaul would," says Ellen, naming another financial analyst.

"Try worsted crepe here," says Liz.

"They already love the gold buttons. And the customers are ready for red-and-white. Marc Jacobs's red-and-white group is doing very well," says Ellen, referring to the twenty-five-year-old designer who is currently designing under his own name and later this year would be appointed vice-president of design at Perry Ellis. "I think this should be major," she continues, referring to the size of the group.

"We now know that our percentages are all screwed up," says Dennis. "We have to have an update. And our Armani suit group fell apart."

The seventh group is Cotton Knit Dressing, accounting for 8 percent of the line. "We use color in a Mondrian way," says Katy, the knitwear designer, as she shows Liz sketches of blue and chartreuse color-blocked clothes.

Liz whistles. "That is beautiful." But then, after a long pause, she says in an apologetic tone, "Color blocking is exciting but you have to be careful because it doesn't go to work. They are not going to wear these colors to work in rayon gabardine. They'll look like Easter eggs."

"Maybe we should do this in black and white," says Liz. "We want seventy-five percent of this line to be go-to-work. Maybe it just has to be Sport that brings in color." She is referring to the Lizsport division.

"Now let's see," says Dennis. "What are we missing? There's a glaring absence of prints because we haven't worked on that aspect of the line yet."

"Anne Klein just delivered beautiful prints," says Ellen.

"The big Anne Klein or Anne Klein II?" says Liz.

"The big one. On challis."

"Challis prints well," says Liz. "That's why they use challis."

"This is the time of year that Adrienne always sells her lightweight jersey with the heavier-weight hand knits," says Ellen, referring to designer Adrienne Vittadini.

"Well," says Liz, "when you have all these patterns it sure ain't boring. You ain't going to fade into the woodwork, even in Saks Fifth Avenue. Checks, polka dots, zebra, ocelot. I think we have to take a few chances. We can't be safe, safe, safe."

"The Anne Klein print is on the front mannequin on the second floor at Saks," says Ellen.

"Let's invest three hundred dollars to see it," says Liz. "Have someone bring it in."

"OK," says Dennis. "We've got to go out and see what's out there. What looks good. We still need ideas. It's gonna be shop till you drop, everybody. Shop till you drop."

Liz Claiborne *April 1–May 3*

The conceptual meeting Liz had with the Collection designers yesterday was the first of many such meetings she will be holding during the first two weeks of April with all the women's apparel divisions in the company. Jay and Ellen Daniel accompany Liz to the sportswear meetings and, with Jay running the meetings, Liz, as she did with Collection, will approve or disapprove of the designers' ideas. Art, whose employees say, is always pacing the halls, keeping an eye on every department, would stop in and say things like, "Did we talk about who we want the consumer to be? You have to picture her first. Step two is to decide what we must provide her with. Too often we go into color stories and messages and overlook what this customer wants every season."

He would also give training speeches to Jay. For instance, at one point during the Lizsport conceptual meeting, Art says to him, "It's time for you to start thinking, 'Where are we going to make this?'"

Referring to a group that consists of only a few pieces, Art continues, saying, "The narrower you are the more dependent you are on each piece. That's where allocation becomes important. You," Art says to Jay, "please don't put it in Antarctica to test it."

Toward the end of the same meeting Art says, "Ellen has noticed some resurgence in the woven-shirt business. You should discuss that trend, whether we're at the beginning of a cycle."

Liz takes a deep breath and says, "We have to get to three more groups by twelve o'clock, darling." Her tone clearly says that he should be quiet and let them get on with things.

"Why by twelve?" he says.

"Because we have another meeting at twelve." And herein lies a major problem at Liz Claiborne. Yes, Liz and Art have to train people, but besides insuring the company's solid future, they also have to make sure that this year its 35 million garments and accessories get designed, produced, shipped, and delivered to the stores on time.

During the last two weeks of April, Dennis will meet with Liz and Art a few times to further hone his division's Spring I concepts. After he gets Liz and Art's final approval, he will tell the fabric studio which fabrics will be used. This studio, which is staffed by seven full-time artists and three colorists, and which is shared by the three women's sportswear divisions, will then instruct the fabric mills on what colors to dye various yarns and will make paintings of the patterned fabrics.

The paintings, made on large squares of white cardboard, will then be cut into two large triangles. (Cutting it into this shape exposes the largest surface area of the print.) One triangle will remain in New York and the other will be sent either to an engraver, if the fabric is a print, or to a mill, if the pattern must be woven into the fabric. Based on which painting is received, the engraver and the mill will analyze how much time and work has to go into the fabric and set a price. Once the price is set, the woven mill will begin dying the yarns that will be used to weave the fabric, or in the alternate case, the engravers at the print houses will make strike-offs of the patterns. The yarns and the strike-offs are then sent back to New York for color approval. Once these are approved, the fabric is printed, or woven, and a piece of it is sent to New York for approval. It is the colorists' responsibility to make sure that all the pieces in a group, which can be made in as many as fifteen different factories, coordinate.

In the meantime, the vice-president of textile research for women's sportswear, will continue making fabric commitments and reserving production space at various mills. Although actual patterns are not yet approved, the base yarns, or in the case of printed fabrics, the base goods, are being bought in their raw states. These goods will be dyed or printed later.

While the fabric department is taking care of its responsibilities, the designers are, as usual, working on four seasons at once. In addition to approving the artists' paintings for Spring I and making preliminary sketches for that season, they are creating samples for their Pre-Spring lines, fitting production samples for Holiday, and reviewing fabric designs for Spring II.

Each of the sportswear woven designers has his or her own sample room. In the case of Collection, this room, located right outside of Judith's office, is staffed with four pattern makers and eight sewers. To meet production deadlines, Judith must design six or seven garments each week and these are almost always designed in the order that they will be manufactured and shipped. After fitting the first samples with her pattern makers, Judith sends these samples, along with a sketch and a pattern, to the production department, located in New Jersey. This department immediately begins making production samples.

Liz, who travels to New Jersey every Wednesday morning to oversee production fittings for the sportswear division, would see these actual bodies for the first time during these fittings. Once these production samples are approved they are sent to the factories, which then begin actual production. Unlike smaller companies, which produce their clothes based on the orders they receive for them, Liz Claiborne, which manufactures such huge quantities of merchandise, begins production before retailers even see the line.

Katy Allgeyer, the knitwear designer, is on a completely different schedule. She works one month in advance of Judith, and rather than designing six or seven garments a week, she tends to design an entire group at once. Instead of using a sample room at the company, Katy sends knit gauge, size and style specifications to the factories that will be producing the knitwear and relies on the factories to make her first samples. (The entire process of knitwear design will be covered in the section of this book on Adrienne Vittadini.)

Since Dennis has slated the Silk Stones knit group and the suits with bright linings for the first delivery, the Collection designers know that they have to design those groups first. Although Judith has not yet designed any pieces of clothing for Spring I, production and mill space is being reserved, base yarns and cloths are being bought, and delivery dates are being established. The next step in the evolution of Spring I is the presentation of this season's concepts to the sales department. We will watch this presentation on May 3, but for now let's turn to Arnold Scaasi, a designer with both a different customer base and a much different method of working.

Arnold Scaasi *April 19*

The press called it the wedding of the eighties when, on Monday evening, April 18, twenty-five-year-old Laura Steinberg married thirty-four-year-old Jonathan Tisch, joining together two billionaire families. She is the daughter of Saul P. Steinberg, chairman and chief executive officer of Reliance Group Holdings, Inc., and stepdaughter of Gayfryd Steinberg, queen of Nouvelle Society; he, the son of Preston Tisch, president and co-chief executive officer of Loews Corp.

Life magazine requested, and was denied, permission to document the multimillion-dollar event. Florists, caterers, and other workers signed confidentiality agreements which could have subjected them to lawsuits for leaking details. Afterward, practically nothing went unreported: five hundred high-profile guests like Donald and Ivana Trump, Henry Kravis and Carolyne Roehm, and Barbara Walters attended the wedding. The evening ceremony was held in a temple, with spotlights set up outside to illuminate the stained-glass windows, and inside to make it seem as if the sun were still shining. The flower bill alone was reportedly $1 million; the wine and champagne tab appear to have been equally staggering. About seventy men worked double time Sunday night to completely redecorate the Metropolitan Museum of Art's Great Hall and restaurant, where the reception was held, and triple time Monday night restoring them.

The details appeared everywhere from the front page of *Women's Wear Daily* to *The New York Times*. Suzy, *The New York Post*'s gossip columnist gushed on and on, reporting that the bride's gown was designed by, as she put it, "no less than Arnold Scaasi," the designer darling of New York's lavish, new-money society.

On the day after the Steinberg-Tisch wedding, it was business as usual for "no less than" Arnold Scaasi. Perpetually tardy, he is no less than an hour late for his appointment at Ratti, an Italian textile manufacturer with offices on West Fifty-seventh Street, just off Fifth Avenue. Here Arnold will choose some fabrics for his spring Scaasi Boutique line of ready-to-wear cocktail and evening dresses.

Arnold designs two made-to-order collections a year (showing them in February for spring, and September for fall) as well as three ready-to-wear collections (comprising Scaasi Boutique). These are shown to retailers and members of the fashion press in April for fall; July for resort; and November for spring—one full season ahead of when the consumers will see the clothes in the stores. This extra time is needed so that Scaasi Boutique has the leeway needed to manufacture and ship its bulk orders.

I arrive at 3:45 and sit down in the reception area to wait. This is only my second meeting with Arnold, but already I sense that he tends to be late. Last week he kept me and a roomful of fashion editors and retailers waiting for over half an hour before he began his fall Scaasi Boutique fashion show in his overheated, nondescript L-shaped beige Seventh Avenue showroom.

Applause is the first indication of a collection's success, and judging by its silent reception, Arnold's—at least in the eyes of fashion press—was a disaster. (Despite this, Scaasi later reported over $2 million in sales for the collection.) Only one person—André Leon Talley (the very tall, very cheerful black fashion writer and editor, who was then creative director of *HG* and would, this summer, become creative director of *Vogue*)—clapped during the show, and that was for only two dresses. He spent the rest of the time sharing jokes with two editors from *Harper's Bazaar*. As the models paraded one by one up the beige-carpeted aisle, the three magazine people barely glanced at them. Instead they giggled and slapped their knees over seemingly endless private jokes. Their rudeness stunned me. I shuddered as I thought about how terrible Arnold must be feeling.

For the five years that I've followed the fashion industry, as a reporter at *Women's Wear Daily* and as an editor at *Harper's Bazaar*, I've met hundreds of people who work in the field. The two things most of them have in common are a love of gossip and a love of laughter. But fashion laughter is not the kind that rings out over a meadow on a joyous summer day. It is a malicious cackle, most closely resembling the braying of a donkey.

A cruel cackle is the sound I remember most from the four years I spent at *Women's Wear Daily*. All the reporters and editors worked in a small newsroom with John Fairchild sitting at a corner desk in the front. He faced his staff so that, like a schoolteacher, he could always see what his fair children were doing. His inner circle of four was crammed into a comically small space in front of his desk, and the five of them were perpetually sharing a joke at someone's expense.

Once a fashion laugh has been turned on you, you never forget it and you do everything you can to make sure it never happens again. It happened to me once, early in my career as a reporter. I had gone to cover a gala benefit for the New York City Ballet for *Women's Wear Daily*'s party page, and after the photographer working with me had taken Anne Bass's picture, I asked her who'd designed her dress. I heard her say, "Yuro." Since I was new to the fashion industry and didn't know many designers I didn't think it unusual that I had never heard of this designer. Because I was representing such an important fashion newspaper, I didn't want to let my ignorance show, and so I wrote down "Yuro" in my notepad and figured someone at the paper would know who he was.

The following morning Patrick McCarthy, Fairchild's dashing young right-hand man, wanted to run Anne Bass's picture on the cover. "Who designed her dress?" he asked me.

"Yuro," I replied.

"Who?"

"Yuro," I said, my heart sinking.

Patrick called over a senior fashion editor and asked her if she had ever heard of Yuro. No. He then asked the paper's editor. She hadn't heard of him either. "It's probably some cheap knockoff artist in Paris," said Patrick. "Forget it. We can't run it on the front page."

I went back to my desk knowing full well that Anne Bass would never wear anything by a knockoff artist and that my short career would be nipped in the bud if John Fairchild ever discovered whose dress she was really wearing. I dug out the newspaper's list of society people's home phone numbers and looked up Anne Bass's number in Texas. I called and found out which hotel she was at in New York. Luckily she was in her room, and luckily she got on the phone and told me that the designer of her dress was Ungaro.

I then had to go over to Patrick McCarthy's desk and, in full view of John Fairchild, fess up to my mistake. The braying and cackling that followed is a sound I will never forget, and now, sitting on my hard little chair at the Scaasi Boutique show, listening to those three fashion editors laugh, while the only other sounds in the room were the rustling of taffeta as the models walked and the intermittent sound of cameras clicking, my heart went out to Arnold Scaasi.

After the show, Arnold came out from backstage. I thought he would look distressed or disappointed, but, as the press and retailers filed past him, he was perfectly composed, as if he'd just invited everyone in for a tea party rather than an exhibit of his talent. Everyone who passed Arnold said hello to him, but no one said the show had been wonderful or fabulous or to die for—the usual compliments given in the fashion industry. The only comment I heard that even referred to the fact that these people had just seen a show was made by one woman who said, "My, how can you design so many dresses?"

I expected the press to publish scathing reviews but soon realized that, unlike movies, fashion shows don't get negative reviews in the consumer press. If they are good they are raved about. If they are bad they are ignored. This lack of editorial scrutiny is based on one fact—many designers spend hundreds of thousands of dollars on advertising, either on their own or on co-op ads run in conjunction with various stores, and the press cannot afford to offend and thereby alienate them.

Basically Arnold's collection was ignored. *The New York Times*, for instance, published these few paltry paragraphs:

"In the pursuit of individuality, Arnold Scaasi decided to eliminate pants from his collection. They were not missed. He did add some daytime styles to his ready-to-wear, including plaid capes over below-knee-length dresses, a length he prefers in short evening styles as well.

"Still, his floor-length, bare-shouldered traditional evening dresses are the mainstay of his collection. The prettiest are in rose-printed taffeta and are accompanied by long satin coats."

The poor response to his collection didn't affect Arnold's ego, judging by his appearance today when, at 4:45, he sweeps into the fabric firm, walking like a little Napoleon, his coat slung over his shoulders like a cape, his gangly male assistant, Timothy Sampson, trailing behind.

"Can I take your coat?" the young woman who will be showing Arnold the fabric line says to him.

Although he says yes, he doesn't hand it to her. Instead, he turns and, with the coat still around his shoulders, walks down the hallway to the fabrics showroom. Against one of the walls is a chest-high wooden cabinet where all the fabrics are draped over hangers. A large, rectangular conference table takes up most of the center of the room and a couch stands at the right side of the door. The woman has followed Arnold into the room, and although she is still holding out her hand for his coat, he ignores her and throws it down on the sofa. "I must use the phone," he says. Arnold stands behind the conference table and waits while his assistant walks over to the phone by the window and dials the number of Arnold's salon.

Once Timothy gets the right person on the phone, he hands the receiver to Arnold, who, in his flat, somewhat nasal voice, says, "Are you near each other?" He's asking whether Patricia McBride, principal dancer of the New York City Ballet, can hear this conversation. She is at Arnold's Fifth Avenue salon, being fitted for a gown to wear to next week's gala opening of the NYCB's American Music Festival at Lincoln Center.

Obviously Patricia isn't near the phone because Arnold then says, "How was the first one? . . . Why? . . . How was the second one? . . . Why? . . . It seemed perfect to me." When he speaks his voice is without inflection, almost deadpan. "Did you call someone in? . . . Which one are you trying on now? . . . Which one did *she* like? . . . It's very important that she look absolutely terrific. . . . That would have been my first choice. . . . All right. I'll call you back."

Since many people will see Patricia McBride at this event and she will be photographed by numerous publications, Arnold wants her to pick a dress that he wants to promote. Although he sometimes lends dresses to model-size women, in this instance McBride is paying for hers, which means that even though Arnold is giving her a great discount, he cannot control which one she will pick.

He looks at the fabrics spread before him and says to the salesperson, "What's the price range?"

"They are nineteen to thirty dollars a yard," says the woman. She takes square yard after square yard of fabric from the cabinet, and Arnold quickly says, "Yes. No. Yes. No. Maybe," as she holds up piece after piece of fabric. "Tell us if we are taking something anybody else has," he says, referring to other designers.

The saleswoman is moving at a rather moderate clip, and Arnold says, "Hurry up. We're in a big hurry." And she picks up speed.

"Where's your mirror?" says Arnold standing up. She points to it and Arnold walks over, holds the fabric against himself, cocks his head, and inspects it in the mirror.

"Yes," he says finally and walks back to the table where the other fabrics he has approved are lying in a pile. Timothy is writing down the style numbers of each approved fabric. "I seem to be picking the same print," Arnold says. "Am I?"

"The same group," she says. As Arnold contemplates the pile, the woman says, "I saw the sketch in *Women's Wear* of the wedding dress. Even though it was only a sketch, I could tell it was quite beautiful."

"Yes," says Arnold in his deadpan voice. "It was a beautiful dress."

He yawns and says, "Oh, excuse me. It was a long wedding. Veerrry long. I thought it would never end. It started at five-thirty and went until one A.M."

As he continues looking at fabrics, Arnold tells his assistant, "I think you should call the office and get a hand on what's going on. Ask if a decision has been made."

The assistant dials and says into the phone, "Has a decision been made? . . . The white tulle with the diamond rosettes and the black with silver?"

Hearing this, Arnold gets up and grabs the receiver. "How does it look on her?" he says. "Which looks better? . . . Are you near her? . . . So cut it off. Cut off the rosettes . . . But everything else fits? . . . But I don't . . . no. I want a very important dress. . . . Well, I like the white but how does it look? It's very important that we have a very important one."

He hangs up and continues looking at fabrics. "I think I'd like to go back to the office and see what she has on," he says, as he walks to the mirror to look at another piece of fabric. "See if you can get downtown on the line. I want to talk to David or Marie. Marie." By "downtown" he means his Scaasi Boutique showroom in the garment center, where retailers are reviewing and, hopefully, ordering the clothes Arnold showed them last week.

The assistant calls Marie and hands Arnold the phone. "How's it going?" he says. "How about the brocades? . . . Leave it at my house. One hundred Central Park South. I'd just like to know where we are so far. . . . Year round. . . . Did Neiman's do those?"

Another phone line rings and the saleswoman goes into an adjoining room to answer it. She comes back and says, "It's for you. It's Anne on line one." Anne, who is working with Patricia McBride, heads up sales at the made-to-order salon. Still talking to his Scaasi Boutique showroom, Arnold says, "I think Saks will do that one. They'll do the group. What about Bergdorf's? Did you do windows with them? Are you sure? They're supposed to be in Thursday, the day after the party. Hold."

He abruptly switches to Anne on line 1. "Which one did she like? . . . How long will she be there? . . . Hold."

He goes back to the other call but the line has been disconnected. He says to his assistant, "Call," and goes back to the other line. "What happened with the white idea? . . . Ravishing? Really? . . . How much? . . . So take a tuck and make a pleat. Think of her. She's going to be on a stage. . . . I don't care about that. That's a lot of shit."

He hangs up and, looking at two similar fabrics, says, "Are these two the same?"

"They're the same color but two different flowers," says the saleswoman.

At 5:25 he says petulantly, "Are we almost through?"

"One more group," she says, and shows him a fabric he doesn't like. "No," he says. She keeps on showing him the same fabric in different colors and, to each piece of fabric, with increasing volume, he yells, "No . . . no . . . no! NO!!"

At 5:27 the phone rings again, and again it's for him. It's Marie from the Scaasi Boutique showroom. "What about the windows?" Scaasi says into the receiver. "OK," he says and hangs up.

At 5:30 he says he has to make a phone call but leaves the room and uses another phone to do it.

He returns at 5:35. "I think I've got to go," he says. He looks into the fabric-filled cabinet lining the wall. "What is this?" he says, pulling out a gingham-check piece. "This is charming." He goes through the hanging fabrics group by group, skipping the gray ones. "I'm just not crazy for gray in spring prints," he says. There are mounds of fabric on the table and the assistant is frantically scribbling the order numbers of Arnold's selections.

"It's a very pretty collection," Arnold says to the saleswoman as he walks toward his coat. "Obviously I like it."

Outside, his chauffeured car is waiting, and just before he and his assistant jump in and speed off to the salon, I say, "Are you always this busy?"

"This is nothing," he replies. "Nothing."

Arnold Scaasi *April 21*

"You should come to this," Arnold tells me hurriedly on the phone. "It's a party for a charity, the New York City Opera, that I'm very involved with. It's for a benefit that I'm doing with Beverly Sills at Christie's in June. The party is at the Kluges'." (John Kluge ranks second on the *Forbes* list of the 400 richest Americans, and his then wife, Patricia, a former pinup girl, is one of Arnold's fifty loyal made-to-order customers, paying anywhere from $6,000 to $15,000 for a dress.)

"A few months before a charity event there will be a cocktail party to get people interested in the event," Arnold continues. "This is the second year that I'm chairman of the opera benefit and I tried to pick a place for the party that people wouldn't ordinarily be invited to. That gets people in the mood for the benefit and makes them feel that they're important.

"John and Patricia are friends of mine," says Arnold, who designed Patricia's wedding dress. "I knew everyone wanted to see their apartment, and that's why I asked them to hold the party there. It's just like last year—I held the opera benefit party at the Steinbergs' apartment because I knew everyone wanted to see that apartment, and everyone came." Arnold gives me the Kluges' address, says, "See you tonight. Five-thirty," and hangs up.

To do business as a high-end fashion designer, one must spin like a dervish on the charity circuit. Since they are primarily selling an image, high-end designers, more so than any other business people or craftsmen, must demonstrate that they are part of the world they service.

Although Arnold has been designing for twenty-five years, his star never rose as high as it did in the 1980s, when his client roster grew to include the publicity-hungry wives of newly, exorbitantly rich businessmen. He provided his customers with what they wanted: a lot of flash for (a lot of) cash.

Many of his new clients also wanted quick acceptance into the New York social world, and as insurance, became active in charities. What Arnold got out of their involvement was the best free advertising imaginable. Whenever his designs are worn by the right women, it's all written up in Suzy's column the next day, and photos of his clients appear in *W*, where a full-page color ad, if Arnold were to pay for it himself, costs $18,400.

Who is wearing what is always news, and the publicity generated by a charity event helps a designer's name and, hopefully, his clothes, to flow into the mainstream. The conduits for this flow are licensing agreements for merchandise that is priced lower than, and is completely different from, the main collections. In these agreements, designers rent their names to other companies for use on a whole slew of items which the designers do not necessarily design, but which they or their staffs approve. In return, designers get a negotiated flat fee and average royalties of 8 percent. It is through licensing that most successful designers earn the bulk of their huge incomes. It is out of a desire to earn more money, to "have an annuity for my old age," that Arnold has recently signed a licensing agreement for a line of furs, is about to sign one for bridal dresses, and is planning one for a fragrance.

Arnold readily admits that his philanthropy is sound business practice. "I support the charities that my friends or clients support," he says. "I support PEN, the writers' group, because Gayfryd Steinberg does. And I support the Girl Scouts because of Austine Hearst and Edna Morris." And he is chairing the New York City Opera benefit because Beverly Sills, who is general director of the opera and a friend of many of Arnold's clients, asked him to.

The address Arnold has given me, 215 East Sixty-Seventh Street, turns out to be that of the Metro Media building. Kluge owns Metro Media, and, at first I think Arnold has mistakenly directed me to Kluge's office rather than his home. But no, the two young black security guards behind the lobby's reception desk tell me that, yes, the Kluges live here. I ask the guards, who have a list of who is to be let into the party, if Arnold has arrived. They check the list, and as I expected, they say, "No. Not yet." Once again I sit down to wait for the designer.

At 6 P.M., a young man and an older woman enter the building. The man says to one of the security guards, "Dr. and Mrs. Levine." The guard scans the list and looks up suspiciously, saying, "Not here."

"Try Moore," says Dr. Levine.

"OK," says the guard, finding the name. He escorts them into a vestibule to the left of the reception desk and unlocks the Kluges' private elevator. After the doors have closed on the couple, the the other guard turns and says to his co-worker, "I can't believe you didn't recognize Mary Tyler Moore."

Another woman walks in, and the first guard carefully scrutinizes her. The woman's back is toward me but I can tell by the guard's face that she is not anyone famous. She spells her name for the guards, " I–t–t–e–l–s–o–n." It's on the list and she, too, is admitted. Then in come Arnold and Parker Ladd, his longtime companion. I join them and Arnold gives our names to the guard. As we walk into the elevator area, he asks me, "Who's here?"

"Mary Tyler Moore, her husband, and Mrs. Ittelson."

"That's it?"

"That's all I saw."

He presses the Door Open button but nothing happens. "How do we get in here?" he mutters.

"The guard has to unlock the door," I say.

Just then Saul and Gayfryd Steinberg walk in, give their names to the guards and are let into the elevator with us. Saul Steinberg does not photograph well, but in person he generates a vitality and sense of power that make him attractive. Gayfryd, meanwhile, who is very tall and has dark, close-cropped hair, looks much younger, slimmer, and prettier than she does in pictures. "Are you re-covering?" Arnold says to them by way of greeting as the elevator rises.

Gayfryd makes the motion of drooping like a wilted flower.

"What's the matter?" Arnold says, instant concern in his voice.

"Motherhood," says Gayfryd. Two of their children, aged four and ten, live with the Steinbergs.

"Is it something a child did to you?" Arnold says, as the elevator rises.

"It's something a child did to another child." Whatever it is, it has her visibly upset, but Arnold doesn't press for details.

We get off the elevator and walk into the entrance hall but it is empty and there is not a sound to be heard. "Is anybody here?" says Saul.

Gayfryd, walking ahead, turns down a long hallway to our left. "No. Not that way," says her husband, so she turns and heads back toward us. Suddenly, as if by magic, like something from the Wizard of Oz, the huge doors behind Gayfryd start to open by themselves, very slowly. "There," I say.

"Gayfryd," Saul calls to his wife, who has already passed us and is heading for the other end of the entrance hall.

"You told me not to go that way," she says petulantly. Walking away ahead of us, Gayfryd heads for the open doors. Inside the large party room, with its marble floors and imposing skylights, a fire roars in the round fireplace. Small groups of people are either standing among the card and backgammon tables, or in front of the bar, or near the piano, or sitting on couches grouped into various conversation areas. The dressed-up folk are holding drinks and accepting hors d'oeuvres from trays proffered by numerous waiters. Arnold notices Mary Tyler Moore and her husband standing by themselves in a corner, looking rather lost. He hurries over to the actress, whom he befriended ten years ago at a dinner party on Long Island, where Arnold has a weekend home in Quogue.

Mary Tyler Moore's face lights up. "What's going on in your life?" she says after they've exchanged greetings. "Let's have dinner."

Arnold pulls an 8½-by-11-inch sheet of paper from his pocket. This sheet of paper, which is updated weekly, has his upcoming two-month agenda on it. He carries this, rather than a pocket calendar, because he doesn't want any bulges in his clothes. "Next week is terrible because of PEN," says Arnold, referring to the benefit that Gayfryd Steinberg is hosting for the nonprofit literary organization at the Pierre the following Wednesday. "How about the following week?" he says. Before Mary can answer, Arnold says, "No. We're in Barbados. What about Monday, the second of May?"

They agree on that date and off goes Arnold, pausing briefly by a couple of women who are talking in hushed tones with Gayfryd Steinberg. He listens for a minute and then is joined by Anne Ford Johnson. "Do you know these lovely ladies?" says Arnold to Anne.

The ladies nod at each other and then Arnold takes Anne by the elbow. "Come on. I'll walk you to the door. They want to talk about children anyway."

The Steinbergs stay for just fifteen minutes, long enough to have shown their support for the charity and to get their picture taken. By 6:20 both they and the Levines are gone, having left separately. For the next hour Arnold kisses cheeks, talks, and poses for the two photographers present; one is from *Women's Wear Daily* and the other is from *Avenue*.

As I circulate around the party I see that many of the people here are not quite sure why they have been invited. Kay Meehan, a friend of Arnold's, strolls around the room by herself and stops to say, "I don't know the people here. I don't even know what this is about. I think it's for the New York City Opera but you better check that. Because of Beverly Sills being here, you better make sure I have the right opera."

The vice-president of public relations from Christie's is equally puzzled. "Who are these people?" she asks me, every time our paths cross. "They all look vaguely familiar."

She tells me that the opera benefit will be an auction held at Christie's sometime in June. For those benefits, she says, "there's a reception at Christie's and then after the reception, after the people get sufficiently juiced, we have the auction, and, having spent the past hour drinking, everyone spends more money than they ordinarily would.

At 7 P.M. Arnold and Beverly Sills stand on the marble steps at the room's entrance, and, clinking silverware against their glasses, they ask for everyone's attention. After a few moments they get it.

"We got you here for a reason," says Arnold.

"No!" yells Patricia Kluge, sarcastically from across the room.

"I thought you got us here because you like us," says Edna Morris, the elderly widow of thoroughbred-racing titan John A. Morris. But she says it quietly so that only her escort and the few people next to her can hear.

"We are having a benefit for the New York City Opera on June twentieth," says Arnold. "We're going to make it a lot of fun this year. A gala, but free. I don't mean moneywise . . ." He pauses until the obliging laughter from the crowd subsides. "I mean free in spirit.

"Please buy as many tickets as you can," says Arnold, "and give what you can. It's an extraordinary institution." With that, even though Robert and Blaine Trump didn't arrive until a few minutes after the sales pitch, the party is basically over.

Arnold Scaasi *April 28*

Last night, at the gala fund-raiser for PEN, Arnold Scaasi stood in the grand ballroom of the Pierre Hotel, happily counting how many of his dresses were waltzing about the room. There was one on Gayfryd Steinberg, who was chairing the event, and there was another on Barbara Goldsmith, and still others on Georgette Mosbacher, Anne Bass, and Charlotte Ford. As always, seeing his gowns in action made Arnold happy, but tonight his happiness was tempered by one sad little fact: he was exhausted. He'd been working and playing so hard that neither activity seemed to be much fun anymore.

Something has to give, he thought to himself, never letting on to anyone in the room that he was having less than the grandest time. I mean, look at what he had to do in this one week alone. Sunday he'd gone to a benefit for Meals on Wheels. Monday he was at a cocktail reception at the Rainbow Room for the Estée Lauder launching of its new perfume, Knowing. After the reception he hosted a party at La Côte Basque for "clients and friends" visiting from Palm Beach. On Tuesday he attended the gala opening of the New York City Ballet's American Music Festival at Lincoln Center, the gala for which he had dressed Patricia McBride. After he leaves me tonight he is going to a dinner party.

Last night, as he watched two more of his creations float by—one on Liz Smith and one on Iris Love—Arnold realized that he's eaten dinner at home just twice in the past three weeks. Ideally, he thought, as he smiled at both ladies, he would give up working and just go to parties, but since that wasn't possible, he decided to opt for the only other alternative. He resolved to absolutely, positively, cut down on his socializing.

But today, as (half-an-hour late) we settle in for a chat in his lovely Central Park South rent-controlled duplex apartment where he's lived for twenty-six years (and where he pays just $1,200 a month in rent), he seems conflicted by his decision.

"These last three weeks have been horrendous, but you have to socialize a certain amount," he says, speaking over the very loud sound of hammering made by workers who are replacing the building's elevator. Something has gone wrong with the sad little fire burning in his fireplace, and it is making the whole room terribly smoky. The fireplace is flanked by two Pedro Friedeberg chairs, both shaped like cupped hands; above the mantelpiece hangs a huge 1962 Picasso; and the wooden ceiling was designed by Louise Nevelson—all visible testaments of Arnold's success. "I happen to like doing that. I'm gregarious. I like people. I like my clients—they are an interesting group of women. I think that . . ." He pauses and then says, "I don't know what I think. I'm too tired."

We are sitting on the blue banquettes that line the walls, facing a beautiful view of Central Park, and as the phone rings, Arnold, whose housekeeper has taken his two dogs out for a walk, wearily stands up to answer it. When he returns, he says, "It's very fulfilling for a designer to go and see his clothes in action. I'm not going to see mine in the streets during the day. I'm only going to see them in the evening so I'm sort of torn. I don't know. Maybe all I need is a rest. I'm going to Barbados and I'll see how I feel when I come back, if I'll keep all my good vows of last night. I mean, if I had my choice I wouldn't work. I would just go to parties. I've got Alzheimer's . . ." Seeing my obvious look of surprise, he says, "I mean, I've got the Alzheimer's benefit. I may have Alzheimer's also, but the Alzheimer's benefit is on May sixteenth. Yasmin Khan is the chairman of that and I am dressing her. And that's it.

"I need time to think about designing, and for that you need some time to yourself. Once you begin to design something it's like writing a book. You've got to do it on your own."

The phone rings again, and answering it Arnold, in his deadpan voice, says, "Yes . . . Yes . . . No . . . That one." He hangs up and comes back to tell the story of how he became a designer.

Arnold Scaasi was born and educated in Montreal, the son of a furrier whose surname was Isaacs. (When he began designing, Arnold turned his last name backwards.) He was the youngest of three children, and while he was still in high school, his sister got divorced. To take her mind off of that ordeal, she decided to visit an aunt and uncle in Australia, and Arnold went with her. "My aunt was a great influence on me," says Arnold. "She was very fashion-conscious and dressed at Chanel and Schiaparelli."

Arnold lived in Australia for a year and finished high school there. He thought about becoming a commercial artist but decided he "hated drawing tubes of toothpaste."

His aunt said to him, "Well, you're always sketching ladies with clothes," and with just that slight push, Arnold decided to become a fashion designer. He went back to Montreal and enrolled at the Cotnoir-Capponi School of Design, which was affiliated with the Chambre Syndicale de la Haute Couture Parisienne in Paris. He was, he says, "their star pupil" and completed the three-year course in twenty-seven months.

While still a student, he created clothes for private clients who discovered his work via the clothes he made for little dressmaker dummies that were then exhibited at his school. "I was a kid, you know," he says now. "I must have been very precocious." He saved his money until he had enough to move to Paris, where he studied for a year at the Chambre Syndicale. "I found I had an extraordinary aptitude," he says. "I was the best in my class and was the most outstanding, uh, student. Whatever.

"But at the Chambre Syndicale I found I was learning what I already knew," he continues. "I went around with my portfolio and ended up working at the House of Paquin for a short time for fifty dollars a month. Then my parents decided I should come home. I came back to America and my parents drove down from Montreal to get me in New York.

"In the meantime, through a friend who was a decorator in Paris, I had an introduction to Charles James in New York." Suddenly, there is a loud crash behind the wall next to us and Arnold stops short to say, "I hope the building doesn't fall down around us." It doesn't and he goes on with his life story.

"Anyway, I had an introduction to Charles James. He was a made-to-order designer who dressed women like Austine Hearst and Babe Paley and the Mrs. Whitney who was *the* Mrs. Whitney at the time. I was to meet him at an exhibit of paintings on Fifty-seventh Street, and while I was waiting for Mr. James to meet me at this art showing, Joan Crawford and Anita Loos walked in. Miss Crawford had on this extraordinary black cocktail coat and a wonderful black hat with long tulle veil. She looked just dazzling and I thought, I am not going back to Montreal. I'm going to stay right here. And I did.

"Mr. James offered me a job and I worked there for about two years." It was at that made-to-order house that Arnold learned the dressmaking technique he still practices today. "Charles James built a dress like you'd build a house," says Arnold. "With a foundation. He sometimes had as many as twenty-five or thirty sections in a dress. That was something I had never seen before, and it's something I still do now. Almost every dress I make today has a foundation of some type."

Arnold decided to leave his job because, he says, there was no place for advancement and because it was a very difficult place to work. He says he had a hard time finding another job, however, because "Charles James was considered so egocentric and eccentric that everyone thought you had to be equally eccentric if you worked there." The phone rings again, and, sighing, he gets up to answer it. Again his conversation consists of quick yeses and nos, and after it's finished, he tells me:

"Finally, Pauline Trigère hired me. I worked for her for ten days until she fired me. Then [in 1956] I designed a collection of suits and coats under my own label for a moderately priced company called Dressmaker Casuals. I did that for a little over a year until I opened my own business."

Arnold had saved two thousand dollars, and with that money he hired a seamstress and a tailor who made a twenty-piece collection of "very high-styled" coats, suits, day and evening dresses, which Arnold launched in 1958 at the Plaza Hotel. The clothes were a success. Many magazines photographed them and they were bought by stores like Neiman Marcus, Saks Fifth Avenue, and Bergdorf Goodman.

Within two years Arnold had won the Coty Fashion Critics Award, along with assorted others. The business flourished as Arnold ultimately sold his ready-to-wear to more than two hundred top specialty shops and department stores; opened a costume jewelry division; and licensed his name for children's wear, furs, hats, handbags, men's sweaters, and ties, as well as a less expensive line of ready-to-wear.

In time, he says, "I found I was very young, had made a great deal of money, and all I was doing was working. I took stock of myself and thought, This is stupid. I've made all this money and I'm not having any fun.

"I had built up a great clientele across the country because of store appearances, and I decided to do the kind of clothes I like to do and to service the kind of people that I like to make clothes for." He stopped designing the ready-to-wear, jewelry, and all the licensed lines, opened his made-to-order company in 1964, and "just had a wonderful time."

"I suddenly started to live," he says. "I designed two collections a year, six months apart. I had all this time to have a life and it was wonderful. I never felt sorry about having given up all the other stuff, although once in a while I would feel I was working so hard getting a collection together and then I would be dressing only fifty women."

In the early eighties, Ellin Saltzman, who today is senior vice-president and director of fashion and product development at Saks Fifth Avenue and would later leave to join Macy's New York, asked Arnold if Saks could sell his made-to-order collection in its branches across the country. Wanting to make the clothes available to women who might not travel to New York, he said yes.

He made personal appearances to promote his collection, and being in the stores and meeting the women (many of whom told him they couldn't afford to spend $6,000 on a dress) made him "pick up the scent" of ready-to-wear again. "I had a big feeling that evening clothes were lacking in that area of the market," he says. "And I know how women want to look when they go out at night." He reopened his Scaasi Boutique ready-to-wear division in 1984. This first collection consisted only of cocktail and evening dresses, and these types of dresses continue to be the mainstay of that line today.

"The most confusing thing for me is keeping the two collections separate," says Arnold. "If you're going to do ready-to-wear and made-to-order, if you're going to do more than one thing, you have to be able to switch off. I can stop everything dead and say I'm going to do only furs this week, and my mind absolutely clicks off to everything else. It's not easy.

"That's why licensing scares me," he says, referring to his imminent fur launch and the other various licensing deals he is researching. "I want to be involved and make sure there are enough hours to click off and on all the time.

"Sometimes," Arnold says, "I will bring a dress into the fitting room and I'll say, 'I don't know what this dress is for. Is it ready-to-wear? Is it spring? Is it made-to-order fall? What is this dress? I don't remember.' Honestly. I'll get confused about all these clothes coming in. I fit maybe four hundred dresses a year and, I mean, you figure it takes a minimum of three hours to fit a dress and it may take two more fittings before you get the dress you want. That's a lot of time that you spend standing there with your arms up in the air trying to fit that model who's six feet tall."

Liz Claiborne *May 3*

What makes Liz Claiborne, Inc., unique, and so extraordinarily lucrative, is that the sales department here has an inordinate amount of input into the final look of the clothes. Since it is they who have the most contact with retailers, it is they who know what retailers and their customers want. Today we will watch as the Collection designers expose their work to the critical eyes of the sales vice-presidents, as well as to Jerry Chazen, co-vice-chairman. Each of these executives will be thinking of only one thing as they view the Collection: How many pieces of each group will sell and what can they do to the product to make it sell better?

Liz, Art, and Jay are not here, and it is Dennis, sitting at the head of the twelfth-floor conference table, flanked by his two designers, who will run the meeting. "Because of our poor performance this season, the line we are about to show you is a very critical line," says Dennis as he distributes the line plan. "We want it to be the best it can be and we want it to be a strong go-to-work line. It offers something for everyone. There are suits, separates, and items. This spring we didn't have enough two-piece dressing or enough color. In the line we're about to show you there are colors, as well as black-and-white and neutrals. We think we've covered everything but I'm sure you'll be able to spot some holes.

"Last year," he says, "we had four groups for the entire spring season and, as we all learned, if you make a mistake with just one group, that's twenty-five percent of your business out the door. This year, to make sure that no one group is going to make or break us, we have seven groups. Sixty-five percent of the units will be delivered in January and the rest in February."

"Do we want to do that?" says Hank Sinkel, senior vice-president of sales for misses sportswear.

"We'll decide everything within the next two weeks," says Dennis. "For now we just want you to think about it and mull it over.

"This year's budget is $45,200,000," he says. "Last year's was $47,181,000, so you can tell we're planning to have less units out there. With that, let's start with the first group, Silk Stones.

"This was Naturally Neutral in pre-spring 1988," he says as the knitwear designer puts sketches of the group on a small upright easel she's placed on the conference table. She passes around a sweater from the pre-spring line so that the salespeople can feel the fabric, and she shows them a piece of paper with cream, gray, and taupe fabric swatches pasted on it.

"This can be go-to-work or novelty-oriented for the customer who likes to wear tunics over her pants," says Dennis.

"What are the prices?" says Jerry. "How are these prices as compared with last year?"

"It's too early to tell," says Dennis.

"This was one of our most successful groups, right?" says Hank.

"Yes," says Dennis.

"We're not talking about quantities at all, are we?" says Kathy Haught Van Eerden, vice-president of sales for Collection and Lizsport.

"No," says Dennis. "We'll do that the next time we meet. For now we just want you to see our concepts and look for any noticeable gaps."

"I think you want to talk about your tops-to-bottoms ratio," says Jerry.

"I think we own too many pants and tunics," says Kathy. "We need more skirts, cardigans, and tops."

"And don't you have to worry about the quota we need?" says Jerry. (In an effort to control imports, the United States government imposes restrictions on the amount and type of certain fabrics and garments that can be imported every year.)

"That's the wonderful thing about this group," says Dennis. "There is no quota on it." (Since silk is not manufactured in the United States it does not fall under any quota restrictions.)

"Right now the pant and tunic ends up being one-third of the group," says Kathy. "That's too much."

"We'll cover that in our next meeting," says Dennis, and he goes on to the second group, Suit du Jour. He puts three sketches of black suits on the easel.

Each of the suits has a bright fuchsia or lime green lining with white polka dots. The women in the room say, "Ahhh." They obviously like what they see.

"Didn't we have a fabulous jacket this spring?" says Jerry, frowning. He is referring to a long jacket in a slubby cream-colored fabric. "We should be in love with that jacket and we should do it again."

"I've heard that our jackets don't sell," says Hank, "so if we've got a good one we should go ahead with it."

"We shouldn't try to reinvent the wheel," says Jerry.

"We're not trying to reinvent the wheel," says Dennis in a tight, controlled voice. "We're trying to rerun great bodies."

"Have we sold those stripes?" says Hank, pointing at a sketch of a pinstriped suit. "We had a dress like that in the dress division and it didn't sell."

"Does anyone have any feelings about the fancy linings?" says Jerry.

"I think they're great," says Kathy.

"Wouldn't that hot pink lining affect the color of the blouse you could wear underneath the jacket?" says Jerry.

Both Dennis and Judith look at him with dumbfounded expressions. They are clearly very proud of this group and surprised that he is finding fault with it.

"Chartreuse with polka dots is begging for trouble," says Jerry.

Judith has been holding up a sheet of paper that has a five-inch swatch of black-and-white pinstripe and a small swatch of chartreuse lining pasted on it. She rests her chin on the paper, looking at Jerry with disappointment written all over her face.

"Wait a second," says Dennis. "Before we jump to any conclusions, let's look at the blouses."

Judith spreads out four pieces of paper covered with black polka-dotted swatches of fabric. On each of these swatches the polka dots are printed on a different base color. The four base colors are chartreuse, yellow, hot pink, and white.

"We will also have solid silk T-shirts in pink, yellow, chartreuse, and black," says Dennis. He looks at Jerry for his reaction, but Jerry is looking down at his copy of the lineup.

"I think our numbers per style are very small," says Jerry. "And we have too many styles. We need tighter groups like the first one you showed. Our ownership is nuts."

"Excuse me?" says Dennis.

"Our ownership is very small per style," says Jerry. The number of styles and the quantity of each style is an ongoing fight between the sales and design departments. Sales would like to see fewer styles made in huge quantities so that the product is less expensive to manufacture, whereas design would like to see more fashion-forward merchandise. The more fashionable an item, the fewer pieces the company makes of it, since most likely it will not sell well across America.

"It's not that different from what we've been booking in the showroom," says Dennis.

"Maybe you shouldn't pay attention to what we're booking right now in the showroom," says Hank.

Jerry angrily points at the sketches on the easel and yells, "This is bullshit. Why apologize for that suit? I would have a lot of trouble with buying that suit, and you have it down for eight thousand units."

In a placating tone Hank says, "We'll quantify it later. Maybe we'll have twelve hundred. We're not finalizing units today."

Jerry launches into a training speech similar to the ones Liz and Art give on their respective areas. "What the sales department should do is make sure that the proportions are accurate and that what we have represents the consumer," says Jerry. "As you look at this, think about what you have been hearing from the stores. Factor in everything you know."

"Well, Jerry, I have a question," says Linda Larson, vice-president of sales in the petite division. "We've been told not to redesign the line. What does it mean not to redesign the line? If we say we don't like the green lining with the polka dots, isn't that redesigning the line?"

"Yes," says Dennis. "It is. Absolutely."

Lowering his voice, Jerry says, "We've been working so desperately to find the right jacket, I guess I'm overreacting, but I can tell you this—by putting in a chartreuse lining you're not going to get *more* women to buy the line. You'll get *less*."

Trying very hard to keep his voice even, Dennis says, "Design loves this concept of classic jackets with novelty linings."

"Take it another step for us," says Linda. "How large a percentage of the entire line is this group?"

"Ten or twelve percent," says Dennis. "This whole line is go-to-work."

"I'm trying to stimulate a little bit of action here," says Jerry, "so I don't hear later from sales: 'How do you expect me to sell a jacket with a chartreuse lining?' "

"That's a valid point," says Dennis. The room is silent for a moment and then Dennis says, "You don't get it, Jerry. Is that what you're saying? You don't get this group?"

"Right," says Jerry. "It's adding something to the jacket that is making it more difficult to buy. My prediction is disaster."

"On that upbeat note," says Dennis, "let's go to the next group, which is soft, two-piece dressing."

"I love it already," says Jerry. He says this although he hasn't seen anything yet because he knows Liz Claiborne customers love to wear matching and/or coordinating tops and bottoms. This group replaces the Armani-inspired rose-colored suits which Liz vetoed on March 31.

The two-piece-dressing group is based on a tropical print, and Judith puts a painting of that print on the easel. "There is a shirt like that in Lizwear," says Linda, looking at the painting.

"Already I don't want to show it to you," says Dennis peevishly. He takes the print off of the easel and puts it into a folder. "There's no point in showing you this group until the prints are all finished."

"Well, is it going to look like that painting?" says Linda.

"Exactly like that painting," says Dennis.

"Then it's going to look like Lizwear," says Linda.

"But Lizwear has only one shirt and we have a whole group," says Dennis.

"It's our job to point out duplications," says Linda.

Just then Jay Margolis, wearing a suit, enters with Dennis's assistant. The assistant asks Dennis to step into the hall. A moment later Linda, who was looking at her line plan and didn't notice Dennis leave, looks up and says, "Where's Dennis? In the hall crying softly?"

"I don't care if he's crying loudly," says Jerry. "Anyway, I have to go. I won't cause any more trouble here." He heads for the door, and Dennis, walking in, says, "No, don't leave."

"I have to," says Jerry. "I have a meeting."

Jay sits down at the foot of the table and, although Dennis has gone on to present the next group, made from the leftover linen, as if nothing were wrong, Jay says, "What's going on? What happened here? I went out for lunch for the first time in months and something happened."

"Serves you right for going out to lunch," says Linda.

"This meeting is different from our usual meetings," says Jay. "I can tell something happened."

The salespeople recount Jerry's point about there being too many styles and not enough numbers behind the styles.

"That's bullshit," says Jay. "He hasn't even seen the product and already he's saying we're over-assorted and have too many SKUs?" SKU is the abbreviation for Stock Keeping Unit, a term that stands not just for the number of styles the company will manufacture, but for the number of different colors each style will come in. For example, if one style will come in four different colors, that style accounts for four SKUs.

"That's nonsense," says Jay. "Don't worry about it. I'll fight with him about that. I'd rather get more good product out there and not worry about being too over-assorted or the numbers."

Jay believes that the greater the variety of merchandise the company shows retailers, the more confidence retailers will think the company has. "Otherwise," he says later, "They'll say, Oh-oh. Liz Claiborne is really nervous. Their line is so narrow."

As Dennis presents the linen group, which he now calls Classics by Liz, Kathy whispers, "That'll be in the Saks catalogue. I can tell already." Following Liz's instructions, Dennis has asked that the gray linen be recolored, and the solid linen colors are now cream, khaki, black, coral, and wintergreen. There are also various cream-colored plaids.

"I like the stripe," says Hank of one of the fabrics. "Can we have more of the stripe?"

"The fabric is eleven dollars a yard," says Dennis. "It's too expensive."

"Are we afraid of a hundred-and-fifty-dollar jacket?" says Hank. "It would cost two hundred and forty on the bridge market." (Bridge is a fashion industry term for clothing whose price points and styling fall between the designer and better markets, thereby "bridging" the two areas. Liz Claiborne is a "better" price designer.)

"Should we change the name from Classics by Liz?" says Hank. "We've already had a group with that name."

"Sure," says Dennis sarcastically. "We can call it Classics by Committee."

Next, Dennis presents the knit group, which was originally printed with Mondrian-inspired color blocks, but now, with Liz's input, has become black-and-white and blue-and-black striped knits. This passes through unscathed, as do the red and navy and the animal-print groups.

After Dennis is finished, Linda says, "Dennis, can we walk through this again?"

He and Judith pin up the sketches and swatches on the wall behind them so that the entire line is visible at once. "What happens," Linda says, "is that our key pieces sell out, and then, once those core pieces are gone, sales slack off. So we do need tighter groups with fewer styles. I, unfortunately, have to agree with Jerry on that one.

"Seeing the line as a whole," she continues, "I think maybe we should do away with the linings. I think those are our only Lady Banker suits on the line."

"I don't have a problem with the dots," says Hank. "I have a problem with the fuchsia."

"How about if we kept the novelty linings but made them more subdued," says Dennis.

"Say it was black with fine lines," says Judith.

"Maybe then the color, and I hate to say it because I love this group, should come from the pocket squares," says the knitwear designer.

"But the whole point was novelty linings," says Dennis. "That was the whole point."

Bill Blass *May 3*

"Where have you been?" says Bill Blass, instantly showering me with his charm as I walk into his office. "I haven't seen you in years."

Those ten little words are a good example of Bill Blass's social graces. Although Bill and I have met only a few times before, always for professional reasons and always briefly, his words make it sound as if I had at one time been a regular part of his life, and as if at all those charity balls and black-tie dinners he regularly attends he's been scanning the crowds, duly noting my absence. His words also make it sound as if the only place to be is wherever he is.

Every weekday morning Bill Blass can be found on the twelfth floor of 550 Seventh Avenue, the most high-profile address of New York's garment center. Despite the fact that he devotes himself to creating beautiful things, he, like most fashion designers, works in one of New York's ugliest neighborhoods, just below Times Square's pornographic theaters, prostitutes, drug dealers, and street crime.

Although the garment center is referred to as "Seventh Avenue," the area actually has two main streets—its namesake, Seventh Avenue, and Broadway—which run parallel and are one block apart. While most of the office buildings lining Broadway house sportswear firms, those along Seventh Avenue are home to dress companies and high-end designer firms. It is from 550 Seventh Avenue that Oscar de la Renta, Carolyne Roehm, Geoffrey Beene, Donna Karan, and, of course, Bill Blass run their empires.

A visit to Bill Blass begins when you give your name to the receptionist sitting behind a see-through plastic wall, then turn left and head toward the glass showroom doors. If you are a retailer, a private customer, or a journalist, you use this entrance. Otherwise you enter, as Bill Blass and his employees do, through a side door that opens onto the behind-the-scenes workings of the company.

It is there that we will be taken. As I wait for Tom Fallon, Bill Blass's advertising and promotion director, to come and get me, I peek through the showroom door. The gray-carpeted floor is usually left clear so that models wearing the latest designs can swirl and pose before customers, but today it is filled with racks of clothes from the fall collection Bill showed last month. A few of Bill's private customers are in there, poking through the racks as if this were a department store.

My look through these doors was prompted by more than casual curiosity. I haven't been in this showroom in three years, and I wanted to see if it had changed at all. No, it is exactly as I remembered it—a sleek, 500-square-foot space with four windows, each of which has a banquette and a small black table in front of it. It is not much bigger or smaller than any other showroom I've seen.

Then why, I wonder, did a new book, *The Fashion Conspiracy*, by a British journalist describe Bill's showroom like this: "The distances involved are so great, and the expanse of grey carpet so enormous, that the horizon melds into the grey of the sofas and the venetian blinds. Every thirty yards or so, like oases in the Empty Quarter, are positioned little black Andrée Putman tables. . . . It would be perfectly possible to smoke an entire cigarette as you journeyed from oasis to oasis, on the route towards Blass's own office."

It's amazing, I think, how even a journalist writing a book with an exposé-like title called *The Fashion Conspiracy* fell victim to Bill Blass's larger-than-life aura and his charm.

You certainly can't blame Bill Blass for the glorification he gets in the press. If you ask him, as I have before, to describe his company he will tell you it is small, with only seventy-three people (including tailors and seamstresses) employed directly by him. If you ask him about his work, he will say, "I don't think of this as a deadly serious business. After all, clothes are meant to be discarded. And I don't like designers who take themselves too seriously, because they are a dreary bore. This is a business like any other." But if you ask him how his deified celebrity status came about, he will be able to tell you exactly how it happened.

William Ralph Blass, born in 1922, grew up in Fort Wayne, Indiana, the son of a hardware store owner. "I had a very typical, normal childhood except for the fact that I sketched from an early age, from the time I was six or seven," he says. "What amazed my teachers was that my drawings were highly sophisticated sketches of ladies in penthouse apartments having cocktails. They represented a world that had nothing to do with my own life."

They represented also what Bill thought was "the most attractive possible life." He was made aware of this life through the fashion magazines his mother kept around the house and through the movies.

"For fifteen cents on a Saturday afternoon a kid could go to the movies," he says. "This was during the Depression when films, curiously enough, photographed the fantasy world that people were not having. They were scenes of the affluent worlds of Hollywood, Paris, and New York."

When Bill was fourteen, he began sending—and selling—sketches to Seventh Avenue manufacturers whose names he saw in fashion magazines. "In those days I would get twenty-five or thirty dollars for a sketch, and a famous evening house wrote me a letter saying they were interested in hiring me. Of course they didn't know how young I was and, of course, I couldn't accept that offer."

But he certainly wished he could. "I always knew that I would come to New York as soon as I was old enough." This happened after he graduated from high school and, at eighteen, enrolled for one semester at the Parsons School of Design.

He left school to take a job at David Crystal as a sketcher. Then World War II broke out, and Bill enlisted and served in the army for three-and-a-half years. "Those years gave me the maturing and toughness that were needed for my later career. I really feel that a great deal transpired due to the fact that I was in the army. I was with an interesting group of men. Art Kane, the fashion photographer, and Ellsworth Kelly, the artist, were in the group, but it was mainly people who, for instance, were tough coal miners from West Virginia. In order to survive my first few jobs with Seventh Avenue manufacturers, who were indeed tough, I really drew on my war experiences and my ability to get along with a wide variety of people. It helped me enormously."

After Bill returned to New York he worked briefly as an assistant to Anne Klein and then went to work for Anna Miller. He began as a sketcher and was eventually named an assistant designer. In those days, Bill says, "Designers were very low on the totem pole. You had to be tough to survive—not to get hurt. We were necessary but we were minor players.

"I grew up on Seventh Avenue during an era when the designer was totally anonymous," Bill continues. "It was an era during which the designer's name was not known—it was the name of the manufacturer that everyone was familiar with. It was an era during which, after he showed a collection, the designer was encouraged to take a vacation and then, after he disappeared, the manufacturer would completely change the line to make it more commercial."

After Anna Miller retired in 1959, the firm merged with Maurice Rentner, a successful Seventh Avenue house which, as Bill puts it, manufactured "staid conservative clothes for fat women." Bill became head designer and transformed Rentner's image into his own more youthful one. In 1960 he was made a vice-president of the company and by 1970 had bought it and renamed it Bill Blass.

Once Bill was named head designer, he did two important things: he began licensing his name and he began inviting his customers to the shows. "I felt that the only way to really succeed in this industry was to follow the examples of Mr. Cardin and Mr. Dior, and that was to diversify, to have a wide cross-section of products. I started out with children's wear, bathing suits, and menswear—products to which I felt my taste could contribute."

As for the shows, he says, "At that time it was considered highly irregular and unusual to have private people at your show. You showed at your showroom on Broadway or Seventh Avenue, not at the Plaza or anything. I would invite my friends—the people I knew who were clients."

Bill says he met prominent, wealthy people "from the moment I arrived in New York. I went everywhere. I went to debutante parties and to every nightclub and café without having any money whatsoever. I have always thought that in New York if you have a dinner jacket and you're an extra man with two legs that's about all you need."

At first, in his travels about the New York evening scene, Bill did not tell people he was a designer. "There was a stigma about Seventh Avenue and about being a designer," he says. "I would tell people something vague, like I was in manufacturing." But then, of course, his friends found out and came to his shows, an action which, he says, "rather appalled the stores. They thought I was selling wholesale, which was not the case, but I felt that the exposure of having your clothes seen by the actual consumer would help the clothes to survive. And, of course, that appealed to Eugenia Sheppard and to *Women's Wear*, who would report on the celebrities and the socialites who came to the shows."

In 1960, the young John Fairchild took over the helm of *Women's Wear Daily,* the trade paper his grandfather had founded. At that time the paper wasn't very well respected and its reporters were seated in the back rows at fashion shows, if they were invited at all. After Fairchild and the late Eugenia Sheppard, who wrote a fashion and gossip column for *The New York Herald Tribune,* began reporting on which designers dressed which social ladies, the trade paper's circulation soared. Both the designers and their customers loved seeing their pictures in the newspaper.

Bill Blass and John Fairchild helped carry each other's social stars into the heavens. Today Bill can't help it if the press, the retailers, and his employees adore him (which most do). Personally, I have found him to be the most accessible, forthcoming, and straight-talking of any of the designers. Bill and Fairchild have built up a relationship over the years by mutually supporting each other—Fairchild giving Bill coverage in his newspaper and Bill reporting to Fairchild, who hates parties, on what happened at the social functions Bill attends almost every night.

But no matter how late he stays out at night, Bill is at work at 8:30 A.M. every morning. He usually walks in with a note in his hand reminding him of what needs to be done that day and gets to work immediately, either fitting a dress on his tall, slim assistant, Laura Montalban (Ricardo Montalban's daughter, who has worked for him for twenty-two years), returning phone calls or sending a note or flowers to one hostess or another. He goes to lunch at 1 P.M. and then either meets with his licensees in the afternoon or takes off to visit antique stores or galleries. (Antiques, he says, are "a passionate interest.")

Tom Fallon opens the door, interrupting my reverie, and says, "Come on in. I'll take you to Bill." We walk through a small area where two salespeople sit, and go into Bill's office, located just next to the showroom.

This office looks more like a den in a country house than the center of power for a business that has an annual retail volume of $450 million. Only a minuscule amount of these sales (about $16 million) comes from his collection. The rest comes from his 66 licensing agreements; 38 in the United States, 12 in the Far East, 10 in Mexico and 6 in Canada. These include menswear, furs, coats, swimwear, scarves, and home furnishings. There is a Bill Blass license for car interiors and there was once a licensed line of Bill Blass chocolates. He has turned down offers for Bill Blass condoms, coffins, and orthodontics. The latter would have involved stamping his initials on braces. Like most top designers, Bill Blass has become far more than a fashion designer—he has become an arbiter of good taste. His opinions on restaurants and hotels are quoted in the press, and his two homes have appeared on television and in magazines. Former President Reagan named him to the President's Council on the Arts and Humanities. His influence on the lives of American men and women goes way beyond their closets, and his workday involves far more than just creating clothes.

Besides being a designer, Bill is also the owner and president of his company, and he operates it with an open-door policy. His door is, literally, always open and, although it is not a revolving one, it may as well be, since an endless stream of people are constantly passing through it.

Bill, who sits at a desk located in the far left corner, says he finds these interruptions stimulating and that he does much of his designing "on the run." "Some designers lock themselves up," he once told me. "I don't work that way. It is not possible for me to get the creative juices working by being chained to a chair and saying, 'All right, now this afternoon we have to knock out this or that section of the collection.' If I attempt to sit down and say, 'OK, I have to do five black short dresses by Thursday,' I can't do it. But then I will be someplace and see something there that will trigger inspiration.

"But," he continued, "the thing that stimulates me most is, when we get going on a collection and while I'm fitting it, I will have twenty phone calls, and then I'll have people walking in and out from production, from sales, from publicity, all asking me questions."

Built into the wall behind Bill's desk are two fake French doors with about two feet of space behind them. Directly behind the doors stand two ficus trees, giving the illusion that a garden stretches behind them rather than the ugliness of Seventh Avenue. This is a perfect setting for a man who creates illusion, who has built a career out of helping less-than-perfect women look as good as they can.

Bill attributes his success to the fact that he has crisscrossed the country many times, meeting his customers in various cities and finding out how they live and entertain. On a smaller and much more exclusive level, he does exactly what Liz Claiborne does—he researches his market and fulfills its needs.

He has long reached the point where, as he puts it, "people will look at your clothes and say, 'Oh, that's very Bill Blass.'" He is best known for designing classic women's sportswear in menswear fabrics, mixing patterns and tweeds and for taking a contrasting, very glamorous approach to evening wear. But he says he gives his customers "a fresh approach each season." That freshness comes from fabrics.

This week Bill, who opened his fall collection two weeks ago will, like all the high-end ready-to-wear designers, be looking at fabrics for his resort and spring collections. These fabrics will be delivered to Bill within six to eight weeks, leaving him about one month to get together his resort collection, which opens on August 11. (Spring, which will incorporate some of the resort designs, will be presented in his fashion show on October 31.)

Besides reviewing fabrics, Bill is currently keeping abreast of and preparing for trunk shows of his fall collection. For trunk shows a designer's entire collection is packed into trunks and taken, by his or her employees, to a store where it is presented to customers. Stores buy only a limited number of pieces from a designer each season, and trunk shows, which account for as much as 40 percent of designers' business, are a way for designers to maximize the exposure their entire collections get to their final customers—the women who will wear the clothes. The first of these trunk shows will take place Monday at Martha's, a Park Avenue specialty shop, where Bill, who, because of time constraints does not attend the majority of his trunk shows, will also make a personal appearance.

Besides preparing for trunk shows, Bill will be designing his fur collection, which he will show on May 16; overseeing the design of an exhibit for an upcoming benefit dinner at the New York Public Library; and putting together a retrospective of his work for the upcoming Drexel University design school graduation in Philadelphia. His menswear licensee is based in Philadelphia and has asked Bill to participate in the graduation. He is doing so because, as Tom later puts it, "It is politic to work with the licensees." Besides busy workdays, Bill has either social or charitable obligations every night this week.

In between taking care of business and pleasure, Bill constantly draws little doll-size sketches on his brown stationery pads. "I'm always drawing," he says, picking up a sketch that was lying on the desk in front of him. "I sketch while I'm talking on the telephone, while I'm in the car, while I'm on the plane. I sketch dresses, shoes, hats, anything and everything that might be appealing as a silhouette."

Bill then enlarges the sketches that he thinks are "valid" for a collection. He matches the drawing to the appropriate fabric and then hands it over to his sample rooms, which, like every designer's sample rooms, make their initial versions of the design in either muslin or in a fabric that is similar to the one Bill has picked for this design. Bill asks Tom to show me the sample rooms. As I follow Tom out into the hall, Bill says, "Come back tomorrow. I'll be looking at fabrics." After I agree to do so, Tom and I turn left and head down the small hallway outside of Bill's office. This hallway is lined, on the right, with three small windowless cubicles where Bill's secretary, Tom's assistant Craig Natielo, and Tom sit. Almost at the end of the hallway, on the left, is Laura Montalban's cubicle.

To the left of that cubicle is a hallway leading into the tailoring room, where a mostly male staff of eight cuts and sews samples for the suits and coats. On the other side of Laura's cubicle is the entrance to the room where dress samples are made. As opposed to tailored suits and dresses, which are cut on a table, evening dresses are draped on dummies. It is a softer approach, and interestingly enough, everyone in this room is female.

"Once Bill approves the samples they get taken into the production department where duplicate samples are made in a real people's size ten," says Tom as we pause for a minute in the entrance to the dressmaking sample room. The fifteen women in the room, all busily fussing with fabric, are used to tours coming through here and they barely look up as Tom continues: "The original and duplicate samples are then shown to Bill simultaneously to make sure they haven't lost some of their expression," he says. "Once the duplicate is approved, patterns are made in various sizes and these are eventually used to make clothes."

"We end up," Tom continues, as we go back into the hallway and turn left, "with an entire collection of originals, which are used for the show, and an entire collection of duplicates, which, along with the originals, are used for trunk shows."

We walk down the hallway, passing a tiny kitchen on our left and coming to the trimming room, a small, narrow space whose walls are lined with shelves covered with boxes of buttons, zippers, and lace. "We own all the trimmings and we feed them out to the factories as needed," says Tom as we peek into this space.

Next we turn right until we reach the fabric room, where all fabrics are delivered and immediately inspected by being run on rollers over a long fluorescent light. Bolts of fabric are stacked on metal shelves that run from floor to ceiling.

"Our single biggest expenditure is in fabric," says Tom. "We own all of it and we always walk a fine line. We may project we'll cut only twenty-five pieces of something. That may be just fifty or seventy-five yards of a fabric. We buy European fabrics, and it takes three months for them to arrive. If we overestimated how much we need, we eat the goods. [The firm actually then sells the fabric to jobbers.] If we underestimated, we lose the business.

"We are a small business," he says. "We don't own any factories. We contract our work out to factories in Manhattan, Brooklyn, and New Jersey. We're paying top dollar because nothing is done offshore, and we don't have any big cutting tickets. I don't know if you've seen any factories, but they usually stack the fabric three hundred pieces deep and cut it. The way we do it, cutting five of one thing, seven of another and then three or two of something else, incurs great labor costs. That's part of what accounts for our price points. Women pay three thousand to six thousand dollars for one of these garments. It's a quasi-custom-made dress, in that a woman can go into Neiman Marcus and, if she doesn't like a particular print that the dress is made in, our salespeople are highly trained and they know which of the fabrics can be substituted. It's quasi-custom-made but it's made in a factory.

"The clothes are cut only as the orders come in. We write up cutting tickets with the style number, description, and the number we need in each size. We send the factory the fabric, lining, trimming, shoulder pads, everything. Once the garments are made we get them back here, inspect them, and ship them to the stores. And that's, basically, how it's done." Basically.

Bill Blass *May 4*

An Italian fabric sales rep named Joanna, who has obviously worked with Bill before, walks into his office, says hello, and immediately unpacks a bag of fabrics and drapes them over the back of the couch. With her is a very nervous-looking Italian man who has just opened a new textile-manufacturing firm.

Bill and Laura begin working, quickly as always. They pick up piece after piece of fabric and hold them against themselves. First they look down at the fabrics draped against their bodies, then they inspect their reflections in the full-length mirror that hangs on the wall by the door, and finally they walk to the window, and examine the fabrics in natural light.

As Bill and Laura crisscross the room, keeping up a running dialogue as they go, Joanna and the textile man circle around them, holding the edge of a fabric here, spreading out another one there. My overall impression is one of random motion—like particles in a chemistry experiment, these four people collide to form a group, and then separate and come together again in a new arrangement.

"I always like plaid but this is a big one," says Bill, discarding a swatch.

"We could do this with this," says Laura, picking up two slightly different plaid fabrics and holding them up against each other. "It's expensive-looking."

"Yes. They like that," says Bill, referring to his customers. Laura places the plaids, along with the other fabrics they like, on Bill's desk.

"Bill, is this too Blassport?" says Laura, referring to Bill's licensed lower-priced line of ready-to-wear as she holds up a brown plaid.

"No, but it's too Armani," he answers. They scrap that one.

"We don't have any stripes like this," says Laura, holding up a beige fabric with a thin blue stripe running through it. She walks to the mirror and drapes it over herself.

Just then a private customer from Washington, D.C., appears in the doorway holding a deep brown gown with very full and puffy sleeves against herself. "How's this for New Year's Eve?" she says of the dress, which is from the fall collection.

"It's perfect," says Bill.

The customer goes back to the showroom, and Bill and Laura walk over to Bill's desk and review the fabrics they have chosen. "You've lost weight, Joanna," Bill says to the fabric rep after they are finished. "I'm so fat I can't stand it."

All of them—Bill, Laura, Joanna, and the nervous man—light cigarettes. Then Bill stands and tells Joanna, "We need dressy fabrics."

"But times have changed now," Joanna says, as the four circle around the desk, tapping their cigarettes over the ashtray that stands next to a half-full cup of black coffee. There are already four cigarette butts in the ashtray. "Who gets dressed up to go to the theater now?" she says. "Or to go anywhere? Life is much more casual."

"There are six parties in New York every night where people dress up and I try to go to two of them," Bill says. "There's a real shortage of evening clothes. Price is no object. Price doesn't enter into it at all. I just can't find what I need. Those women who go south have loads of daytime pants and skirts and sweaters but when it comes to six o'clock they need evening clothes. I'd like a group of evening pajamas and I'd like to make long evening dresses out of white linen," he says.

Every year, Bill starts creating spring by designing a resort collection for "the women who go south" to wear on warm-weather vacations. Comprised of about forty-five pieces, it is offered only to his biggest customers—stores like Neiman Marcus, Bergdorf Goodman, Saks Fifth Avenue, and I. Magnin.

"What?" says Joanna, in a tone that says she disagrees with Bill about the use of white linen. "They'll get so wrinkled."

"It's a great idea," says the textile man, who has not yet developed the relationship with Blass that Joanna has.

"In New York, Chicago, and Dallas they want evening clothes," says Bill. "It's hard to buy from Italy because they have such a different lifestyle from us. This has been a season where it's very difficult to buy."

"I had a feeling when I came that I didn't have the right things," says Joanna.

"Well, honey, you didn't. Maybe you can scout around for us some more. Try some of the smaller people."

"The smaller people don't know how to deal with the export market," she says. "You don't need problems."

"We already have problems," says Laura. "We're going to be stuck for the first group." By this she means resort.

"Come here," says Bill, leading Joanna and the nervous textile man out into the showroom, where six racks of fall clothes are hanging. "Look," he says. "Four racks are cocktail and two racks are daytime. That shows you how important evening is."

After Joanna and the mill owner leave, Bill tells me, "Evening is always a problem. There are no textile designers left in America. We have to rely on the Europeans, who often have no concept of what American life is like. We've seen almost every fabric house, and still there is a shortage of evening."

Just then another fabric salesman, carrying an overstuffed canvas suitcase, is shown into Bill's office. The man says hello, quickly heads for the couch, unpacks his suitcase and drapes the fabrics over the back of the sofa. He, too, has apparently worked with Bill before, since he doesn't waste time on small talk. The one thing he does say is that the fabrics are very expensive.

"Price is not the issue here," Bill says. "All I care about is quality and whether or not anybody else bought it. Price doesn't matter." If only Liz Claiborne could hear such a thing, I think, but then, Bill is designing for a whole 'nother world.

Liz Claiborne *May 6*

Having changed the line to comply with the sales department's requests, Collection's designers are now ready to show the results to Liz. They will also show her their preliminary concepts for Spring II, which will be in the stores in March and April of 1989.

Besides polishing the Spring I collections, they have spent this past weeks looking at fabrics for Spring II and will, today, begin conceptualizing that next Collection.

At 10 A.M. Liz, carrying a Styrofoam cup filled with black coffee and wearing faded jeans and an oversized white turtleneck, walks into Dennis's sleek, black-and-white office followed by Judith, Katy, and Cheryl Rosenthal, vice-president of textile research for women's sportswear. All sit at the small, round conference table, and Judith updates Liz on the changes they've made on the line. "The linings in the suit group are now black and white," she says.

"We don't have to do black and white," says Liz. "We don't have to run away from the idea of bright linings. I think we should just tone them down. I think a red-and-white dot would be acceptable to the world."

"Jerry just made everyone so nervous," says Dennis.

"I know," says Liz. "But no one is against bright linings. He's just against lime green and big dots. It was a very brave thing for us to do."

Dennis shows Liz some new fabric swatches he's chosen for blouses. As opposed to large dots, these have tiny pindots. Pointing to a fuchsia swatch, Liz says, "I'm even worried about that color as a blouse. We should make it red."

"So we'll do white with red pindots," says Dennis.

"No," says Liz. "Red with white dots."

Liz changes some other colors and fabrics and then says, "This is going to be communicated to the right people? If it's in Taiwan I'm particularly nervous. We must see swatches."

"We've done this fabric before," says Cheryl.

"That's not good enough for me," says Liz. "I'm getting very difficult in my old age. We have to see swatches."

They discuss some other changes and then start working on Spring II. "This is delivered March first, right?" says Liz.

"Yeah," says Judith, who then reviews how this year's Spring II line sold in the stores. Any runaway best-sellers would be repeated in a slightly altered version. "The navy-and-cream group was good; City Linen was not so good; White Out was good and Wood Block was so-so."

"Wood Block has done well in more sophisticated stores," says Dennis.

"What surprises me is that the cropped white shirt has done well on its own," says Liz. "Cropped!"

"What fabrics do we want?" says Judith.

"We don't want stretch," says Liz.

"I think we need a major linen group," says Dennis.

"That's where we can have color," says Liz. "Anne Taylor had these great bright things in their window that looked so great. They just took them down.

Every time I passed them I thought they looked fabulous. Let's think of who we're competing against—Finity, Jones."

"What does Finity run at this time?" says Judith.

Liz doesn't answer her directly but says, "Certainly Finity's goods went up in price."

"I've been inquiring about linen," says Cheryl. "Prices have skyrocketed."

"We've never run linen in summer before," says Dennis. "I like the idea of a small, tight group for summer based on the selling Saks is having now on the special linen we did in red, white, blue, and black. We shipped it to them on April fifteenth. That's the tail end of Spring II and in New York you can't even wear linen yet." The weather has been unseasonably cold, adversely affecting sales of many of the warm-weather clothes that are in the stores now.

"Well, that's unusual," says Liz.

"Saks is selling twenty-five percent of our linen group a week. The jacket is ninety-six dollars and the finish on it is great. Whatever that finish was."

"We can never be there again," says Liz, referring to the low cost of the jacket. "We used to make fabric purchases way in advance so it cost us less."

Katy shows Liz a knit vest she bought in Paris. "Could we do something like this?" she says. Liz feels the fabric and nods.

Judith walks out and returns with an assortment of bright yarns she brought back from Europe. "Maybe we could do a couple of knit groups?" says Judith, placing the fifteen different yarns on the table.

Liz places pieces of green, yellow, and lavender yarns next to each other. "These colors you could get in polyester," she says. Indicating the bright blue and orange, she says, "These Howard Johnson's colors you never would."

"What do we think of print dressing?" says Judith. "Is that Spring II?"

"Yes," says Liz. "The customers understand it.

"What could be our new color to match with white?" says Liz. "Forest green and white is beautiful."

Judith shows Liz an ad from a foreign magazine that features a man in a white shirt and pants reclining on an Oriental carpet. "Yes, those could be our colors," says Liz, referring to white combined with strong solid colors in the Oriental rug.

"We need a cotton group," says Judith. "Cotton is important."

"Is it?" says Liz.

Judith leaves and returns carrying a jacket and skirt made of a black, gray, and white small floral-print fabric.

"Oh, that's fabulous," says Liz. "I think this is new, a printed cotton suit group. She doesn't have this in her closet. There's nothing wrong with having a black-and-white group."

"Never," says Dennis.

Liz feels the fabric. "It's a Claude Barthalemy," says Judith.

Jay walks in, and, looking up, Dennis says, "We're noodling."

"Good." says Jay. He sits down and says, "You need two colors that work well together. When you have five colors like this"—he picks up a bunch of yarn in his hands—"and we make it work in the showroom, it never works out on the floor. Just two colors, like navy and white, are great because each piece works with the others."

"What did you decide about the print?" he says. Liz and Art had talked about changing some of the colors in the tropical print. "My philosophy is, when you have to work on something for so long and it's so tortured, you should move on."

Liz says, "Why don't we take the background of the tortured print and put . . ."

"I'm gonna die if you change that print," says Dennis, cutting her off. "Come hell or high water I want to show it to you the way that it is because it's gonna be a winner."

"It's got to be," says Jay rather ominously.

Between designing and fitting Spring I bodies and conceptualizing Spring II, the Collection designers must also put together the key looks from their holiday line for two upcoming presentations. The first will be held for the benefit of the company's salespeople who—two hundred strong—will fly in from around the country in two weeks. The second, a runway fashion show for press and retailers, will be held on May 27.

At the sales presentation four models will wear the most important outfits, and the sportswear division heads will present every single piece on their lines in every color in which the pieces will be available. The salespeople will then ask questions about the line so that they will know how to pitch it to the retailers. After this presentation the holiday line will be turned over to the sales department, which will practice its pitch.

In the meantime, the designers, in conjunction with the Liz Claiborne Creative Resources department, which handles the firm's advertising and public relations, will prepare the runway show. This means they will choose models and accessories and decide the order that the outfits will be shown on the runway. Then, three or four days before the show, Liz and Jay will review the proposed runway presentation. It is only on the morning of May 27, at a dress rehearsal for the show (held an hour before the real thing), that anyone will actually see the models in the clothes. It is on this morning that we will once again see the Liz Claiborne design team.

As the designers attend to specific details, Liz is making herself available to the different divisions as needed. Plus, she and the other senior corporate executives are preparing for the firm's annual meeting on May 19. We will catch up with them then.

Arnold Scaasi *May 13*

Knowing that Arnold is easiest to reach at home in the morning, I called him yesterday at 10:15 A.M. He got on the phone and said he's been busily fitting furs and that he has a final fitting with Princess Yasmin Aga Khan tomorrow for the dress she will be wearing to the Alzheimer's benefit. "I'm not sure if she'd want to be named in your book," he said. "She's very private. My clients are funny about publicity. They feel used. Like I just got a call on May fourth from Laura Steinberg saying she was angry that I had released a sketch of her wedding dress to *Women's Wear Daily*. I'd *cleared* that with her and Gayfryd when they were here for a fitting. I sent it over to *Women's Wear Daily* and they agreed not to run it before the day of the wedding."

"They didn't run it before the *day* of the wedding," I said. "But they did run it before the wedding itself."

"Whatever," said Arnold. "My point is, the wedding was when? April eighteenth? I've seen her three times since then and she calls me on May fourth to complain? You just never know how someone will take these things." With instruction to "not let on as to why [I'm] there" he told me to come to his salon at noon today and "just sort of sit there."

The rather small salon is on the fourth floor of 681 Fifth Avenue, the building right next door to Fortunoff's. The waiting area is lined with banquettes and, on a cabinet by the rear wall, stand framed photos of brides (Patricia Kluge and Patty Davis Raynes among them) and clients (Elizabeth Taylor and Beverly Sills) in their Scaasi dresses. Their dresses evolved in much the same way as Yasmin Khan's.

Six weeks ago, knowing that she needed a special dress to wear to the Alzheimer's benefit, Yasmin called Arnold and made an appointment to come and see his made-to-order collection. She ended up picking one of the most complicated dresses in the collection. Made of skintight silk taffeta, it was draped from top to bottom with minuscule folds of fabric. The original sample, however, was lime green and fuchsia, and sleeveless. Yasmin wanted hers to be pink and yellow, and she wanted sleeves.

Her measurements were taken and a fitting dummy was padded to those same measurements. Working with the dummy, a draper made a muslin sample for the dress's slip. (A slip is always sewn into a dress like this, because the draping, consisting of many pieces of fabric, must be attached to something. Obviously it can't be sewn onto the person, so the slip is used as a second skin.) Following the muslin as a pattern, a cutter cut out the slip and then a sewer put it together. A fitter fitted the slip on the dummy and then it went to a dressmaker, who corrected the slip after the fitting. At this point Yasmin came in to fit the slip with a fitter and the salon's female director, who wrote down what changes were necessary. Corrections were made and then the sleeves and the bottom of the dress were basted onto the slip, and Yasmin returned for another fitting.

At this point Arnold stepped in and altered the dress's proportions. He changed the direction of the draping so that it had a more flattering line and made the flounce on the bottom back of the dress wider so that it dragged on the floor slightly, making the dress appear longer.

For Yasmin's next fitting, the entire dress was basted together. Corrections again needed to be made, and the dress was taken apart and pieced together again by a dressmaker and a finisher, who does meticulous sewing by hand. With the dress almost finished, Yasmin had another fitting. Still more corrections, until finally, today, she and Arnold will take a last look at the finished product.

According to Arnold's somewhat generous estimates, three people worked full time for twenty days to make this dress. Each of the workers earns $20 an hour, which means the labor cost of the dress could be as high as $9,600. "Wow," Arnold said, after he tallied the labor costs. "I'm going to raise the price of my dresses." While not revealing how much Yasmin paid for the dress, he said the price could be as high as $14,000.

But, he added, "Yasmin's dress was very complicated to make, with all those little tuckings for the draping being done by hand. That's very time-consuming." The other dresses don't involve anywhere near that type of labor.

Quite curious about this dress, which sounds more like a work of art than a garment, I follow Arnold's receptionist down a short hallway lined with four doors, three closed and one open. Outside the open door on the right, a tray of costume jewelry stands on a table. Inside, Arnold is on his knees, pinning the hem of a yellow-and-black plaid dress worn by an older blond woman whom I don't recognize.

Arnold doesn't introduce me to his customer, but she and I say hello. I stand in the doorway watching him hem the dress and listen as Arnold advises his customer on what clothes to take with her to a ranch in August. As the woman inspects her dress in the full-length three-way mirror, Arnold looks at me and points at the door across the hall. It is behind this door that Yasmin Khan is being fitted.

A seamstress walks out of Yasmin Khan's room and Arnold says to her, "Tell them I want to see the dress before she takes it off." He leaves the blond woman to try on her next outfit and heads across the hall, motioning for me to come with him.

Inside the room there's nothing much to see—just a beautiful wealthy woman wearing a beautiful, intricately draped, very tight, slim pink gown that is long in the back and short in the front. The short front reveals the yellow fabric lining the back of the gown.

As he inspects the dress, Arnold tries to make small talk with Yasmin, but she seems startled by both his and my presence.

"Have you finished seating?" Arnold says to her of the benefit.

"No," she replies. "We were seating this morning and we'll seat this afternoon."

She seems very uncomfortable with my being there so I avoid eye contact, squinting at the dress and taking notes as Arnold says, "I want the back panel to stick out." I'm trying to act like one of his assistants. As I stare at the dress, I realize how amazingly intricate it is, how difficult it would be to get all of this draping exactly right.

"Have you worn your pantsuit yet?" Arnold says.

"What?" Yasmin answers, very nervously.

"You've gotten your pantsuit, you know."

"Oh. Yes. I know." She picks at the fabric around her stomach as if it's too loose. The meaning behind this gesture is immediately and correctly interpreted by Arnold. "It's a dress, you know," he says teasingly. "It's got to move a little." He pats her lightly on the hipbone and fixes the draping that she's displaced.

Later he says to me, "I think a lot of designers think doing made-to-order is easy; that if you can design ready-to-wear you can design made-to-order. It's not true. You have to have a very special personality to do made-to-order clothes because your contact with the client is very important. You have to put up with her foibles, with what she needs and wants."

These wants go beyond a desire for skintight dresses. Most women, for instance, demand exclusivity, something that even Arnold, as a couturier, cannot always guarantee, since all the custom-made clothes are available to all of his customers. What he can offer, however, is his knowledge of who bought what dress, in what color, and where the customer is planning to wear it. On the day before an important event, his salon becomes information central, with the ladies calling up to find out who will be wearing what.

Carroll Petrie, wife of mega-philanthropist Milton Petrie, prefers to wear Scaasi made-to-order dresses because, she says, "He's pretty careful that two people who know one another don't dress alike. He's very diplomatic. I've rarely seen two of his dresses in the same room. I like Bill and Oscar but I'm reluctant to buy from them because their dresses are going into department stores all over the country and I don't know how many times I'll see myself coming and going in them."

As far as his ready-to-wear is concerned, Arnold says, "I can't tell who's going to wear what where. I can't control it. But for made-to-order they ask me, 'Can I wear my blue, red or green dress, or is someone else wearing it?'

"I have a policy of letting our clients know who will be wearing what. If someone had a dress specially made for an occasion, we will call the other women who have that dress and ask them if they could wear something else."

The women, according to Arnold, usually say, " 'Oh, thank you for letting me know. I would have died if I had seen someone else in my dress.' I mean, they're very nice ladies.

"The only time someone said no," he chuckles, "was when Patty Raynes, poor girl, had the same dress as Barbara Walters and Barbara said, when she had the dress made, 'I'm going to wear it to the big museum party in December.' " This party is an annual benefit held at the Metropolitan Museum to benefit its Costume Institute.

"I knew Barbara planned it to wear it there," Arnold says, "and that her husband had bought her a piece of jewelry for it, so I called Patty and said, 'Would you wear another dress?' and Patty said, 'No. I won't. You've sold this dress to so many people. Three of my best friends have this dress and they all call me and say, 'Please don't wear that dress because I'm wearing it. If I don't wear the dress to this I won't be able to wear it for the rest of the season.'

"So I said, 'OK, you wear it.' So they both wore it. I told Barbara Patty would be wearing it and it turned out fine because they never saw each other. They were on opposite ends of the room. The only time it ever came out that they were wearing the same dress was when *W* printed photographs of them, but not in the same pictures. But it was funny. It wasn't a terrible thing." Other women, however, might not have been amused.

Liz Claiborne *May 19*

The Liz Claiborne annual meeting is being held at the company's large, modern production facility in North Bergen, New Jersey. To make it easier for stockholders and executives to get here, the firm rented shuttle buses to transport them from, and back to, Manhattan.

After being let off at the main entrance, stockholders walk through a mazelike series of hallways, with employees stationed at each turn telling them which way to go. Their final destination is the building's cafeteria, where lime green, red and yellow plastic chairs have been set up in rows to face a raised platform. By the entrance stands a table piled high with cookies and coffee. While guests help themselves, Jay Margolis and Jerry Chazen work the crowd.

At 2:55, Jerry comes over and says they had expected more people, based on the number of calls they got asking for directions. Of the three hundred chairs set up in the room, half are empty. "Well," he says, as he heads for the podium. "That's show biz."

At exactly three o'clock Liz, Art, and Harvey Falk, executive vice-president, enter from behind the podium and join Jerry behind the raised table. Liz, wearing an orange jacket, lime green T-shirt, and taupe pants from the Dana Buchman collection, walks to the microphone and opens the meeting. After stockholders approve the election of two new directors, Liz sits down, and Harvey Falk walks up to the microphone. "The company has been in existence for seven years," he says, referring to the firm's life as a public company. "It has been a time of celebration and 1987 was no exception as sales and earnings hit an all-time high.

"But," he continues, "for the first time, our shared pride is mixed with frustration because of the level at which our stock is trading. Around this time last year, our stock was in the low thirties and was seen as a growth stock like The Gap and The Limited. Last June our stock hit an all-time high of 39⅛.

"Then," he says, as the stockholders sit in total silence, "starting in mid-

August, specialty stores fell out of favor. Liz Claiborne shares were painted under the same brush and then came October nineteenth. Our stock, by October twenty-third, had fallen to sixteen and a half, less than one-half of its level a scant four months ago. Because of an overall erosion of confidence, we expect the second quarter of 1988 to be down from our record second quarter last year. The remainder of 1988 remains a concern, with a number of factors influencing it.

"It's no secret that some of our divisions had some problems, and it wasn't just the hemline issue. We also had excess inventory. Retailing is in a state of tumult. There is a momentary climate of uncertainty as all these consolidations take place.

"As a company we feel we've turned our product around. We see 1988 as a year that will turn our business around." He pauses for dramatic effect and says, "We face disappointed shareholders. Many of us have been hurt by the stock's low level. I can assure you that at every one of our board meetings we've looked at our stock price and talked about what to do about it."

Harvey then proceeds to detail the performance of, and changes at, various divisions. Women's sportswear, he says, is the largest group of divisions, accounting for 70 percent of the company's business this year. He stresses that Collection will receive greater acceptance because of its approach for the working woman.

"The company has opened five First Issue stores," he says. "They are in Manhasset, Woodbridge, Paramus, Georgetown, and outside of Atlanta." Plus, he says, the firm is developing product for the large-size market and is planning to open a lingerie division. Then he opens the meeting up to questions. Immediately, hands shoot up in the audience.

Q.: *What is the purpose of First Issue, as opposed to The Gap?*
ART: Our competitors have buyers that shop the markets and then adopt or knock off the merchandise. Our designs are our own and we are able to track them throughout their production cycles. We want to fall into the gap between The Gap and Anne Taylor.
Q.: *How will the trade bill before Congress affect you if it passes?*
ART: We live constantly in an uncertain trading environment. The odds are against such a bill passing but we'd be kidding ourselves if we thought we were home free. We are diversifying our sourcing base, going into such places as Central America, the Caribbean, and increasing our domestic sourcing. We will be considerably less adversely affected than our competitors. Our strategy is to create a global sourcing base so that we are not too reliant on one country.

Q.: *How will your Liz Claiborne stores differ from First Issue and where will they be opening?*

JERRY: We are opening prototype Liz Claiborne stores to, in a larger sense, show retailers how to present our merchandise and better serve the customer. No locations have been signed yet.

HARVEY: They will house the same Liz Claiborne merchandise as is in the stores. It is different from First Issue.

Q.: *Won't you basically be competing with department stores for existing customers?*

JERRY: The main purpose will be to help retailers do a better job. We do have a role model out there in Ralph Lauren. He opened a store on Madison Avenue and that store helped the business at nearby retailers. Our merchandise is sold in 3,500 doors.

ART: We are very aggressively seeking to open Liz Claiborne stores offshore. We see them in the Far East, West Germany, and the EEC. It's something we call Project Consumer.

Q.: *We're not seeing your clothes made here.*

HARVEY: Ten percent of our production is domestic. We are a billion-dollar company. That means that one hundred million of our product is produced here.

Q.: *I heard that clothes are being taken to North Carolina and dumped or sold off-price.*

The executives look stumped for a moment. Finally Harvey stands up and, attempting to look serious, says, "I would hope that it is not Liz Claiborne because that is not one of our distribution policies."

Q.: *Do you have any plans to franchise?*

JERRY: No. [Behind me a woman whispers to her friend, "They want to control it themselves."]

Q.: *What do you see as the fashion trends for the coming year?*

LIZ: To the knee and lower; the more formal approach to career dressing, which we are really concentrating on. Lizwear is being cleaned up and pressed. Color is being injected in a much stronger way. The dress division is offering career and dressier dinner dresses.

Q.: *Have you been approached by anyone who wants to take over your company?*

HARVEY: No.

Q.: *With the new administration it looks like we might run into a recession. Is it wise for us to be spending this much money on expansion?*

HARVEY: We try to estimate, as best we can, what the buying power of the consumer will be and act accordingly.

ART: These are in-house start-ups so there is a minimal capital investment on our part. We have large sizes, First Issue, and we're looking into lingerie, but it's all being done in-house.

HARVEY: I'd like to take some more questions, but what's going to happen is, as it gets later, you're all going to hit traffic going back through the Lincoln Tunnel so I think we'll just take only one more question.

"That's terrible," says the man next to me. "He shouldn't cut off questions like that."

One stockholder, the man who asked about the dumping of clothes in North Carolina, stands up and says, "I'd like to congratulate you on a job well done and to say that I believe with God's help it will continue." He claps and the other stockholders follow suit as Art laughs and says, "Everything that's happened, has happened with God's help."

The same stockholder then says loudly, "Bless this house, O Lord we pray. Keep it safe by night and day." He then says, "I think Liz deserves a nice round of applause."

Liz smiles, raises her hand in acknowledgment, and the show is over.

Bill Blass *May 19*

Traffic is, in fact, pretty light on the way back to Manhattan. At home, with some time to kill before going off to meet Bill at 7 P.M. at the New York Public Library's Ten Treasures Benefit Dinner, I thumb through the new (June) issue of *Vogue*, which arrived in today's mail. Inside the magazine I spot a photo of Bill standing between Annette Reed and Sharon Hoge. Sharon, wife of *Daily News* publisher Jim Hoge, and Bill made up one of the ten teams who were asked by the library to create tableaux around one of the library's ten most treasured books, maps, or prints. They are posing next to a book placed on a large pedestal, with oversized books scattered on the floor in front of them. The accompanying story by William and Chessy Rayner is about the Ten Treasures benefit. Happily, I settle in to read about what to expect tonight.

As I read, my happiness turns to dismay and then to horror. Not only have the Rayners written the story as if the Ten Treasures benefit has already happened, but they say it has set a whole new standard for entertaining for the people who "not long ago" forked over hundreds of dollars for tickets to charity dinners and then were forced to eat food "sure to run a close second to that on a no-frills flight" and endure waiters who "would clash the dishes together as if they had received their training playing cymbals in a marching band."

But, they write, things "seem to be changing for the better" . . . if the party "held in May for the New York Public Library . . . [is] any indication." Calling the library evening, as well as another party that also has not yet taken place, "the heavy metal of social events" they say these two gatherings "set the standard by which all other events are judged."

Lying through their teeth, they tell the 1,202,471 *Vogue* readers that the library benefit's menu "by Glorious Food [was] superior, the service impeccable, and the decorations perhaps unmatched since Francis I entertained Henry VIII on the Field of the Cloth of Gold."

"To call the exhibitions the library mounted for its evening 'decorations,'" the story says, "is as inaccurate as to say that Cheops's pyramid was really built to embellish a package of Camel cigarettes. Indeed, they were among the most creative efforts ever undertaken."

Now mind you, since magazines work three months in advance, this story for the June issue had to be filed by the Rayners in March. The exhibitions were just set up in the library this week, so there's no way in the world the Rayners could have seen these "most creative efforts ever undertaken."

The story goes on: "The caterer served a superb dinner to twelve hundred in two of the city's most beautiful public rooms. Those who had the strength stayed after dinner to dance in the hall named after one of Vincent Astor's forebears."

How could *Vogue* have printed this story? I think, and why? Since Chessy is the stepdaughter of the chairman of Condé Nast (which owns *Vogue*, as well as *Mademoiselle*, *Self*, *Glamour*, and *The New Yorker* among many other publications) and Bill is editorial business manager of *Vogue* and Sue Newhouse is general chairman of the evening, the answer to the first is pretty clear. The answer to the second, however, will not become apparent until later in the evening.

Tonight's cocktail hour is scheduled to start at 7 P.M. and, although people tend to come to these parties an hour late, Bill, as usual, is one of the first to arrive. He heads immediately for the tableau he and Sharon Hoge had party designer Robert Isabell create for them. Called "Maps: Voyages on Paper," it is located in a small corridor on the first floor of the library. The corridor was transformed into a ship deck by fake walls with portholes, showcasing the library's collection of rare maps, and a woven net ceiling. To give the exhibit the feeling of a cruise ship bon voyage party, the floor was covered with confetti, and now champagne is being served, noise-making poppers are being handed out, and two male photographers dressed in beige trench coats and old-fashioned reporter's hats with *Daily News* cards tucked into the brims are pretending to take everyone's picture.

"There were supposed to be copies of *Traveler* here and there aren't any," Bill says, looking around trying to find copies of the Condé Nast publication.

"Did you happen to catch the Rayners' piece on this party?" I ask as he paces the length of the exhibit, looking for the magazines.

"Yes," he replies. "She wrote it as if it already happened." The fact that *Vogue* gave it such a glowing review doesn't faze him in the least, and he goes off to take a quick look at the other exhibits before the crowds start pouring in and he must stay near his tableau to greet them.

The location of Bill's exhibit isn't exactly prime. Next to him is Sue Newhouse's display, inspired by the library's copy of *The Wonderful Wizard of Oz*. In this magical-looking tableau, under extremely hot spotlights, the Wizard of Oz sits on a golden throne surrounded by green balloons, gold streamers, and red poppies. Recordings of "Follow the Yellow Brick Road" (which sounds like it's being played at too high a speed) and "Ease On Down the Road," play, over and over and *over* again.

Bill returns to his spot just as, drinks in hand, crowds start flocking toward this exhibit. Most of the crowd stands on a slow-moving line, waiting to receive one of the big red plastic hearts, silver medals, and paper diplomas that the Wizard is handing out.

The line, unfortunately, cuts right into the tiny main area of Bill's bon voyage party, and the spotlights set up on the floor in Bill's area to illuminate the Wizard are making the space scorchingly hot. While Bill, somehow, chats above all the noise, Sharon hands out the poppers, shaped like champagne bottles, and says, "Pull the string!" When they do, the little bottles go "Pop!" and Sharon and the string-puller yell, "Yeah!" as the photographers flash their very real flashbulbs.

Now I've got to tell you, at first glance—or first experience—this is very cute. But, as the night goes on, and as more and more people crowd into the line to see the Wizard, and as the same two songs play over and over again, and as the spotlights get hotter and hotter, and as the photographers flash their strobes over and over, and as Bill repeatedly mops the sweat pouring down his forehead with a white handkerchief, the scene begins to lose its charm. Bill, however, is as charming as ever. Bill's eyes never stop scanning the room, taking notice of everyone near him. Every time he sees a camera pointing in his direction he slowly turns so that he is facing it. He knows that the photographers are there to take his picture. Unlike some other public figures whose business success depends on name and face recognition, Bill is never coy.

As I stand here, getting more and more claustrophobic, I think about how the pictures in tomorrow's papers will most likely make all of this look like so much fun. Right now, though, I'm wondering how Bill can stand it. I have to leave intermittently to get some air, but now that the crowds are here, Bill doesn't leave his spot once.

The rest of the party, by the way, really is magical. Orchestra music drifts through the library's spacious marble hallways as obviously amused people dressed in black tie stroll around, drinks in hand, looking at the ten exhibits that are scattered over the building's three stories.

On the second floor, Ralph Lauren, who designed a huge Indian tepee filled with American Indian treasures, stands, almost shyly, with his wife. They talk to anyone who comes up to them, but mostly they talk to each other. Also on this floor is Carolyne Roehm's 19th-century tableau. Inspired by the library's autographed Franz Liszt manuscripts, it is set in a drawing room where a pianist is playing Liszt. Carolyne herself doesn't arrive until a short time before dinner is served.

I head up to the third floor where I am shocked to see a tableau designed by Mica Ertegun and her business partner, Chessy Rayner, the co-author of the *Vogue* article. Nothing like tooting your own project's horn in your own column, I think.

As I walk back to Bill's exhibit I leaf through the evening's press kit and see that the Condé Nast corporation was one of the evening's sponsors. Its overeager promotion of an event it was so closely involved with is somewhat excusable only when one considers that the evening raised $1.5 million for the library. Still, what ever happened to truth in the press?

Bill Blass *May 23–August 25*

Item: *Women's Wear Daily* reports that Bill Blass is having tea today with Nancy Reagan in Washington. Will he be offering her advice on what to wear for her upcoming trip to the Soviet Union? the newspaper asks. "Only Billy and Nancy know for sure."

We leave Bill now for a few months and pick up with him again on August 25, at a time when he will be designing spring. Later this month he will head for Vienna. His workrooms will be closed for the month of June, and Bill himself, when he gets back from vacation, will make a few store appearances promoting his early fall line. On June 13, for instance, he will attend a trunk show at Neiman Marcus in Dallas with a *New York Times* reporter in tow. (For the story that ran in the *Times* on June 22, a Neiman's executive told the reporter that Bill's charisma "adds twenty to twenty-five percent to our sales.")

Overall, however, things will be pretty quiet until after July 4, when the workrooms will reopen and Bill will start designing his resort collection. He will open this resort collection to the stores in his showroom on August 11 and will incorporate its most successful pieces into his spring line. But more on that on August 25. As we leave Bill preparing for his vacation, let's cross the street and see what's happening at Liz Claiborne.

Liz Claiborne *May 27*

In the Collection and Lizsport showroom, on the seventh floor of 1441 Broadway, a runway has been set up along its length on one wall. The other side of the runway is bordered by rows of about 250 plastic chairs. At 9 A.M. these chairs are filled with Liz Claiborne employees who have come to watch the dress rehearsal for the Holiday fashion show. The actual show is scheduled for 10 A.M. Since we will be in Chicago with Bill Blass on the day of Liz Claiborne's spring show we will watch the Holiday presentation to see how shows here are handled.

For Jerry Chazen, the company's annual meeting represented "show biz." For the sportswear designers, however, that is what today is all about. As music plays, and the models, dressed first in Lizwear, then Lizsport, and, finally, Collection, walk up and down the runway, Liz, wearing faded blue jeans, a white shirt, tan belt, and white sneakers, sits in the front row, writing the things she doesn't like about the show on her lineup. She scribbles furiously as a model, who is obviously not wearing a bra, walks out with her jacket flung open and the outline of her erect nipples showing through her T-shirt.

After the dress rehearsal, Liz, Ellen, and two women from the Creative Resources department walk into a small office backstage. "We have to speed up the show or eliminate some things," says Liz. "My real problem is with the models. They come out looking like they've just rolled out of bed. I feel like putting a firecracker under them."

"Tell us what models you don't like so that we don't use them next time," says the stylist from Creative Resources.

"'Don't like' is an understatement," says Liz. She looks at her lineup and names three models.

"They are print models, not runway," says the stylist.

"You can tell," says Liz. She tells the stylist which outfits to drop and which to restyle with new accessories, and then she says, "And tell them to put their jackets on. They tend to wear them too far back. Poor Al Lohn (a senior vice-president of production) had a heart attack when he saw those jackets. And this one," says Liz, pointing to the braless model's name on the lineup, "she needs a bra."

"I thought that was the highlight of the show, personally," says Jay.

Liz rolls her eyes at him. "Margaret needs blush," she says of one of the models. "They all look like they're dying from hunger. They all have scrawny necks."

All walk into the larger office, which has been turned into an extremely crowded makeshift dressing room for twenty-four models and their twenty-four dressers. The models are changing into the first outfits they will wear in the show and the stylist starts implementing the changes Liz has asked for. Liz, meanwhile, sends someone to get a man's tie from another division, and someone else to find colorful pocket squares and black belts that will replace some brown ones.

The models who do not need changes look bored. Some are reading magazines, but most are chitchatting with one another. The room is very claustrophobic and it is hard to hear the directions the stylist is calling out. "Will everyone please be quiet," Reggie yells. Most of the models listen but some continue whispering to each other as they sit on the floor and wait for the show to start.

At 10:15 Jay comes back in and says, "Are we almost ready? Start lining people up. We're really late."

Liz adjusts a jacket on a model. "The shoulder pads should be on your shoulder," she says. "You also wear a white coat, don't you? Make sure it's on you."

As the girls start lining up, Liz says, "Go out there and have fun! These are fun clothes. This is a fun show. Fun, fun, fun! Even if it's not fun for you."

The models look at her with blank faces. For the first time I understand the origin of the phrase "cattle call." This is how magazine editors refer to the sessions that models call "go-sees," when they all show up and are looked over to see if they fit the look that the company wants. The girls are looking at Liz with the wide, blank eyes of cows grazing in a pasture.

Judith, who has already designed 25 percent of the spring line, and Dennis do the first check on the girls, then the models check themselves in a full-length mirror (usually three at a time, staggering their positions so that each of them can see). Then they go on to a final inspection by Liz, who is standing just inside the exit to the runway.

The show starts at 10:18. At the last minute Liz notices that three models in one group are wearing the same color pants and sends one of them back to change into a different color. "She won't make it back in time," says Reggie, looking very worried.

"If she comes, she comes," says Liz calmly. "If not we'll drop it."

The model returns and and checks herself in the mirror. The other girls have gone out already. "Come on, you look terrific," Liz says, putting her hand on the model's arm. The model impatiently shakes off Liz's hand and looks at herself one more time.

"Oh," says Liz, her voice indicating surprise and affront.

"Let's go," says the stylist, and the model, finally satisfied with the way she looks, goes out.

The other girls are coming back from the stage, taking their jackets off as they go. "Who sings this?" says one.

"Suzanne Vega," says another.

"Right." Other models dance as they wait for their turn to walk onstage.

Liz looks at a model wearing a black bomber jacket with a white scarf and she tucks one end of the scarf inside the jacket saying, "This makes it softer, less aviatorish."

The model who had brushed off Liz's hand comes out and says, "I'm sorry. I can't walk out without looking in the mirror."

The braless model with the erect nipples now has her jacket buttoned. As the show ends, the designers line up for their bows. "Hi," Liz says to knitwear designer Betty Bentsen, kissing her on the cheek. "When did you roll in off the plane?" Katy, the knitwear designer for Collection, is still in Hong Kong working on sweaters for Spring.

The designers walk onstage for their bows, but Liz and Dennis stay backstage clapping loudly. Dennis leans against a wall and, slapping his palms together slowly, says, "I feel like I'm the clapper on *Laugh-In*."

Liz laughs as the two of them applaud their own work.

On the way out of the store buyers who viewed the show grab the huge chocolate-covered strawberries set out on the table by the elevator. (There are also sticky pastries and coffee.) On the way down, three buyers are eating strawberries, holding them by the stems as if they were ice-cream pops.

"Hmmm."

"Sweet."

"I missed those," says another buyer, eying them hungrily.

"Well, I ate your share."

"I thought this line was much better than their last one," says one strawberry-less buyer to another. "How are your stores doing with Liz Claiborne?"

"Good now."

"We're taking a bath."

On the way out, the strawberry stems are deposited in the ashtrays in the lobby. They lie there, as the buyers walk out through the revolving doors, the green stems with bits of red, reminders, like ticket stubs on Broadway, of the fact that on one floor in this building today's business was show business.

Women's Wear Daily's review of the show appeared a few days later, saying, "Liz has done it again. Consistently good looks."

Arnold Scaasi *June 8*

Item: Liz Smith's *Daily News* column reports that when Elizabeth Taylor, whose Passion perfume has been nominated for several awards, attends the 16th Fragrance Foundation Awards at the Waldorf Astoria tonight, she will be wearing a Scaasi gown.

"Miz Liz went to see her old friend Arnold Scaasi this week," writes Liz Smith, "and she'll be wearing a new white off-the-shoulder organdy dress with violet thistles and green and violet satin ribbons. Scaasi had to drop everything in the midst of his launch of designer furs for Maximilian. [His fur show was on June 6.] But he is nothing if not obliging for stars of the Taylor and Streisand ilk and also the stars of society."

"We did three fittings on that dress during the week she was in town," Arnold later told me. "It was less intricate than Yasmin Khan's dress, but still, we worked a lot of overtime on it."

Full-length pictures of Elizabeth Taylor, in her (nonexclusive, made-to-order) Scaasi dress appeared in many publications, and, although Arnold says just one woman later came to him wanting "the dress that Elizabeth Taylor wore," he adds that "all publicity generates sales, if not directly, then indirectly. The fact that someone like Elizabeth Taylor wore one of my dresses could only help business."

Adrienne Vittadini *June 8*

When it came to designing her spring/summer collection, things went from bad to worse for Adrienne Vittadini, the beautiful blond knitwear designer who is also chairman and chief executive officer of the company that bears her name. Having just finished a huge holiday/cruise line, she'd used up not only her best ideas—she'd used up *all* of them. If you are a designer who creates ninety-five pieces a season (the average number shown in a fashion show), running out of ideas is a bad thing. If, like Adrienne, you must come up with close to one-thousand pieces at a time, it is a disaster.

This disaster was compounded by the nature of the medium in which Adrienne primarily works. Although she does use some woven fabrics like cotton and linen, most of her designs are knits, and knits have to be created earlier than wovens since they have to be made from scratch. In the case of wovens, Adrienne, like all designers, works with preexisting fabrics so that the pattern and design are visible to her before she starts working. For knitwear, the pattern still has to be created with the yarn that Adrienne will be purchasing. Adrienne places orders for yarn through her production agents in Hong Kong and Italy. The spinners that these agents buy from ship the yarn to the garment factories that Adrienne has contracted to manufacture her garments.

Adrienne then telexes to these factories sketches that include the size, pattern, tension, and gauge for each item. Since all her manufacturing is done overseas, she will not be able to check on the progress of her samples and will not see them until August, when she and her staff (and we) will go to Hong Kong to find out which of their ideas worked and which did not. It is at that point that Adrienne will discard the clunkers; out of one-thousand pieces only six-hundred will remain.

Her trip to Hong Kong is only eight weeks away, and not only has Adrienne not purchased any yarn but she hasn't sent her factories a single sketch. The longer she delays in designing, the shorter the period of time her factories will have to make her thousand samples, and the greater the chance that they will not finish all the garments before Adrienne arrives to check and correct them. The corrected, finished garments must be in New York by September, since that is when stores must buy the collection to insure that the clothes will be made and delivered to them in time for spring selling.

In a worst case scenario, if Adrienne doesn't begin designing soon, her con-tracted factories will have nothing to knit, Adrienne will have nothing to sell, and retailers will have nothing to hang in their Adrienne Vittadini departments. Rare is the designer who has not had a nightmare in which his or her racks hang empty in a store. In Adrienne's case this would account for a lot of empty floor space.

The thousand garments that Adrienne and her staff are about to design will be divided unevenly between her two sportswear divisions: the Adrienne Vittadini Collection, a line of dressy sportswear appropriate to wear to the office, and the much larger and more prosperous division, Adrienne Vittadini Active, a line of casual, usually cotton interlock or jersey sportswear.

Besides this, in-house there is a dress division and a petite division which downscales some of the larger-size pieces. There are also licensed lines of swimwear and coverups; loungewear; accessories (gloves, hats, and scarves); travel cosmetics bags; socks and tights; handbags; belts; and a new license for home furnishings. The total wholesale volume done by her clothing lines and licensed products in the U.S. is about $100 million. (Since the firm is privately held it will not reveal exact volume figures.) Besides its domestic business, the company also distributes its products in Canada, Japan, Australia, Europe, and Mexico.

Of course Adrienne has assistants to help her create all of this, but two of her assistants have just quit to take higher posts at other companies, and the six who remained ran out of steam. Adrienne asked them to present her with spring design ideas and liked only what one of them showed her. She hired another assistant but soon fired her. This, of course, was demoralizing for the rest of Adrienne's young design staff. They began wondering when and if the ax was going to fall on them.

They knew Adrienne was disappointed with them and they weren't feeling too great about her either. They needed more direction than she was giving them. They wanted *her* to tell *them* what to design, so that they could then go out and research fabrics, patterns, and silhouettes. They told her so, but her response was, "I just can't keep having it revolve around me like this. I go from executive meeting to executive meeting and have to make personal appearances and give interviews. I was in a store only once in months. I don't have the time that you do to be exposed to ideas. You're the ones with the time on your hands."

But still, the buck stopped at her desk, and, with no ideas forthcoming from her staff, Adrienne tried, as she puts it, to stimulate herself. She went to antique shops and bookstores, and looked through numerous magazines, hoping that something—maybe the corner of a picture or the color of a wall—might trigger inspiration. She looked through numerous home-design magazines, which, she says, are a wonderful source of ideas for prints.

In the meantime Adrienne wondered how she could effectively delegate some of her design responsibilities. Lately she had been at work from ten in the morning to almost ten at night, and that was too long. She decided it might help if she promoted her Collection designer, Odile Laugier, who has worked with her for seven years, to more of a teaching position as head designer, and moved Kristina Salminen, who had designed swimwear, loungewear and socks to be the designer of Collection, under Odile's tutelage. Adrienne, meanwhile, would be training Odile to step in for her in other areas. Odile is also a blond, and has adopted her boss's soft-spoken demeanor, a demeanor under which, for both, lies an iron resolve.

After Adrienne promoted the two young women, she then turned her thoughts back to designing. The ideas still weren't coming and she did the only thing left to do: she panicked. Finally, out in the Hamptons, where she and her husband have a weekend home, Adrienne went to see *White Mischief,* a movie about stylish expatriates in colonial Kenya in 1940 and 1941. She watched, mesmerized, thinking, "I love those clothes. I love that style. That is how I want people to look." The following Monday she told her staff that she wanted to do forties-inspired clothes, and they began researching the predominant silhouettes, patterns, and fabrics from that period.

They scouted antique shops and looked through vintage magazines and coffee-table books on the thirties and forties, particularly those that showed the work of photographer Jacques-Henri Lartigue. In an antique shop they found two men's ties—one printed with miniature polka dots and the other with miniature Scottish terriers—and brought the ties back to the office so that they could copy the prints. The Lartigue books inspired them to do blue-and-white stripes in various sizes, as well as a classic cable-knit tennis sweater.

They went to the library at the Fashion Institute of Technology and found more prints; they called in representatives from antique-print houses and bought fabric designs from them; and finally, things began to roll.

The bulk of the forties-inspired ideas will be for Collection, which, unlike the larger Active line, centers its twenty-two groups around one cohesive design statement. Active, on the other hand, consists of thirty different groups built around interesting patterns and ideas that are not necessarily related. Adrienne continued searching for more Active ideas. Leafing through *Elle,* she was struck by a picture of a girl in a crisp white shirt sitting on a horse that was covered with a Mexican-print blanket. This picture gave her the inspiration to do a Mexican group. Months ago she had bought the artwork for a Mexican print from a textile house in Milan, simply because she loved the way it looked, and now she decided to build a group around it.

Earlier in the year she had bought the artwork for some other prints that had caught her eye, and she now began figuring out how to slot them into the Active line and whether she would have them made into knits or wovens or both. (Although the bulk of her business is in knitwear, this season Adrienne will be offering more coordinating wovens to wear with the knits.)

While still searching for more ideas, Adrienne then took all of her existing fabric colors and patterns and, dividing her time between Collection and Active, began putting them into cohesive groups, thereby deciding which colors, patterns, and fabrics would be delivered at the same time. The merchandise that is delivered at the same time must make a cohesive color-and-style statement on the sales floor. "Otherwise," says Adrienne, "your department will look schizophrenic."

Today she will be reviewing more fabrics, since there are still many holes in Active, and slotting these fabrics into groups. Sarah, Adrienne's young (also blond) secretary shows me into Adrienne's airy sun-drenched office. With its parquet floor, fresh flowers, and two huge walls of windows filled mainly with sky, it feels more like a beach house than an office. Adrienne is behind her desk, her back to the windows, leaning over a red sweater that is spread out flat on the desk. Working with a production assistant, she is correcting production samples from the Holiday line that have just begun to arrive from Hong Kong. Always, the finishing of one season overlaps the conception of the next.

"Can I tell you something?" she says in her soft Hungarian-accented voice to the assistant who is working with her. "The shoulder pads should be bigger and more out and the sleeves should be longer. It should be one-quarter of an inch bigger all over. These all shrank."

The assistant writes down the corrections Adrienne wants made on this and other Holiday pieces. They do this for an hour. After the assistant leaves, Adrienne tells her secretary to call in David Witkewicz, chief assistant designer of Active. While she waits for him she takes a phone call from June Weir, executive fashion editor of *Harper's Bazaar,* who is calling to invite Adrienne to lunch. The two women pick a date, time, and place (Bellini), and then Adrienne says, "Could you leave a bit of time? If I could entice you, I'd like to show you the new collection: Holiday/Cruise." (Cruise, or Resort, is delivered after Holiday, but Adrienne designs the two seasons at the same time.)

June agrees to come see the clothes. Next, Adrienne returns a phone call from her husband, Gigi. He is co-chairman of the company and treasurer and had called earlier from another floor in the same building. "Two events for tomorrow?" she says to him over the phone. "I don't want to go. I'm adamant about it. I'd have to get my hair done, go home and get dressed. No."

Adrienne was supposed to go to a tea at the Park Avenue home of John and Laura Pomerantz, where, under the auspices of a fashion organization called The Fashion Group, Laura and her friends Ivana Trump and Gayfryd Steinberg would speak about their charity involvements. The other event was an AIDS fund-raising dinner at the Hilton Hotel at which Burton M. Tansky, president of Saks Fifth Avenue, would receive a humanitarian award. "I won't be able to make it," she says to her husband. "I don't have time."

Just then, David walks in. He appears to be in his early twenties and is wearing a black-and-cream striped shirt, matching socks, and black pants with black suspenders, as well as a small gold hoop earring in his left ear.

David and Adrienne have had one meeting prior to this during which they began slotting various fabrics into different groups. Based on what they decided then, David has pasted magazine photos and some fabric swatches onto concept boards. He now spreads twenty of these concept boards out on the floor by the window and covers some of them with piles of fabric whose patterns they may want to duplicate.

Both David and Adrienne sit on the floor and stare at the boards, but Adrienne seems to draw a blank. "We have so many groups in Active," she says. "Refresh my memory." After David does so, Adrienne says to me, "This is the hardest part. I look at this and my instinct is that I hate everything. But I have to be loose and just start. I don't know if a writer works like that—you start just so that you get your hand into it and then, once you're well into it, you go back and rewrite the first chapter."

Ornella Vittadini, Adrienne's sister-in-law and the director of production, walks in. "Sorry for interrupting, but I have to show you these," she says in a very heavy Italian accent, as she hands three woven fabric swatches to Adrienne. "This is Japan, this is Japan, and this is Italy," she says of the respective swatches. "But we have to order the piece goods. . . ."

"Immediately," says Adrienne as she runs each swatch through her fingers. As soon as Adrienne decides on a fabric or a knit pattern, Ornella has the company's overseas contractors start working on its development. "How much is it a yard?" Adrienne says of the first swatch.

"Four dollars and ninety cents," says Ornella. "We'll do it in Hong Kong, right?"

"That's affordable," says Adrienne. "But I tell you, the other one, the one with the little dogs, will be from Korea." Then, alerting Ornella to another fabric she has decided on, Adrienne points to a blue leaf print on one of the boards and says, "I would go ahead and print that immediately."

Ornella leaves, and Adrienne and David continue looking at fabric swatches, first for a batik group and then a tie-dye group. Suddenly Adrienne looks up and says to me, "Am I the latest? Has everyone else picked their fabrics?" Adrienne wonders what stages of design everyone is in and then, as she will often do, questions how Liz Claiborne has managed to structure such a mammoth organization. Adrienne already doesn't have enough hours in a day and she doesn't know how she will handle the growth that the retail stores she is opening across the country this year are sure to bring. This past March, Adrienne opened her first store in Beverly Hills. Her first franchised store will open in St. Louis in August, with the second opening in November in Costa Mesa, California, and the third in San Francisco in early 1989. A total of nine more will open by the end of 1990 and five more in 1991.

Although her success seems like something to be envious of, Adrienne quite honestly and quite frequently dreams of chucking it all because all this hard work has cut into the quality of her life. Having not been raised to be ambitious, she has mixed feelings about her success.

Adrienne was born in Hungary, and although she won't reveal the date, it was somewhere around 1945. She was the eldest child of a physician, and as she says, "Doctors had a very special privilege in Hungary. They were like little kings there. My father had a car when no one else did and he never belonged to the Communist Party. I always grew up with housekeepers and I had a governess who spoke many languages. Languages were very strongly stressed. I felt very privileged as a kid."

In Hungary, she says, "Fashion was not a priority. You can't get beautiful clothes in department stores there." Drawing, rather than fashion, was her first love, and she credits her father for exposing her to art. "He would show me the beautiful colors in a painting and explain why an icon is beautiful," she says. "He turned over Oriental carpets and taught me how to tell what makes them precious, the fine weave and whether it's a silk or woolen weave. He taught me the art of looking."

When Russia first occupied Hungary in 1945, all of Adrienne's family's land and homes were taken away. Adrienne's father became active in an anti-Communist organization and supported the revolution in October 1956, during which the Hungarian people regained control of the government. When Russia reoccupied the country one month later, Adrienne's father feared he would be imprisoned, as many of his friends were. He fled with his family to Austria, and then to the United States.

Adrienne spent her teenage years in Philadelphia, where she studied at the Monroe College of Art. She had planned to become a fashion illustrator, but after taking a few fashion courses as a freshman, decided to become a fashion designer. Her affinity for the fine arts remains apparent in her collections. At various times, the patterns in her clothing have been derived from works by such artists as Alexander Calder, Picasso, Miró, and Max Bill.

In college she worked part time as a model at the Saks Fifth Avenue branch store in Philadelphia. As a junior, in 1965, she was awarded a fellowship to travel to Europe, and Saks arranged an internship for her with Louis Ferraud, who was one of the New Wave designers of the 1960s and designed hip clothes for models and actresses, of whom the most celebrated was Brigitte Bardot. Adrienne worked for him for four months, and it was there, she says, that she "learned the importance of paying attention to details" and was exposed to "all the cuts, structure that went into clothes."

After graduation, her first job was at a sportswear company called Sport Tempo, where she was one of many designers and created woven suits. Two years later, in 1968, she joined the Rosanna division of Warnaco where she designed SW1, a line of contemporary knitwear.

In 1971 she took a sabbatical and went to Europe. She skied. She sailed. And, in Italy, she met Gianluigi Vittadini, who was at that time executive vice-president of a large pharmaceutical company started by his great-great-grandfather. She married him the next year and settled in to enjoy "the Milanese pace of life."

But soon Adrienne realized "you can only go to so many luncheons." To alleviate her boredom she began a working relationship with Warnaco, whereby she traveled to Hong Kong and designed there part time while Warnaco sold the goods in New York. Her mother-in-law was horrified that she was going to be working. "She thought I should be chaperoned in Hong Kong," Adrienne recalls, laughing. But her husband supported her in her activities, even though he didn't take her work seriously. He thought of it as a hobby. "Let her play," he told his mother. "She'll create less problems."

In time the Vittadinis established a dual residency in New York and in Milan, and Adrienne joined the Kimberly Knits division of General Mills as a merchandiser. But she found it "difficult to relate to the clothes," which were staid and stodgy, and she missed designing. "It was very frustrating for me to merchandise something that I couldn't correct from the beginning to end," she says. "Changing just a button or a shoulder didn't make a difference."

She persuaded the company to let her design her own line, as part of this division. The line, Avanzara, was well received, but Kimberly Knits was losing money, and in 1978 the company went out of business. Adrienne decided that rather than go work for another company she would go out on her own.

Simultaneously, Victor Coopersmith, a vice-president of another clothing company, was also feeling an entrepreneurial itch. A mutual business associate introduced Adrienne and Victor. The two became partners and opened AVVC, Inc., in January 1979. They took advantage of "the wonderful, loyal factories

Avanzara had developed in Hong Kong," says Adrienne, and they produced a line of knitwear, primarily sweaters.

Continuing to source its knitwear in Hong Kong as well as in Italy, the company grew to approximately $12 million in three years. Like many apparel firms that grow so quickly, AVVC went through growing pains, particularly in its third year, when it passed the $10 million mark. Adrienne and Coopersmith had all sorts of delivery problems and began not to see eye to eye on how to take the business forward. Victor wanted to key in on items and keep inventory tight while Adrienne wanted to design more extensive collections. She strongly believed that knitwear could be more than just sweaters; it could be a total look.

In 1982 the two decided to part and Adrienne, with the financial support of her husband, Gianluigi (Gigi), bought out Victor, who today is president of Coopersmith Enterprises, which developed the Andrea Jovine and Rebecca Moses businesses. Until this point, Gigi had been advising Adrienne, insuring, for instance, that she kept all rights to her name. He would come in once a week to see that, as Adrienne puts it, "financially, everything was running," but he continued working in his family's business.

"Gigi was commuting between Milan and New York and that was a big strain on our life," says Adrienne. "We kept a small apartment in Milan and we knew we had to make a decision. Either I had to move with him to Milan or he had to move here. When we made the decision to buy out Victor, Gigi decided to leave his family company, which was eventually sold, and he stepped into my company." Gigi became co-chairman, with Adrienne, and treasurer.

The two began a search for a president and, after interviewing sixty prospective job candidates, hired Richard Catalano away from Evan-Picone, where he was president of its sportswear and petites divisions to be the president of her company, a post he retains today.

Adrienne credits Richard with much of the increased visibility and business success she and the company have enjoyed. "Richard changed our entire method of working," she says. "He saw all the loose ends. He restructured our shipping, moved our warehousing to New Jersey, installed a more sophisticated computer system, hired new people, and said we should have fashion shows to increase our visibility."

Richard, thirty-four, grew up in the garment center. His father was the elevator starter at 1407 Broadway, a building a few blocks down from the Adrienne Vittadini headquarters. As a child, Richard would often ride the elevator with his dad, who retired in 1988. At the age of thirteen Richard lied about his age and got a job as a delivery boy at a coffee shop in the lobby of the same building.

Throughout college, where he majored in physical education, Richard spent his summers working as an elevator operator in that building. That was how he met the man who was then president of Evan-Picone. The executive would greet Richard by asking, "So when are you going to come work for me?" Richard, however, was determined to become a physical education teacher. But when faced with the necessity of attending graduate school to reach that goal, he changed his mind and joined Evan-Picone as a sales trainee in 1975. He rose through the ranks until he left to join Adrienne in December 1982.

At that point Adrienne was designing only one collection and had one assistant, Charlotte Neuville, who today is designing sportswear under her own name. That same year Adrienne took up tennis and needed "great, active-looking, natural-fiber clothes but everything out there was polyester and not tasteful." She designed a group of active apparel and the clothes were accepted so well that she and Richard decided to open a separate division, called Active. By 1984, the year she launched the Petite division, the firm's annual volume more than doubled, to $25 million. Then she won the Coty award, began licensing her name, and saw her company begin to reach the astonishingly rapid growth that demanded she work practically around the clock.

Four years ago Adrienne was based in a small office across the hall from Richard's on the thirtieth floor of 1441 Broadway. In 1985 the company leased extra space on the ninth floor of 1441 to use as its Petite showroom and a design studio for Adrienne. The Collection and Active divisions remained on the thirtieth floor. In 1986 Adrienne opened a dress division, and she and her ever-burgeoning design and production staff outgrew their space on the ninth floor and took the entire twenty-first floor in the same building.

This is where she is working today. As Adrienne stares at the Active concept boards, one of her licensing design assistants walks in and hands her a bunch of fabrics saying, "I went to the flea market last Sunday." One of the fabrics has light blue morning glories printed on a white background. "I love that for sheets," says Adrienne, who is currently developing her first line of home furnishings. She places the fabrics on the floor next to her and she and David turn to a boldly striped group which was inspired by a beach towel Adrienne bought in Paris this past spring. The towel had a white base and blocks of multicolor, multisize stripes. On the concept board for this group David has pasted three different cards painted with three different widths of stripes. These cards are surrounded with various magazine photos of striped clothes.

Adrienne gets up, walks to her desk, and retrieves a green pocket square. It is from her own wardrobe and she has brought it to work because it is the exact color green that they want to use in the stripes. As she cuts the pocket square in half she says, "You know, we go shopping and buy things we like and think we are going to wear them but they always end up here. They were never intended to be samples, but somehow they get cut up."

"That's why all of Adrienne's clothes have holes in them," jokes David.

"That's why I save everything," she says. "I need a closet as big as a city block."

They go on to a gray-and-cream striped group, and Adrienne says, "You sent these off to Raoul? Can he do them?" Raoul is the man who owns their main factory in Italy.

"I didn't send it," says David.

"You didn't? Why not?"

"I forgot."

He goes into the studio to get something and Adrienne looks at me and whispers, "He forgot? How could he forget? He's lucky you're here."

The same assistant who had gone to the flea market walks in with a small piece of white cardboard on which a tiny black terrier (the same terrier that was on the antique tie) has been painted. A few days ago Adrienne had asked this assistant to paint a new design in which this black terrier would be repeated over and over, covering the whole piece of cardboard. This type of design, which takes a character—be it an animal, a person, or a flower—and repeats it over and over again, is referred to as both a character and a conversation print. "I didn't do it," says the assistant.

"Why not?" says Adrienne.

"I just didn't. You took it back one day and I thought you were going to have someone else do it."

"Paint it up," says Adrienne. "Don't spend too much time on it because it might not work but I just want to get it out of my system." She is speaking very softly and gently, trying hard not to lose her temper. She knows a certain amount of human error and misunderstanding is inevitable but she doesn't have the time or the patience to deal with it now.

David comes back and Adrienne says, "Send the stripes out to Raoul to see if he can do the group. There's such a shortage of heather yarns that he may not be able to do it."

Group by group, Adrienne and David continue to make decisions on which patterns to group together and which yarns and fabrics to order. They stay with it until 10:30 P.M., since, after all, yarn and fabric for thirty groups is a lot of yarn and fabric.

Adrienne Vittadini *June 9*

Even though Adrienne doesn't have the time or the patience for human error and misunderstanding, she is being besieged by it. For instance, she learned yesterday that Donna Cristina, who is Adrienne's vice-president of public relations and one of her best friends—and who had just returned from a trip to Monte Carlo, where she was overseeing the photography for Adrienne's fall ad campaign—had misunderstood the types of pictures Adrienne wanted.

Last month, when the campaign was being conceptualized, Adrienne, pressed for time, was not very accessible to either Donna or Benita Cassar Torreggiani, the campaign's free-lance art director. An advertising campaign is the very last thing a designer approves each season. In Adrienne's case, she was already deeply involved in Holiday/Cruise, and trying to come up with ideas for spring, when it was time for her to conceptualize the fall ad campaign. Instead of using numerous pictures to illustrate the mood she wanted in her ads, Adrienne had expressed her desires with the words "city, reflection, café, France." Yesterday, as she looked at the pictures for the first time, Adrienne learned that those words evoked different images for Donna than they had for her.

Adrienne hated everything that Donna and Benita showed her. The model, who had gained ten pounds but had promised to lose them for the shooting, hadn't done so and it showed. Besides this, the mood in the photos was too harsh and slick for Adrienne's liking. She asked the art director to trim the model's thighs in the photographs and to somehow soften the mood in the pictures.

Today, they will meet for lunch in a windowless conference room that is practically filled by a round conference table and five brown leather chairs. The table has been set with white china plates, peach-colored quilted place mats, and matching cloth napkins.

Adrienne has left Donna and Benita for a few moments, being needed elsewhere. While Adrienne is gone, Donna and Benita spread the photos on the table. Most of the pictures are of the model but some are purely scenic shots. The opening shot for the entire ad portfolio is one in which the model is wearing a red dress, a red scarf over her head, and black gloves. The dress has buttons on the shoulder and one shoulder has been left unbuttoned, exposing her skin. To soften the mood of this slick photo, Benita proposes placing a full-page mood shot next to it and moves a photo of sunlight streaming through a window next to the picture. Then Benita lines up four more photos of the model in different poses and outfits. The photos feature the sportswear from the collection and Active divisions: dresses, handbags, and other accessories. Benita plays with the order of the photos and decides that she likes the accessories photo in the center. This photo—a closeup of the model with a flower in her hair—is a generic mood shot for the overall concept of Adrienne Vittadini accessories. The flower isn't actually for sale.

Next Benita pulls out clear plastic strips printed with different colored versions of the Adrienne Vittadini logo. She lays the various colors on the photos one at a time, and she and Donna try to decide which colors look better where. Just then Adrienne's voice is heard in the hall and Donna nervously says, "Stash it." Benita quickly pushes the photos into one pile and, turns them over just before Adrienne enters.

"Have we solved the problem?" says Adrienne as she walks in and walks around the table to take a seat.

"I think so," says Benita, as she slowly lays out the opening fashion picture and the sunlit window photo to its left. Then she lays a blue Adrienne Vittadini logo on the window picture.

"I like the blue," says Benita.

"I do too," says Donna.

"I don't like the blue for sure," says Adrienne, and this sets the tone for the rest of the meeting. She does not like a single thing, basically, that has been done so far.

As Adrienne reaches for a sandwich, Donna lights a cigarette. Putting the sandwich on her plate, Adrienne looks at the first picture of the model, the one in which the buttons on her shoulder are unbuttoned. "This is slick," she says. "And this picture," she says, pointing at the sunlit window, "doesn't enhance anything. She looks like she was photographed in a studio, and that is outdoors."

Adrienne keeps staring at the first picture of the model. Finally, she says, "No matter what, her foot is going to be cut off?"

"Yes," says Benita. "The photographer didn't get the foot in the frame."

"I don't like this picture," says Adrienne. "It's so slick. So studio."

"But it was photographed outdoors," says Donna. "That window is exactly the light she was standing in. That's the window of the bar in Colombe D'Or."

"Donna, you being there, have the mood of the place. I don't. To me it looks like a studio picture that was taken with a flash. The light looks like harsh reflected light."

Benita lays out the rest of the pictures, one by one, in a row. Adrienne points to a picture of the model standing in an airy light-suffused room. The model is wearing a short black dress and has placed her arm inside a blue stocking, the way a woman would if she was checking her hose for runs.

"I'd like a little more off the thigh," Adrienne says.

Ornella comes in, apologizes for interrupting, and says, "Dianna in Italy is panicking. She says we're so late she's never going to be able to get things done on time." Dianna is the woman who oversees the manufacturing of the Adrienne Vittadini Collection in Italy. Although Active is Adrienne's largest business in the United States, that merchandise is not available in Europe.

"Tell her to come next week," says Adrienne. The Italian licensee needs to have the sketches for spring even earlier than Hong Kong because she opens the line in Italy two weeks sooner than Adrienne does in the United States. Plus, all the factories in Italy are closed for the month of August. This means she needs to get all of her samples made by the end of next month.

Adrienne's secretary brings in some individual-size bags of potato chips and Adrienne asks her to please ask Richard and Gigi to come and look at these pictures. Adrienne stares for a long time at a picture in which the model is sitting on a bed and is draped in what looks like a navy blue towel but is actually a piece of clothing from the Active division.

"What we need is an aesthetic shot that looks like an image ad and also sells clothes," Adrienne finally says. "We've seen we sell clothes from the ads so it shouldn't be just a naked back."

Richard and Gigi walk in and Adrienne says, "What do you think?"

As if he'd heard Adrienne, Richard immediately points to the picture Adrienne has just commented on and says, "I don't know what this is. I don't know what she's wearing. And I don't like this one," he says, pointing to the picture where the model has draped the stocking over her hand. "This is the first picture I've seen of Rachel where she doesn't come alive."

"Let me say that I am major disappointed in the ads," says Adrienne. "I've already told Donna and Benita that I am disappointed in it and in them. It was supposed to be French and it isn't. I felt city, reflection, café, France, and this looks to me like a studio shot." She points to the opening photograph of the model. "It's everything I despise. I hate slickness, sleaziness. That's the one I would take out. When do you ever see me unbutton my shoulders like that?"

Then she points to the photo all the way at the right in which the model is wearing a lime green jacket and has a brown handbag in front of her.

"Odile doesn't think this looks like a handbag ad," says Adrienne.

"What is it?" says Richard.

"It's a handbag ad," says Donna.

"It's a handbag ad," Richard repeats angrily. "It's a handbag ad because you *think* it's a handbag ad. You shot it with that intention but the woman walking down the street might think it's an ad for a lime green jacket."

"What is this?" says Gigi, pointing to the one in which the model has her hand through the stocking.

"Dresses," says Donna.

"I thought it was for Trimfit," says Gigi. Trimfit is Adrienne's sock licensee. "You look at the hose in the picture, not the dress. And why does she have blue hose on her arm? She would never wear blue hose with a black dress. It doesn't make sense."

"She looks like a dead fish," says Richard. "Rachel is best when she's moving, smiling. Not just standing there like that. There's no life in that picture."

"Donna, that is not us," says Adrienne. "I am a fanatic for the healthy look. I want blond, happy, airy, cheerful."

"She's ugly," says Gigi of the model.

"No," says Richard. "She's beautiful when she moves. But she's huge. Look at this." He picks up the hose shot and points to the model's thighs.

"And that's already scaled down," says Adrienne. "She gained ten pounds, which she promised she would lose, but she didn't."

"Before the shooting was over she got hysterical," says Benita. "She started crying."

"Why?" says Gigi.

"No one knows," says Benita. "She just flipped out. She just didn't want to have her picture taken anymore. She's a very difficult girl."

"We need to find someone else," says Adrienne, "but there's no new face around. Anyway, this is getting destructive. We have to decide what to do about these pictures. When is our deadline?"

"Tomorrow for the mechanicals," says Benita.

"My problem with this," says Adrienne, "is the whole impact that isn't made. Color and layering was the whole essence of the collection."

"They had on tight pants in the show," says Benita.

"Where was this taken?" says Gigi.

"Monte Carlo," says Adrienne.

"Why did we go to Monte Carlo? These could have been taken in 1441," he says, referring to the building in which their offices are located.

"This is Renoir's actual studio," says Benita, pointing to the hose picture. "No one has ever been able to photograph in Renoir's studio before."

"But who knows that?" says Adrienne. "You tell me this, and then I read things into the picture, but other people don't know."

"Why did we go there?" says Gigi.

"Because we photographed in some of the most expensive hotels in the south of France. This chair," Benita says, pointing, "is from the Grand Hôtel or the Hôtel du Cap in Cap Ferrat. We must have looked at every chair in the south of France."

"But," she continues, "if you don't like these pictures I don't think you should run them. It's expensive to reshoot but..."

"But it's less expensive than the placement," says Richard. "What are our deadlines?"

"We're to get the mechanicals to the separators tomorrow," says Benita.

"Where are these running?" says Richard.

"*Vogue, Elle, Vanity Fair, Town and Country,* and *W,*" says Donna.

"Why don't you take them home and play with them over the weekend?" says Gigi to Adrienne.

"We don't have time for that," Adrienne replies. "The deadline is tomorrow. Let me just keep them for tonight," she says to Benita. "I need to get it straight in my own mind."

"Maybe we should reshoot," says Richard. "This is $150,000 worth of placement and $10,000 worth of photography."

Adrienne doesn't reply. She shuffles the pictures around and then focuses on the hose picture. "I saw this as very Audrey Hepburn," she says, staring at the picture for a long time, while everyone silently looks at her. Finally Adrienne looks up, sighs, and says, "I'm baffled. I don't know what to do. Ideally I would like to use black-and-white photos because it's much newer but I am all about color. I have to play with it in my head."

She turns to me, sitting on her left, and, ever the gracious hostess, says, "May I offer you a coffee?" She walks back to her office with Gigi and on the way in says to her secretary, "Do you want to go talk to Donna and Benita? I think they might need a glass of wine."

Arnold Scaasi *June 9*

Item: *Women's Wear Daily* reports that Arnold Scaasi was the only man invited to the baby shower Barbara Davis gave at L'Orangerie for her daughter, Patty Raynes, Wednesday. It was Arnold and fifty-eight women. "Teddy bears dominated the festivities," reports *WWD*, and "Davis wore a teddy bear print Scaasi dress."

Why was he invited? "They love me," Arnold tells me. "They called and said, 'Would you come?' and I said, 'I'd love to,' and they said, 'Well, you'll be the only man,' and I said, 'That's an honor, I think.'"

Adrienne Vittadini *June 14*

Although she wasn't happy with the ads, Adrienne decided to let them run as they were. Even if there wasn't such a tight deadline for their completion, Adrienne couldn't afford to take the time to oversee a reshoot.

Already she's been spending too much time away from designing—she's been meeting with some of the major retailers viewing her just-opened Holiday line (this afternoon Bloomingdale's took up two precious hours); talking to reporters (something she is ceaselessly asked to do); and interviewing prospective assistants.

She worked on the Collection this morning and only now, at 4:30, does she have the time to go back to it. I follow Adrienne into the room situated between her office and the large area where all the design assistants sit. In this middle room each of the three divisions gets a wall of its own where it hangs up concept boards from its current line in progress; the fourth wall is one of huge windows. Walking into this room is the closest one can come to being inside Adrienne's creative mind. In here one can immediately see how the three main divisions are developing.

If you stand with your back to the windows, the wall on your right has the concept boards for dresses pinned on it, the one on the left has the boards from Active. Since, unlike the main collection, these two divisions don't need a unifying theme, their concept boards are covered with pretty, but unrelated, prints. The wall directly across from the windows holds Collection's concept boards and most of these are covered with magazine pictures and swatches of fabrics very similar to those which appeared in the movie *White Mischief.* I recognize the red carnation, the blue carnation, and assorted black-and-white prints that Greta Scacchi wore in the movie.

Adrienne introduces me to Kristina, the new designer of Collection. She has fine chin-length brown hair, a self-effacing, gentle demeanor, and an Eastern European accent. Then Adrienne walks past the women, who are sitting in chairs facing Collection's wall, steps over the extra concept boards and magazine pages scattered on the floor, and finally, like a teacher in front of a blackboard, stands in front of the wall.

Crossing her arms, she stares at it and then says, "I want to tighten this because we're really overboard. We have too many groups. And we're very heavily woven for summer." Starting at the left side of the wall, she walks alongside it, pointing to group after group, saying, "Woven, woven, knit, knit, woven, woven, woven, woven. . . .

"Let's see what we have to have," she says and points to one of the boards: "The Mexican Group." She points to another and says, "The tie-dye I love. That could be bread and butter for us, although it may conflict with Active." She continues walking along the wall, pointing at different boards as she goes and saying, "This I think is beautiful . . . beautiful . . . beautiful . . . beautiful . . . beautiful."

"OK, Ornella," says Adrienne. "Tell me the spring deliveries. What do I need?" This "need" is dictated by the sales and marketing division, headed by Richard Catalano.

Ornella's accent makes her a little hard to understand as she reads, very rapidly, from a sheet of paper. "For February delivery you need six groups: two wear now, and four spring, with one of them being base career and one that will relate to all groups. So, the navy and white story is good for that."

Ornella begins to say, "For March . . ." but Adrienne interrupts her. "Tell me, what do we need for April and May?"

"For April we need five groups: two fashion forward, one impulse buy, one irresistible, and one complementary groups. For May we need two fun and whimsical, one dressy, one pretransitional, and one other."

"See," says Adrienne, looking at the wall. "We definitely have too much for summer." The April and May deliveries consist of summer merchandise, while February and March are spring.

"For February we need two wear now," says Ornella, returning to their first delivery.

"That we definitely don't have," says Adrienne. The term "wear now" refers to clothes the consumer can wear in February, as opposed to pieces that will be saved for the warmer spring months. "In the spring we're competing with all the career companies like Ellen Tracy and Anne Klein II. That's when people buy their work clothes, all those very structured looks, and some of those should be wear now. But I wouldn't want to force it, if we don't feel for wool."

"Why are we coming out with wool if we ended the January delivery with cotton?" says Odile.

"The cotton is for people who take cruises," says Adrienne as she takes a sheet of white poster paper and cuts four 4-inch squares out of it. She picks up a red Magic Marker and writes February, March, April, and May respectively on top of each. "Tell me, again, what we need for February," she says to Ornella, who repeats the groups, and Adrienne writes down in pencil what Ornella said about February, the first square.

"Now continue to March," says Adrienne. They cover all the months, and Adrienne pins the four cards up on the wall, starting with February on the left, leaving an equal amount of space between them.

Adrienne walks back to the wall and moves the tie-dye concept board all the way from the left to the right, placing it under the May sign.

"I have an idea," says Adrienne. "A brainstorm hit me. We can do linen with a stripe."

"It's very *White Mischief*," says Kristina about the white linen group.

"Oh, you saw it?" says Adrienne. "When?"

"Saturday," says Kristina.

Adrienne thumbtacks four other concept boards under the May sign and then, although the answer to her question is written on the white card she has pinned to the wall, she says to Ornella, "Tell me again, what was April?"

Ornella tells her and then leaves to take a phone call. The other women sit and stare at the wall. "What do you think, Kristina?" says Adrienne. She is concerned that, since Odile is present and since this collection was Odile's baby for so many years, Kristina may be letting her sensibilities be overshadowed by Odile.

"I would put all the soft groups together," says Kristina, pointing at the left corner. "The carnation and stripe is too harsh to go with the others. I would put that with the black-and-white story."

"Talk to me," says Adrienne. "What do you mean?"

Kristina repeats herself, pointing, and Adrienne says, "Yes." She moves the boards around saying, "So this is feminine and goes together."

She moves the five soft groups under the April sign. "This looks right to me," says Adrienne. "It's all demure and feminine." All the groups delivered to a store within the same time frame should somehow be related to one another.

Adrienne steps away from the boards and says, "Here we have five groups for April and five groups for May. So we have summer."

Adrienne and the designers work on the groups they are slotting into the remaining months, changing the color of some fabrics and dropping others. In a very general way they begin to talk about the kinds of silhouettes they would like to do. "Once we have these concepts tight, the sketches will be very easy," Adrienne says to me.

Ornella returns and Adrienne explains to her what has been done so far.

"Do you see anything that you don't like?" says Adrienne.

"I'm not sure about those two together," says Ornella. "The red carnation print with the red-and-white stripe."

"I see this," says Adrienne, pointing to the carnation-print group, "with long skirts, white socks, tucked-in T-shirts. It's a forties mood, and this—" she points to the stripes—"is a forties mood too. It's the same woman. They can be designed to work together. It can be a *White Mischief* summer." Indeed, in that movie actress Greta Scacchi wore a red carnation print with red-and-white stripes.

Ornella shrugs.

"We were craving red-and-white," says Adrienne. "Where is that fabric?"

Kristina finds the bolt of red-and-white striped fabric in a basket at the side of the room. Adrienne holds it up for Ornella to see, then asks Kristina to cut a piece of the fabric. Odile holds the bolt while Kristina cuts off about a yard. Adrienne lays the striped fabric next to the carnation print, steps back to look and says, "Then we can deliver our black-and-white story at the same time." She lays a piece of wide black-and-white stripe fabric next to the red-and-white stripes.

At 6:15 Adrienne sighs and says, "It's so hot."

"It's after six o'clock," says Ornella. "They turn off the air in the building."

"If you don't need me anymore," Ornella continues, "I'm going to telex Dianna about gabardine."

"Ask her if she can find a wool-and-cotton blend for us," says Adrienne.

"Ods," says Adrienne to Odile, "we need two concepts for March." They bat around more ideas and, at 6:20 David (Active's designer) comes in and says, "Did you want to work with me later tonight?"

"No. I don't think so," says Adrienne.

"Because I have something to do at seven," says David.

"Fine," says Adrienne. "Go ahead. I'll work with you tomorrow."

"This," Adrienne says after David has left, "is the only company I know of where six P.M. is like noon."

We leave Adrienne now for three weeks, during which time she will go to Europe to oversee the manufacturing of her spring and summer lines in Italy. She will spend three days in Milan, meeting with Dianna, explaining all the details to her, and overseeing fabric and knit swatch development. She will meet with her contractors and with Guy Aulenti, the architect who designed the Adrienne Vittadini stores. Also she will visit bookstores, where she will buy many books on Mexico.

Then she will travel to London, where she will comb book and clothing stores looking for more ideas that she can apply to spring. A mandatory stop will be Saint-Tropez, an area that almost every single contemporary designer and retailer flocks to in the summer in search of trends. This year, however, Adrienne will find only "the same little French tourist in the same short white boots and short skirts." Then she will come home, where, much to her consternation, on July 6, the sales department will ask her to add six more groups to the Active line.

Since Active is such a large business, with many accounts, the company needs to have a broad selection of merchandise to offer these accounts. This is done to insure that two stores in the same city can carry the popular Active line without carrying the same styles. Since Adrienne will not see the actual clothing until we go to Hong Kong in August, and will not know until then which groups will have to be dropped because they didn't look as good in reality as they did on the drawing board, the sales department wants to make sure that they are amply covered with different styles.

We will pick up with Adrienne when she gets this bad news. Now, let's turn to . . .

Arnold Scaasi *June 20*

Since we last saw Arnold, he has busily been trying to get people to donate items or services for tonight's New York City Opera auction benefit at Christie's. He convinced the "Concorde people" to donate a flight on the Concorde, and Marina B to donate some jewelry for the auction. For the party itself, he contacted the Bronfman family and got them to supply Seagram's liquor, and he persuaded a florist to donate the flowers.

Apart from the benefit work, he signed a licensing agreement to design a bridal collection for a company called Eva Haynal Forsyth. His first collection, for spring, will be available in September, with retail prices starting at $1,800. The collection, he tells me on the phone, is "very natural" for him to do, "since bridal dresses are so similar to my evening dresses."

But tonight, bridal dresses aren't what's on his mind. He's more concerned that everyone he's invited to the benefit have fun. "My main role as chairman of the event is to make sure everyone has a good time," he says. "Otherwise, they won't return next year."

He is so anxious to be a good host that he is actually on time, having arrived at 5:30 P.M., to greet his guests in a large room on the second floor, where the items available for the silent auction are displayed either in glass cases or on the walls, and, in the case of clothing, on live models, who are slowly circulating among the guests. As they walk, the models hold up cards that identify the designers of their garments, as well as listing the lowest bid accepted for the clothes. Below this information, those who are interested in the items will write their names and the price they are willing to pay for them.

The room is crowded and I am surprised at the large number of press people who are here. There are three reporters from *The New York Times* style section, as well as Bill Cunningham, a *Times* photographer who, along with his camera, is a ubiquitous presence on the New York social scene. All the ladies know him and most greet him by his first name. He is a tall, skinny man with side-parted gray hair, a ready grin, and a quick darting glance. He glances now at Edna Morris, who is talking to Arnold. Bill scurries over, gives them a little wave and a smile, and raises his camera.

"Oh, Bill," says Edna Morris. "Wait! Let me get rid of my drink." Bill takes a picture without waiting for her to put down her wineglass. Resigned, she stands, drink in hand, and both she and Arnold smile at the camera. "I tell you," she says to Arnold as Bill takes their picture, "I never go anywhere without this man."

She is referring to Bill and, although no one is exactly sure what she means, everyone laughs, and for posterity Bill captures Edna Morris and Arnold Scaasi sharing a joke that *New York Times* readers can only wonder about.

"A very good newspaper you're with," says Arnold, as the photographer is about to turn away.

Richard Buckley, the editor of *Women's Wear Daily*'s "Eye" gossip page, who by next summer will join the staff of *Vanity Fair,* and Eric Weiss, a free-lance photographer, pass by. "There's Ann Slater," says Richard. "She's my favorite." Eric takes a picture. "Only one picture, Eric?" says Richard. As Eric follows her to take another picture, Richard steps up to another woman and asks her name. She tells him and watches him write it down.

Richard says to me, "So often I'll ask women for their names and then, under their names, I'll write down a description of them so I remember what they look like when I look at the pictures the next day. You know, I write, 'Fat lady in ugly print,' and then they look in my notebook as I'm writing and see how I've described them."

While Richard goes off to find Eric, I take a stroll around the room. Recognizing only Mary Tyler Moore and some blue blood society types, I head back to the room's entrance where a crowd of reporters and photographers stand, waiting to check out new arrivals. Among the press, Richard Buckley is chatting with Michael Gross from *New York* magazine, while the three *Times* reporters are huddled together. Next to them stands Mary Hilliard, a free-lance photographer whom the Opera Guild has hired to photograph the event.

"Someone said Mary Tyler Moore is here," says a waiter to Mary Hilliard.

"I already photographed her," she replies. She is more concerned with the fact that someone seems to have stolen a camera she left by the door.

"I don't see her," says the waiter.

"She has short hair now," says Mary. "She's hard to recognize. You probably gave her a cheese puff and you didn't even know it."

"One time Mrs. Howell from 'Gilligan's Island' came to a party and it was unbelievable," says the waiter. "The Queen of England could have walked in and you wouldn't have known it. Imagine. All this fuss over Mrs. Howell."

At 6:15 Saul and Gayfryd Steinberg arrive. One of Arnold's PR people tells Mary to make sure to get a picture of Arnold with the Steinbergs.

Next, Blaine Trump arrives and kisses *New York*'s Michael Gross hello.

At 6:30 Arnold comes up and says, "I don't know where everybody is."

"It looks to me like everybody's here," I say, but he has walked away.

The beauty editor of *Women's Wear Daily* arrives wearing casual clothes. She is with a photographer who, without even glancing around the room, goes to work setting up a tripod and a reflector near the far wall.

"What are you doing?" I ask.

"We're shooting a story on the perfect evening look and we needed a party," says the beauty editor.

Just then, Claudia Cohen, society reporter for WABC-TV, and wife of Revlon chairman Ron Perelman, arrives with a cameraman. With small, delicate features, she is much prettier than she looks on TV. She and her cameraman go right to work, too, as the cameraman turns his bright light on Mary Tyler Moore. Claudia and Mary speak very softly, and the noise in the room is too loud for me to hear anything they are saying. For the first time I realize how incredibly sensitive a TV microphone must be.

Claudia scans the room and picks Arnold as her next interviewee.

"A lot of people are here because they love to wear your dresses," Claudia says.

"They're also here because they are my friends," he replies.

"How much do your dresses cost?" she says.

"Six thousand to fifteen thousand dollars."

"How many of your dresses are here today?" she says, asking a question for which Scaasi always has a ready answer. At most parties he will divulge that information to reporters without their asking.

"About fifteen to twenty," says Arnold. Among the women wearing his dresses are Blaine Trump, Gayfryd Steinberg, Kimberly Farkas, and Austine Hearst.

At 6:40 Claudia interviews Beverly Sills while Arnold walks around the room saying, "The auction is starting. Come on, we're going in now." In an adjoining room, the live auction is about to start.

Arnold and Beverly Sills go onstage and Arnold says, "Hello. We're going to begin the live auction. I want to thank all of you for being here."

"I want to thank all of you, too," says Beverly Sills. "And I want to remind you that you're not supposed to get a bargain here. You're *supposed* to pay more than it's worth."

As the auctioneer takes over, Arnold and Beverly Sills come down from the stage and sit next to each other in the front row, facing the stage. Nan Kempner, who has just arrived, kisses Arnold hello and sits on his left, and Blaine Trump sits on Nan's left.

The auctioneer opens the auction by saying, "Bidders are requested to pay immediately." He is reading from a piece of paper and he holds it up saying, "*Immediately* is underlined here and written in big, bold letters."

Obviously bidders did as they were told because the evening raised $250,000 for the opera.

Arnold Scaasi *June 21*

Today Arnold will make a personal appearance on the third floor of Saks Fifth Avenue, where his Scaasi Boutique line is regularly sold. As it did with all designers, Saks actually invested in just a fraction of Arnold's fall collection. The rest of it will be shown to customers today at a trunk show. Whatever orders are taken will be credited to Saks's account and the dresses will be shipped to Saks, unaltered.

If you remember, the Scaasi Boutique show, the one where three magazine people exchanged jokes throughout the entire event, was held in late March. About seventy styles were shown at that time. In the two weeks following the show, retailers from across the country picked the styles they wanted to sell in their stores. About fifty-five dresses were chosen. It is those fifty-five that will actually be made and it is those fifty-five that Arnold and his staff will be showing women today.

In front of the escalator on the third floor, a sign says: *Here today at Saks Fifth Avenue. Come meet Arnold Scaasi and Trunk Show.* On this floor there is one main aisle separating the departments, and Connie Cook, the model, is walking up and down it. She is wearing a Scaasi Boutique dress and holding a sign with Arnold's name on it. She tells me Arnold is with a customer in his department's dressing room. I walk past the racks of fall dresses in the middle of his department, and as I reach the dressing room Arnold comes out. He is walking behind a customer who is wearing one of his purple gowns, and he's saying, "I love that color on you. I love it. Please get it. It's wonderful for your coloring."

The woman, who is looking for a dress to wear to her daughter's wedding, inspects herself in the three-way, full-length mirror on the sales floor. "And look how thin it makes you look, and it's not even zipped up yet," says Arnold. The woman is quite thin without the dress's help but Arnold knows what women like to hear.

He leaves this woman with a saleslady and goes back into the dressing room to see another mother of the bride, who is wearing another purple gown. It's huge in the bust and she is squinting into the mirror, trying to imagine what the dress would look like if it fit.

"This is the color of the bridal party," she says, pulling a lavender swatch out of her purse and showing it to Arnold.

"Well, this is perfect with that color," he says. He leaves the woman with her saleslady and goes out onto the sales floor. At 12:30 senior vice-president and director of fashion and product development Ellin Saltzman, wearing all black and carrying her lunch in a white paper bag, stops by to see how the trunk show is progressing.

"How'd you do last night?" she says to Arnold.

They walk away and have a short, intense, whispered conversation in the aisle. As they walk back toward the department, Ellin says, "We sold six yesterday and three today." She is referring to a Scaasi Boutique dress that was featured in a *New York Times* ad last Sunday. The dress retails for $995.

"It's a great dress," says Arnold.

"It was a great ad," says Ellin.

After she leaves, Arnold says, "Ellin was absolutely rude to me last night. I said, 'What's the matter?' and she said, 'Did you like your ad?' and I said, 'It was fabulous,' and she said, 'Well, I didn't hear about it,' and I said, 'I didn't want to call you on Sunday. Every time I call you on Sunday you're in a foul mood,' and she said, 'For something good you can call me.'"

"She just apologized to me for being rude," he continues. "I said, 'I've known you for twenty-seven years. You can be rude.'"

Tomorrow Arnold is leaving for Paris to look at fabrics for his fall made-to-order line, which like all made-to-order is presented right before the actual season, and which he is showing in September. After Paris he will vacation in Capri. "I'll be back July twentieth," he says. "Give me your address. I'll send you a postcard. But if I don't you'll understand why."

A postcard never comes, but later Arnold tells me how he spent his time in Europe. He and his companion, Parker, arrived in Paris on June 22 and checked into the penthouse suite at the Hôtel Crillon. Although it was close to midnight there, Arnold was still on New York time. For him it was 5:30 P.M. and he went to work, immediately opening the suitcases full of fabrics that various French,

Italian, and Swiss textile and embroidery firms had left for him.

Working with a free-lance assistant, over the next three days he made his fabric choices, picking those with unusual textures, colors, or embroidery—things he would not be able to find in the United States. Because Paris was so pretty, he stayed for another two days, just for fun, and then he and Parker traveled to Capri, where they stayed at an old villa that had been turned into a hotel. Although this was supposed to be a vacation, Arnold met with an Italian fabric representative here and continued to have fabric swatches from various houses delivered to him. From Capri he placed the rest of his European fabric order. Now that his fabrics were chosen, the shape of his fall made-to-order collection began germinating in his mind, side by side with the resort Scaasi Boutique ready-to-wear, which he was showing in less than a month.

He and Parker returned home via London, where they stayed for a few days. Back in New York, Arnold took a couple of days to "do normal things" and then went to work on his resort Scaasi Boutique collection, which was opening on August 11, for which he was designing a lot of chiffon dresses.

Like all the other American designers, he took his cue from the July fall couture shows in Paris, where a lot of chiffon was shown. But, he says, the Parisian dresses "didn't look modern. They looked like chiffon dresses from past decades. I wanted mine to look new, so I picked bright colors and made the shapes very young."

On weekends he climbed into bed at his house in Quogue and sketched for hours. In New York, he created other dresses in his salon by draping fabrics on Connie. As usual, as the day of his show approached, his temper got shorter and his workdays got longer. After it was over, his resort collection got a much better reception than the previous one for fall. Even *Women's Wear Daily* called it "a major improvement."

Before and after his work on resort, Arnold continued working with his private clients, designing, for instance, an exclusive lime green, pink, and white draped gown for Mary Tyler Moore to wear to the Emmy Awards at the end of August. He also worked with Patricia Kluge on the extra-special royal blue gown she will wear to her fortieth birthday party in September. The dress was being made to match the sapphire-and-diamond necklace her husband had given her as a present and the party is to be an elaborate gala, "a Belle Epoque ball in the Viennese style," in the grand ballroom of the Waldorf Astoria that a party planner worked on for fourteen months. In September, gossip columnists will devote reams of space to this party, to be attended by such friends as John and Susan

Gutfreund, Saul and Gayfryd Steinberg, Carroll and Milton Petrie, Henry Kravis and Carolyne Roehm, Katharine Graham, Happy Rockefeller, Empress Farah Diba, and, of course, Arnold Scaasi.

Also in September, Arnold will have to design and show his fall made-to-order collection and his bridal collection, as well as get started creating samples for his spring ready-to-wear, for which, like all designers, he's already ordered fabrics. Since his samples are made on his premises he, like Bill Blass and Donna Karan, can start creating them later than designers like Liz Claiborne and Adrienne Vittadini, who do so much work overseas.

We'll pick up with Arnold again later. For now let's return to June 23. Besides being Arnold's first full day in Paris, this Monday is also the day on which the designers of Liz Claiborne Collection will be presenting their work for spring to Liz, Art, and top executives from the sales department. . . .

Liz Claiborne *June 23*

In the twelfth-floor conference room, the Collection design team will present its entire spring collection to key sales executives, as well as to Liz, Art, and Jay. Remember that since its lines are so much larger than any of the other designers, which means that manufacturing, shipping and delivering is much more complicated, Liz Claiborne works much further in advance than other companies.

At this point, 85 percent of its women's apparel lines are designed, which means that sketches for this merchandise have been done and sent, along with first samples, to the production department in New Jersey, which, in turn, is making production samples and, with sketches and patterns, is sending these samples out to contractors around the world. At this point, however, anything and everything can still be changed.

Dennis, Judith, and Katy sit at the head of the table. Liz is in her usual seat by the door, the strap of her pocketbook slung across her chest. Ellen is on her right and Art is on Ellen's right. Jerry Chazen sits across from Art, and the rest of the seats are taken up by executives from the sales, fabric, and petites divisions. Two models stand in front of the room, ready to put on anything they are asked to put on.

Silk Stones, the first knit group, hangs on the wall across from Liz. "I think you have to be quite brave to wear the striped top with the striped bottom," says Liz, opening the meeting. "I'd like to give them the option of wearing a solid bottom with a striped shirt."

"This is a big deal group," says Art, looking at his line plan.

In a defensive tone, Dennis says, "The numbers are the same as . . ." But Art interrupts him, saying calmly, "No, no. I'm just saying, this is a big group."

"A ten percent group," says Dennis, meaning that the group accounts for 10 percent of the line.

"Dennis," says Jerry, the co-chairman who heads up marketing and sales, "is there a reason why the price went up so much?"

"Yes," says Dennis. "We're doing many more jackets and we're doing more constructed suit looks. The price of fabrics went up, and some of the items have more details, which are more expensive."

"I think you should let people know that our prices went up because the price of fabrics went up and because there are more details on the clothes," says Jerry. "The balance of the line doesn't mean anything when it comes to pricing. The buyers are gonna compare last year to this year, shirt to shirt and pant to pant. Alan MacNeary in the dress division told them prices went up because there were more jackets in that line too, to go with the dresses. He shouldn't have even given them that information. That's not the reason our prices went up."

They go on to the group featuring suits with bright linings. "This will be delivered simultaneously with the knits," says Dennis, "so we'll have a nice assortment on the sales floor."

Judith hangs four outfits, composed of jackets and skirts or pants, on the wall behind Liz and then hangs a group of blouses and sweater-blouses on the wall behind Dennis, saying, "Not all of the pieces are here yet." Liz looks at the two jackets hanging on the wall behind her and says, "Are they the same jackets?"

"The pinstripe jacket is more fitted," says Dennis. "It's more of a fashion statement, which is reflected in our ownership." What he means by this is that there are fewer units of this jacket than of the other.

"As far as blouses go," says Jerry, "what's the percentage of black to white?"

"It's sixty percent white, forty percent black," says Dennis. He looks at Jerry and says, "Jerry wants more white. He likes white blouses."

"They're not going to wear black blouses with black suits," says Jerry defensively.

"They're not black suits, Jerry," says Dennis. "There's one black jacket." Indeed, the other jacket hanging on the wall is a white-and-black plaid.

"Jay," says Jerry. His tone says, 'Help me out.'

Jay looks at Jerry and raises his eyebrows, but he doesn't say anything.

"Are you listening?" says Jerry.

"I'm listening," Jay replies.

"Dennis, when are you supposed to be finished designing?" says Art.

"In two weeks."

"Do you have time for refinement?" says Art.

"Yes," says Judith. "We're right on schedule."

"Should we add more color?" says Jay. "And what about the number of long sleeves we have versus the number of short sleeves?"

"It's a good time to have long sleeves in the south," says Ellen.

"You think the south would want long sleeves?" says Jay.

"For the look," says Ellen.

"Do we want more longer-length jackets?" says Jay.

"We have one that's long," says Dennis. "That's the jacket that's not here yet."

"How long was the one that did so well?" says Jay.

"Much longer," says Liz.

"They're only gonna buy one suit," says Jerry.

"Two," says Dennis, thinking that Jerry is referring to the stores.

"No," says Jerry, "the consumer. She's only gonna buy one."

"I think we should lengthen this one," says Liz, standing up and walking over to the black pinstripe jacket.

"Make it twenty-seven, twenty-eight inches?" says Dennis.

"Twenty-eight," says Liz.

"This part of the meeting is critical," says Art. "We have to make sure we haven't gone too uptight and serious throughout." It's nine o'clock, and Jay walks out of the room.

The salespeople aren't sure whether they like two of the blouses, and Dennis asks the models to put them on. The models leave the room and one returns wearing a yellow short-sleeve V-neck blouse with a scalloped collar and scalloped sleeve bottoms.

"That's not a suit blouse," says Jerry. "You're much better off if you give the customer the option of buying two blouses that work under suits instead of throwing in one that doesn't. That's the type of thing the stores yell at us about. "Why don't you give us more suit blouses?" he says in a whining voice meant to imitate a complaining retailer.

"This is a great item blouse," says Liz, "but it doesn't work under the jacket." She points to the black-and-white pinstripe jacket. "It gets squashed." Dennis sends the model out of the room to put on a black-and-white knit suit from the first group.

In the meantime the other model has returned wearing a short-sleeve sweater. Liz calls her over and pushes the sweater up under the armpit. "It's too low here to wear under a jacket," she says. "There's too much fabric."

"We have a color problem," says Dennis. "This yarn will not take the red dye."

"They can't do it in Hong Kong but they can do it in Japan," says Liz.

"No," says Katy. "They tried it in Japan. It didn't take."

"I think we should look at the whole line," says Liz, not addressing Katy's comment. "Somewhere we should have a collarless jacket. I don't care where, but we should have one."

The first model returns in the knit suit. It's tight, and Jerry says, "Liz, how do you feel about the knit suit being fitted because of the way it pulls on a typical consumer if it's just a little tight?" He is saying that the typical Liz Claiborne customer has bulges and will look awful in this outfit.

Liz fiddles with the jacket, trying to figure out how to make it fit better.

"This is the first prototype," says Dennis. "It won't be tight when we're finished."

"It will be, on most consumers," says Jerry. "When you try to make a suit jacket in a knit it becomes a very difficult thing. It pulls."

"How committed are you to it?" says Art to Dennis.

"Not at all," says Dennis, meaning that they haven't booked production time for it yet.

"It may be the kind of item that you don't need to anguish through for just ten thousand units. Tell John it's iffy," Art says, referring to John Listanowsky, senior vice-president in charge of knitwear production.

"OK" says Art, joking. "Let's increase the units a little and go on."

"And raise the price," says Jerry, laughing, as he names the second thing that the company regularly tries not to do.

The next group has two tropical prints, one with an olive background and the other with a black background. This is the print that Dennis refused to let Liz change back in April. "Everybody," Dennis says, as he places two color Xeroxes on the table, "these Xeroxes don't give you a true sense of what the colors are. The real colors are very bright."

Judith hangs up one jacket, two blouses, three skirts, and one dress. None of them is made out of the tropical-print fabric, since that fabric has not yet been printed. The production department made these samples out of a fabric that has exactly the same fiber content as the tropical print will have so that the design department could see how the fabric would tailor. This is what Judith is showing the sales executives right now.

"Why do you need the black background?" says Jerry, looking at the two Xeroxes.

Liz sighs and raising her voice, says, "This is why I don't like these meetings. I'm sorry, Jerry. We have red [pieces in the group] and we have royal [blue pieces in the group] and they go well with black. The black is going to outsell the olive," she says.

"Did anyone tell anyone that?" Art says angrily to Liz. "The line plan says fifty-fifty. You're depending on supportive staff to think inside your head. What does the print order look like?" He is asking whether, based on Liz's projection that black will outsell olive, the company has ordered more of the fabric with the black background than with the olive background. According to the line plan, the fabric is being bought in equal numbers.

No one answers and Art says, "Will someone please call Japan and find out? Say, 'Look, fellas. Don't print it fifty-fifty.' I'll call if nobody else will." He stands up and heads for the phone in the corner.

"I'll do it," says Cheryl Rosenfeld, vice-president of textile research for the sportswear division. She walks to the phone and calls her department to find out whether this fabric has been printed yet.

"No one is going to buy two colors," says Jerry.

"They are two different statements," says Liz. "And we're hoping one store will buy one and another store will buy the other so we don't look like a cookie cutter out there. The olive in higher price points is considered a classier color."

Art says to Cheryl, who is still on the phone, "Tell them you want to see the goods before they print."

"Alison is over there," says Liz, referring to the woman who designed the fabric and who is overseeing its production in Japan.

"Tell them we want to make sure no one prints a goddamn thing until we see the first strike-offs," says Art. "They'll say to themselves, 'We're not very busy right now,' and they'll take any opportunity to print."

"Alison will be back on Monday with all the strike-offs?" says Liz. Cheryl nods.

Art picks up a bunch of green striped and dotted fabric swatches. "Is this D and D?" he asks, referring to an expensive process called dye and discharge that saturates the fabric so completely that it can be difficult to tell which side was actually printed.

"Yes," says Dennis.

"Goddamn it," says Art, throwing the swatches down on the table. He is cursing under his breath, imagining the expense of this mistake if it is indeed a mistake. He gets on the phone himself and calls the fabric department. After a quick conversation, which I can't hear, Art hangs up the phone and sits down again at the table.

"It's shoddy," he says, banging his fist on the table. "It's a lack of attention to detail." Again he bangs his fist. "You know they're not busy now." Again, the fist. "You know they'll go ahead and dye it." (Bang.) "You can bury a group as important as this just because of a lack of attention to detail." (Bang.) "You should always, in writing, tell them, 'This is a tentative assortment. Do not print.'" (Bang.) "'Do not dye.'" (Bang.) "'Until New York gives final approval.'" (Bang.)

"I thought assorting reserves space," says Dennis.

"But the minute our people approve it, it goes," says Liz.

They go on: "I think jackets drive our business," says Jay. "There's an opportunity for jackets."

"But," Liz says, "if you look at how well—" here she stops, looks at me, and hesitates—"how well what's her name on the West Coast did with two-piece dressing." She is obviously referring to Carole Little.

"I think there's a lot of conversation going on here that will not be relevant once we see the goods," says Art. "You have about ten to twelve variables that can change. That's why I'm so upset. We almost painted ourselves into a corner."

"But the silhouettes have to be done," says Liz angrily.

"But you may have to change how much we own of the prints," says Art, also angrily. "I'm referring to the fact that these should never be approved and printed before we see the goods. That almost happened because we ignored the fundamentals of the game. Incidentally, Japan hasn't printed, so you can see the whole thing on Monday. But pick up the phone. I shouldn't have to be the one to do it. Once you see the prints you may decide you want to change the balance. You may decide you want to make a different silhouette once you see the prints."

"As far as assortment and printing goes," says Jerry, "is there some way to put it into the calendar so that we make sure it's done, because there are so many new players here? It could easily fall through the cracks."

"These new people are managing the company," says Art angrily.

It's 9:30 and Jerry asks, "Where's Jay?"

"He's in an interview," says Art.

"Why did he schedule an interview that conflicts with this meeting?" says Jerry.

No one answers him and they go on to the group using the leftover linen. Again, Judith hangs the pieces on the wall. Many of them are black, and Jerry says sarcastically, "I think it's a good thing black is such a terrific color this year."

Dennis ignores him, and Jerry, pointing to one of the jackets on the wall, says, "That double-breasted cardigan jacket—have we ever had an odd jacket like that sell?"

"It's one of Anne Klein II's best jackets," says Ellen.

"But as a suit jacket. That's not a suit jacket. It's an odd jacket."

"Where is it from?" says Art.

"Korea," says Dennis.

"Dennis," says Art, "make a mental note to yourself that you need a hangtag."

"That says the slubs are part of the silk Honan fabric," says Dennis.

"Slubs, rips, tears are all a part of the fabric," says Art.

Speaking at the same time, Judith, Ellen, and Art all ask Liz questions. "I'm sorry," she says, slightly annoyed. "I can't hear everybody at once."

She answers their questions, one by one. At 9:50 Jay returns. He has to pass behind Art to get to his seat. Art stops him and the two of them hold an intense whispered conversation. Annoyed, Jerry says, "The rest of the meeting is, uh . . . over here." Art and Jay stop talking and, along with everyone else, they look at a group of eight sweaters Katy has hung on the wall.

"Are we going to edit this now?" says Art.

"This is the only opportunity we're going to have to edit them with wovens," says Liz.

"We have to figure out what will hang with what," says Art. "If it ain't obvious, we're only kidding ourselves."

Nodding at a cardigan sweater, Art says to Katy, "You'd better deliver that one early, honey."

"Well," says Katy, "it's Shanghai. I don't know."

"It's Shanghai?" says Art. "Then we'd better make sure it's half-knitted now, even though we don't know what we're knitting yet."

They choose the best styles and go on to the black-and-blue and black-and-white striped jersey group.

"What makes this a Liz Claiborne Collection group?" says Jerry. "No one is going to wear this to work. It looks like Lizsport."

"It's a fine cotton yarn," says Dennis, "which adds a different flavor. It's a less expensive way of putting yourself together for work."

"It's only a five percent group," says Jay.

"We decided that since everything at retail has been so tailored and career that we would take a fly and do something sporty," says Art.

Jerry gives him a blank stare.

"The look on your face!" says Dennis.

"I don't know if he's kidding or what," says Jerry.

"I'm serious," says Art.

"Sport is nipping at the heels of Collection and Lizwear is nipping at the heels of Liz Claiborne and Lizsport," says Liz. "By Spring 1989 I don't believe everyone is going to want to dress in these uptight suits."

"But this is not an alternative to a suit," says Jerry. "This could be in Sport. That's why we have a sport division. I'd rather see elegant, dressier, country-club type clothes in Collection than this."

"Sport would not have the details this does," says Liz. She looks at Dennis, expecting him to support her case, but Dennis throws up his hands in an "I don't care" gesture and says, "I'm not fighting anymore."

No one takes the argument any further, and it's understood that this group will remain a part of the line. It is 10:25, and they go on to the group with both red and navy gold-buttoned suits. Judith hangs up the suit pieces on one wall and the coordinating blouses and thin knit tops on another.

Dennis says to Judith, "Show Jerry the fabric."

"Why me?" says Jerry defensively.

"Because everyone else has seen it," says Dennis.

"This is a crepe Jerry's familiar with," says Liz. "It's Burlington's worsted crepe. It's a beautiful crepe."

"And they did it just for us?" says Art, who has been on the phone.

"Yes," says Liz.

"Jerry," says Jay, "this was Spiegel's favorite group."

Jerry nods, and almost to himself he says, "The balance of blouses and sweaters is off."

"We need more blouses than sweaters," says Ellen.

"I just commented quietly on that," says Jerry.

"The blouses are so strong," says Ellen. "I love the polka dots and the tattersall."

"We have to talk about line balance, items, and we haven't even looked at delivery rotation," says Jerry.

Jay points at two of the sweaters hanging on the wall. "Those are really blouses," he says. "They're worn under a jacket."

"As we go over the totality of the line, we have to see where we want to adjust," says Art.

"If we have twenty-five thousand or thirty thousand units of something," says Jerry, "it should be a blouse and not a sweater."

"But you're being inconsistent," says Jay. "We've had a lot of conversation about the opportunity for sweater-blouses."

"There's an opportunity for blouses too," says Ellen. "Evan-Picone is over-priced. They're priced at eighty dollars for a polyester shirt. So is Jones New York. That means we have an opening."

"We moved away from blouses," says Jerry. "When we move away from something everybody else moves away."

"Just because we're idiots doesn't mean everybody else is an idiot," says Art.

"We're not idiots," says Jerry, stating the obvious. The look on Dennis's face says that he might beg to disagree, but he doesn't, because, in the end, the philosophy of giving the customer what she wants, even if it isn't what Dennis Gay wants to give her, has paid off in a big way for Liz Claiborne, Inc.

Adrienne Vittadini *July 6*

Having been told by the sales department that they need to add six more groups to the Active line, Adrienne and David are sitting on the window ledge in the design room trying to meet that request. The room is extremely cluttered. All the walls are covered with concept boards, and spread out on the floor in front of Adrienne and David there are swatches of fabrics and small piles of clothes that appealed to Adrienne and that they may knock off.

Adrienne, who looks exhausted, is starting to panic. "I don't know what to do," she says. "We already have so many groups, since we're designing spring and summer at the same time, and we haven't sent a stitch to Hong Kong, and in one month we are going to be there editing. Last night I was up from two o'clock to four thinking, 'How are we going to do this line?' I took a sedative that could kill a horse."

"We can work over the weekend," says David.

"I hate working weekends in the summer, David, I can't. I've sacrificed too many weekends already. But the deadline for our sketches is next Friday." She turns back to the fabric swatches in front of them and, picking up a green one, says, "Can I tell you this? I would layer that color over that one so that it becomes a better tone. How can I explain it? This green bothers me."

Ornella comes in and tells Adrienne she wants to try a factory in Turkey.

"What can they do?" says Adrienne in a very controlled voice.

"I'll come back later," says Ornella, who turns on her heel and leaves.

Francesca, or Frenchie, as Adrienne calls her, comes in. She is a skinny girl with bobbed brown hair who is responsible for developing prints for all the divisions, as well as for tracking the progress of the home furnishings and Accessory Street licenses. There's a real feeling of tension in the air as the three of them sit down to review fabrics.

"I went through every shelf of every bookshop in London for ideas," says Adrienne. "This morning at the sales meeting they said I have too many stripes. We have ten striped groups and I still feel for one or two more."

They decide on a type of emblem they will use in one of the groups and Adrienne says, "Are these going out tonight?"

"Tomorrow," says David.

"Tomorrow?"

"It's six o'clock."

"It's six o'clock? Oh, God, where did this day go?"

They are looking at tiny prints, one of which is a miniature elephant, and Adrienne says, "Didn't someone in the past use elephants? Someone like Agnès B?

"You know what I heard today that a buyer from Nordstrom's said?" she continues. " 'Adrienne must have fallen asleep in the fields with all those butterflies and daisies she has on the resort line.' " This line is currently being sold in the showroom.

"Yeah," says Francesca. "We're really sleeping in the fields."

"It's so hot in here," Adrienne sighs. David opens the window onto the terrace and they go back to looking at color yarn swatches.

At 6:10 Ornella comes in again, and Adrienne says playfully, "What are you doing here?"

"I just need the number of this board," says Ornella. She writes down the number and leaves.

At 6:35 Donna comes in and says, "I need you to do an interview with *Newsday*."

"Now?" says Adrienne, looking up. "Donna, we are in the most painful part of designing. I had a meeting with sales this morning and they wanted me to come up with six more groups."

"Well, this will make you work faster," says Donna. "It won't take long. They just need fifteen minutes on the telephone. How about tomorrow morning?"

"I have the dentist and then a licensing meeting." (She will be meeting with executives from Fieldcrest to present them with her color and pattern choices for her new line of home furnishings, which are being made under license by Fieldcrest. They, in turn, will tell her if they agree with her choices, will analyze these choices to see if they conflict with any other designs already on their line, and will tell her if what she wants to make is technically possible on their machinery.

"Friday?" says Donna.

Adrienne nods and looks back down. "I'm so frazzled. I'm designing six groups at once."

Donna points to a faded navy blue crew-neck T-shirt with a dark green neckline. "This looks like one of Gigi's old shirts," she says, referring to Adrienne's husband.

"I adore it but I don't think Americans will understand it," says Adrienne.

"They won't," says Donna. "Not unless you trim it in white."

"And," Donna continues, changing the subject, "*The New York Times* wants pictures for that magazine thing with Carol Vogel." The *Times* magazine section is preparing a story on interior designer Guy Aulenti and wants to photograph Adrienne's Aulenti-designed stores.

"This is not Anne Marie Schiro?" says Adrienne naming another *New York Times* reporter who is preparing an article on Adrienne.

"No. This is the magazine. And there are people waiting for you in your office to have a meeting about licensing."

"Now?" says Adrienne.

"I'm only kidding."

"Donna," says Adrienne, holding up the color Xeroxes of three different prints, "which do you like? The elephants, the fish, or the bugs?"

"The elephants or the fish. The bugs look like something you did already."

Adrienne nods and puts the three back on the floor. "Francesca," she says, "see if there is anything in the books I brought back that we can pull for some wonderful hand-embroidered Mexican T-shirts."

Francesca brings in a stack of hardcover coffee-table books, and she and Adrienne leaf through them while David cuts out a piece of fabric from a brown sweater to use as a fabric swatch. "This is what we're missing," says Adrienne.

Ideas are, obviously, the first step in the fashion cycle. Bill Blass conceives a large part of his collection behind his desk, where he can be found every weekday morning.

The problem with designing, however, is that designers' workdays encompass much more than just creation, a fact well illustrated not just by Donna Karan's expression, but by the clutter on her desk as well.

For Arnold Scaasi, as for all designers, sketching serves as a form of note-taking, helping him and his staff to visualize what he has conceived. Sketching begins as soon as ideas occur and continues almost to the day a collection opens.

Bill Blass reviews fabrics with his assistant Laura Montalban. The selection of fabrics is an important part of the conceptualization process since it can often trigger ideas.

Arnold Scaasi checks on the progress of a muslin sample. Garments are first sewn in muslin so that if an idea does not translate well into reality, expensive fabrics will not be ruined.

Draping fabrics on a live model to see how they fall and take shape is an important part of Arnold Scaasi's design process.

Donna Karan giving a seamstress the sort of specific, detailed instructions that must be given on a regular basis. As samples are being made, constant communication between designers and their workrooms is a must.

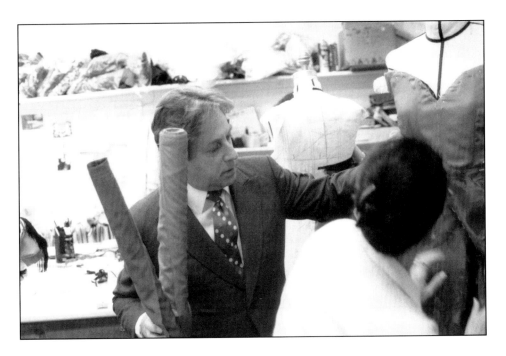

After muslin samples have been approved, the workrooms then make the garment in its actual fabric. Arnold Scaasi checks on the progress of one such garment.

Once ready-to-wear samples are made in the right fabrics, they are then adjusted on standard-size eight fitting models. Once these are fit, patterns are then made and graded up and down to fit standard sizes four to fourteen. Here, at the company's production facility in New Jersey, Liz Claiborne adjusts samples.

Donna Karan adjusting a sample which has been made in the right fabric for the first time.

Just before their fashion shows, at which they show their collections to fashion magazine editors and store buyers, designers put together press kits that explain the concept behind their collection and describe the clothing that will be shown. Here Peter Arnell, whose firm Arnell/Bickford handles all of Donna's advertising, takes pictures of Donna as she reviews a press release.

Bill Blass checking a model backstage at his fashion show.

Backstage at her fashion show, Adrienne Vittadini reviews Polaroid pictures of the outfits that are being shown today. These Polaroids help her and her stylists remember which accessories go with which outfit.

Adrienne Vittadini gives models a final inspection before they head out on the runway.

Arnold Scaasi with Barbara Bush wearing the gown he designed for her to wear to the inaugural ball. Having someone as prominent as the First Lady choose you to design a dress for her to wear to something as important as the inauguration is the best accolade any designer can receive.

"Black-and-white conversation, which would be the elephant print; Mexican; and turquoise."

At 7:30 David and Adrienne start taping fabric swatches onto six boards. "We still have to come up with Mexican prints," says Adrienne. "I see flouncy skirts. I love it red with turquoise and some touches of white." Then she sighs, "It's so hot."

"And it's only going to get hotter," says David. "It's supposed to be a hundred degrees for the next ten days."

"Dianna called from Italy and said it's so hot there that they can hardly work in the factories."

Francesca carries in seven hardcover books on Mexican costumes. The phone rings in Adrienne's office and Adrienne yells to her secretary, "If that's Gigi, tell him I'm not coming home tonight." She's kidding, but she sounds as if she means it.

She sits on the floor by the boards and David and Francesca walk over to her. Adrienne's secretary comes in and Adrienne says, "Sarah, call the Mexican embassy tomorrow and ask if there are any stores for Mexican folk art, and send this telex to Jimmy: 'Dear Jimmy, about your so-called revised sample....'" Jimmy is the head of one of the factories Adrienne uses in Hong Kong, and her telex to him details everything that was wrong with a sample she has recently received from him.

At 8 P.M. Sarah says to Adrienne, "Are you going to work with dresses tonight? The designers are waiting."

"No," says Adrienne. "They can go." I'm beginning to see that a working day here could easily extend into the wee hours of the morning.

Adrienne Vittadini *July 20*

For the past two weeks, Adrienne and her designers have been working until 10 and 11 P.M. drawing the one thousand sketches they need to send to Hong Kong. Now that all those sketches are finally in the hands of their factories, the news that Adrienne has been fearing came this week—no way, nohow, were the samples going to be ready in time for her scheduled trip to Hong Kong on August 3.

Now she is sitting in her office with Donna Cristina and with Shasha Boyd, who is vice-president of sales for Collection. The three are trying to figure out what a later trip to Hong Kong would do to Adrienne's vacation plans and to her business obligations for early fall.

Donna reads a list of Adrienne's upcoming personal appearances: one in mid-September at Macy's in Tyson's Corner, Virginia, and another a few days later at Adrienne's own store in St. Louis. Plus, Shasha says, Adrienne needs to design something for Bloomingdale's upcoming Hong Kong promotion. Speaking of Bloomingdale's, Shasha says, Kalman Ruttenstein, vice-president of fashion direction at that store, wants to feature a black-and-white striped group from Adrienne's holiday line in the store windows for a week beginning October 23. "I said they won't have the merchandise by then, that it's a November delivery," says Shasha, "and they said that's OK."

"They've done that before," says Adrienne, who then picks up the phone and calls Richard, the president of the company. "I have a list of problems," she says to him. "Kal first. I've been talking to him every day. He wants to do windows on October twenty-third and have me make a personal appearance on the twenty-fourth, as well as go to a press luncheon. Donna didn't think that was prestigious enough. She wanted a charity gala. He would be happy with samples for the windows but Shasha said that if we shipped them early we would have to ship everybody early.

"Two, do you know anything about a personal appearance that I committed to in Virginia? I don't." She listens and then says, "I did? Oh, boy. This is crazy.

"Three, Saks," she says. "I wanted to call Mara [Urshell, senior vice-president and general merchandise manager at Saks Fifth Avenue] and say I want a wood floor in our department, maybe a couple of Guy Aulenti chairs. Richard, I would love to put some pressure on Mara. We could split the costs. I'd love to have a meeting with Mara, Tansky, and Jacobs. [Burt Tansky is the president of Saks and Mel Jacobs is the chairman and chief executive officer.] They're renovating the floor and that area looks so shabby. It would be in their interest. And I'm also upset that they're only putting us in fourteen stores. You are aware of that? What about the balance? Our figures are so great, I don't understand." She listens and then goes on to the most pressing problem.

"Richie, I fell asleep last night and forgot to call Monica," Adrienne says, referring to the woman who oversees their production in Hong Kong. "They won't be able to have samples in time. How is this affecting you? . . . I haven't had a summer. Saint-Tropez was sheer work. I spent just half a day at the beach. If we go to Hong Kong later it will be cold in the Hamptons by the time we get back." She listens to Richard for a long time, as Donna and Shasha slip out of her office and Odile and Adrienne's secretary, Sarah, take their place. Finally Adrienne hangs up, resigned to going to Hong Kong later. She doesn't have a choice.

With Odile and Sarah, Adrienne tries to figure out when she, Odile, Richard, Ornella, and the assistant designers should arrive in Hong Kong. Odile will get there a few days before Adrienne to fix obvious errors in the clothes.

"When does Active open?" says Odile.

"It was to be September nineteenth," says Adrienne. "He's delaying it to the twenty-sixth." These are the dates that the line will open for selling in the showroom, giving the factories only one month to manufacture and ship final samples of the line.

As the three women stare at their respective calendars, Brenda Perenti-Holland, a young red-haired woman with freckles and a squeaky voice who is vice-president of production, comes in with pictures of some fit models for Adrienne to review. Adrienne will be taking a fit model to Hong Kong to fit samples on her. As Adrienne looks at the first girl's picture, Brenda says, "She has good measurements for a fit model, thirty-five, twenty-seven, thirty-seven. She's worked for Bern Conrad and Cathy Hardwick.

"This second girl I liked but she was too chatty," Brenda continues. "She's worked for Liz Claiborne and Bonnie August." Adrienne hands the pictures back to Brenda without making a choice.

"When are you going to Hong Kong?" Brenda asks Adrienne.

"She's not going," jokes Sarah. "She's going to the Hamptons with me."

"Great," says Brenda. "We'll go and take over the company."

"Be my guest," says Adrienne. "I'll wash my hands of it."

"The novelty of Hong Kong has worn off, hasn't it?" says Odile. "Although, my next door neighbor thinks it's cool and my mother wants to go. Maybe I'll send her in my place."

"My father wants to go, too," says Adrienne. "They can go together."

"If they only knew what it's really like," says Odile. "If they only knew."

Adrienne Vittadini *Hong Kong*

Hong Kong, the world's largest exporter of garments, is a country in transition. In 1997 it will once again become a part of China, with unforeseen consequences. Right now, however, it remains a city where most top American designers manufacture a large portion of their collections. In 1988 Hong Kong exported U.S. $3.9 billion worth of garments and accessories to the U.S.

Hong Kong is a country of contrasts. It is a place that has more Rolls-Royces per capita than any other nation, yet 50 percent of its approximately 2.8 million people live in high-rise, government-subsidized housing projects, easily identified by the laundry draped over their balconies. In these projects the typical Hong Kong family, which consists of six to seven members, lives in a one-room, 400-square-foot apartment, sleeping on bunk beds and hanging its belongings in baskets suspended from the ceiling.

Because their apartments are so small, Hong Kong residents spend a good part of their free time outside—on the sidewalks or in restaurants or movie theaters. Even I, a native New Yorker who is used to Manhattan's crowds, found Hong Kong horrifically claustrophobic. Adding to this feeling was the fact that it was terribly hot and humid, and it poured rain during every single day of Adrienne's stay. After I had done some initial exploring, I could well understand why Adrienne and her employees rarely ventured outside the walls of the Regent Hotel.

The Regent is a calm, cool, marble oasis. Personally I found the hotel over-serviced. The Regent's service staff will interrupt all conversations—no matter how impassioned—to greet you as "Sir" or "Madame," and they will make a great show of apologizing for getting on the same elevator as you. Despite the truism "Good help should not be noticed," at the Regent, you cannot help but see that lurking around every corner is a white-jacketed employee waiting to attend to your every whim. I soon learned to flip the switch that turned on the Do Not Disturb light in the hall every single time I entered my room, to keep out the housekeeping crew, ever eager to fold my clothes or line up my shoes in neat little rows.

This very fact, however, is what American designers love about the Regent. Since Adrienne always works morning, noon, and night in this hotel, she welcomes the service. It will make an almost unbearable crush of work a little more pleasant. And she doesn't have to think about anything but clothing.

The first Adrienne Vittadini employee to check into the Regent was Odile, who arrived on August 6. She visited the factories and corrected many samples before Richard and Adrienne arrived—he on the night of August 9 and she last night.

This morning, the factories making clothes for the Collection, Active, and dress divisions delivered to the hotel what they had finished so far. Adrienne has no control over what she will see when. She has to take the merchandise when, and only when, the factories are ready to show it.

The bulk of what came in this morning was for the Active division, and for that reason Adrienne chose to start editing Active, leaving the initial edit of the other divisions to the assistants for those divisions. Adrienne is working with Richard, Ornella, and David in her room, a corner room with a view of both the harbor and the Peninsula Hotel across the street. Richard, wearing crocodile loafers without socks, and a heavy gold chain around his neck, is sitting on the bed next to Ornella. The five groups of clothes hang on a rack by the window, and Adrienne and David hang the first of these groups on the armoire next to the bed.

While Adrienne and David are looking at the clothes from a creative standpoint, Ornella is checking for potential production problems and Richard is making sure the line is shaped in a way that would best appeal to store buyers. It is better, he told me earlier, not to give the buyers too many choices. "That tends to frustrate the buyer," he said. "Adrienne will do two V-necks and think they're different, but the buyer will say, 'Why do you have two V-necks in this group?' and then you have to go through this whole explanation that only a creative person would understand." Also, he says, superfluous styles are costly, since the company makes fourteen samples of every piece it plans to produce. It needs samples for its New York showroom, plus for its four sales representatives in different parts of the country and its licensees.

Each concentrating on his or her own area of expertise, the four look at the group of blue-and-white printed knits hanging in two rows on the armoire: shirts on top, skirts and pants on the bottom.

Yawning, Adrienne points to a short-sleeve printed T-shirt that at the moment has a white neckline. "Do we like it with white or blue?" she says of the neckline.

"Blue," says Richard. "White is too sporty."

David writes this down in a black reference binder that holds all the production sketches. He and Adrienne will later communicate this and their other changes to Monica, the young Chinese woman who is employed by Adrienne's agent here, Lark International, to oversee all of Adrienne's production. Monica, in turn, will communicate these changes to the appropriate factories.

"Think about long sleeve," says Richard. "We need a long sleeve, and do we have a sarong?"

"Yes," says Ornella.

"Great," he says. "This is hot."

"Adrienne," he continues, "Think private label. I mean, exclusive. That's a good Neiman's group." By "exclusive," Richard is referring to a trend in the industry where stores, in an effort to differentiate their sales floors from those of their competitors, are asking designers to provide them with merchandise that is theirs exclusively. "Private label," on the other hand, refers to items that the store itself designs.

"Richie, wait a minute," says Adrienne, who does not want to limit the group's distribution.

"Adrienne, the heat for exclusives is getting hotter and hotter. Everybody wants exclusives."

"Do we want a straight skirt?" she says, ignoring Richard.

"No," he says.

"If someone wants it we can merchandise it in," she says.

"I love that sundress," he says. "I'm glad sundresses are back. I love sundresses."

"There are four groups here," says Adrienne. She means that the blue group will be delivered with three others—"tie-dye, the stripe story, and color block."

She describes to Richard which groups they have planned to deliver in the spring, and what they will deliver for summer.

Replacing the blue group on the rack by the window, David and Adrienne hang a cream, heather, and blue group in its place on the armoire. "David, who's the factory on this?" says Adrienne, yawning again. "It looks really shitty."

"This does look bad," says Richard. "It's too yellow. It looks old and washed out. But there are some cute styles, some cute silhouettes. That's a cute logo."

Richard points to a tank dress. "Are we going to wear this with a T-shirt underneath, or bare?"

"Bare," says Adrienne.

"Then we have to be careful under the arm. We have to make sure it's high enough so it doesn't reveal too much. The ladies are uptight when it comes to that."

They put this group away and hang up another one. "OK," says Adrienne.

"Let's pick out the dogs." She stares at the clothes on the armoire but doesn't make a move to remove any of them. Richard, David, and Ornella watch Adrienne as she stares at the clothes, until finally she says, "I'm exhausted. My brain is like a marshmallow."

"You need some sugar," says Richard. He goes to his room and returns with a complimentary plate of candylike cookies that the hotel sends each member of the Adrienne Vittadini contingent every day. For some reason Adrienne's cookies have not yet arrived. Adrienne eats four of them.

"I was in Beverly Hills and I was getting feedback that our clothes are getting too big," says Richard. "People who are fours and sixes are having trouble buying our clothes."

Adrienne doesn't respond to his comment. Instead she says, "I don't like the chopped ones," as she points to a pair of stretch pants that are navy on top, beige in the middle, and navy on the bottom. "How could we have done this?"

"We didn't," says David. "They're supposed to be beige. The factory ran out of fabric."

They take the "dogs" out and go on to the next group, which is cream-colored with white embroidered crests.

Richard walks to the wardrobe and feels the cream pants. "These are great first samples," he says. "Look at the details. Who did these?" David tells him.

"These are great," says Richard. "These could put us in business."

"Providing the price is right," says Ornella. Prices will not be set until after Adrienne is finished editing the line and correcting the pieces that remain.

Adrienne goes into the bathroom carrying a pair of white pants. She comes out wearing them, and David says, "They look nice."

"David," says Adrienne, in an anguished voice. "These buttonholes are horrible. And there's not enough hip. They fit me perfectly, and I have no hips. They will not fit most women."

She goes into the bathroom with another pair of pants. "These, on the other hand," she says, as she comes out wearing them, "have too much hip."

At 12:25 a bellboy delivers a plate of candy. "Your daily delivery of sweets," says Richard, who is now barefoot.

"Good," says Adrienne, who is also barefoot. "More to get fat on."

"You need a full skirt and pant in this group," says Richard.

"And a slim skirt," says Adrienne.

David writes these down, and they go on to the next group, which is taupe-and-cream striped.

"How many groups are we making here?" says Adrienne.

"Twenty-five," says David.

"And only two with Raoul?" says Adrienne, naming the owner of the main factory they use in Italy. David nods.

"Quota has come down a lot," says Richard. "It's going to make this place a big value again." In an effort to keep down the level of clothing imports, the U.S., working in terms of quantity rather than quality, has allocated a set amount of quota per apparel category. This quota is purchased in the country of origin for the merchandise (in this case Hong Kong) and its price fluctuates according to demand. Since the apparel business is so bad right now, almost all American firms have cut down on the amount of clothing they are manufacturing, thereby freeing up more quota. This decreased demand has resulted in decreased prices.

Without commenting, Adrienne tries on a taupe-and-beige sweater. "This is great," says Richard, referring to the group. "Can we make this career? Not sporty?"

"But there is safari with this. And riding pants," says Adrienne, referring to other merchandise that will be delivered at the same time.

Adrienne calls Monica, the production liaison, who is working with Odile on Collection in Odile's room. Adrienne tells Monica to have lunch and says, "After lunch I'll explain everything to you."

As they return to editing, Richard voices many opinions while Adrienne is slightly undecided about much of what she sees. "See," says Richard, "it's better when I get here a day before you."

"You're sharp, and I'm so out of it," says Adrienne.

At 1:30 they decide to break for lunch. "I think we should have our first family meal," says Richard. He calls the coffee shop downstairs to reserve a table for twelve but is told they do not take reservations. I go downstairs with him. We walk through the marble lobby, with its absolutely spectacular view of Hong Kong harbor, and down a flight of stairs to the coffee shop, which has the same spectacular view.

The hostess tells Richard he'll have to wait for a table. There are two empty ones standing next to each other in the middle of the floor close to us, and Richard says, "Why don't you just move those two tables together?"

"They are reserved," she says.

"What do you mean they are reserved?" he says angrily. "I just called and was told that you don't take reservations."

"The concierge must have given you the wrong information," she replies. "We do not take reservations for breakfast but we do take them for lunch."

He goes on complaining but is told to sit and wait. We sit on one of the two benches in the large, airy space.

"That reserved table is probably for Bo Derek," he says. "I saw her yesterday in the elevator. You know what would make a good book? Exploring what John Derek has going for him. Think about it. First Ursula Andress, then Linda Evans, and now Bo Derek."

The entire Vittadini group makes its appearance two by two. When we are finally shown to a table, we sit six on one side and six on the other. I am sitting next to Richard, and over lunch he tells me that there is subtle competition between the designers to get their work out first. He says Odile is very competitive and David is very charming. "That's how he gets his way with things."

After lunch Adrienne and Ornella go to place personal clothing orders with a tailor, one of their few forays out of the hotel. I tag along with Richard to his tailor, located on the ground floor of the Regent Shopping Mall. Afterward, he gives me a tour of the Regent Shopping Arcade. The tour includes a white marble staircase that appears to be hanging in midair and has a handrail made of black lacquer. "They scrape this lacquer down every two months and refinish it," says Richard. "And they polish the brass on the doors every day." He is as proud of the Regent as he would be of his own home, and as the days unfold I come to understand why he has this affinity for it. Almost all of Adrienne's samples are delivered here to be edited and fit, and this hotel becomes like a womb for them.

As we walk, I ask Richard where the good shopping is in Hong Kong, and he says, "I don't know. In all the time I've been in Hong Kong I've never taken a tour. Maybe someday I'll bring my family and then I won't be in such a hurry to get back home." In fact, everyone is in a hurry to get home—not a day passes that someone doesn't say that maybe he or she could leave earlier than scheduled. Already it is quite clear to me that for these designers Hong Kong is nothing more than a place they must visit to get their work done.

Adrienne Vittadini *August 12*

This morning Adrienne had breakfast with Ira Kaye, head of Lark International, the company that sources her production in the Far East. By 11 A.M. she is back in her room making specific production changes, with David and Jean Vercillo, who oversees production for Active, on the pieces that survived yesterday's editing session. It is pouring rain outside, and the room is so dark that they have set up a much-needed spotlight to shine on the armoire, where the clothes are hanging.

All three are sitting on the bed, and Adrienne is yawning repeatedly. "My body's falling apart," she says. "It's revolting. It's saying, 'I don't want to come to Hong Kong anymore.' You know how many times I've been here?"

"Let's see," says David. "The company's ten years old. Three times a year. You've come here thirty times since you started this company."

"Thirty?" says Adrienne. "No. In the beginning I used to come five times a year. But I've been coming here since 1969. Can you imagine?" She yawns and points to a garment, saying, "I would do an edge stitch here and a two-inch hem. The horizontal opening is too wide." As Jean writes this down on a yellow piece of paper and pins the paper to the garment, Brenda and the fitting model walk in. After Adrienne is done making stylistic changes, the production people will fit the clothes on the model, making them a standard medium size. Adrienne's factories make her clothes in three sizes—small, medium, and large—and they will use these medium samples to give them the proper scale for the other sizes.

Brenda seems chipper enough, but the model says she couldn't sleep at all last night. Adrienne offers to give her a "light pill," saying, "There's such a thing as overtired."

"No," says the model. "I might end up sleeping through the next day."

Adrienne points to the pants she tried on yesterday. "I have no hips and these fit me perfectly, so you should add some width in the hips."

"Do you have your pads?" David says to the model.

"I don't have them on but I have them with me," says the model, who needs to pad her hips to bring them out to the proper size.

They finish up the cream group and go on to a navy blue one. Adrienne dictates corrections, and again using the yellow paper, Jean writes down what

Adrienne says and then pins these pieces of paper to the appropriate garment.

At 11:30 Monica, the production liaison, arrives. She is a thin, fashionably dressed Chinese girl with long, wavy dark hair and a tasteful, but noticeable, amount of gold jewelry.

"How are we doing?" says Adrienne.

"Good," says Monica, with a slight Chinese accent. "We will be finished with everything by tomorrow night." She means the thirty-six groups for Active.

"Everything?" says David.

"Yes," says Monica.

"Monica, let me ask you," says Adrienne, "do you favor David?" Her question is a loaded one because, in fact, Monica does favor not necessarily David, but David's division. She had told Odile, who in turn reported this to Adrienne, that she would rather work with Active because Active is the division that does big numbers. Active will do twenty-five thousand pieces of one item while Collection will make, say, a thousand pieces of an item. Monica, in Odile's opinion, doesn't want to bother with just a thousand pieces. She'd rather work with the big numbers, as it is the big numbers that are most profitable.

This preference shows up in the fact that almost all of Active's groups are ready, while, as of yesterday, only one of Collection's thirty-four groups was totally complete. Pieces of other Collection groups had arrived at the hotel, but they were indeed just pieces, and Adrienne can't make any final decisions about them until she sees the rest of those particular groups.

Monica ignores Adrienne's question but David says jokingly, "I pay her off, but it's worth it. I get to leave early."

"Do you?" says Adrienne.

"No," he says. "My flight is next Sunday, which is ridiculous."

Adrienne finishes correcting the navy group and leaves David, Jean, Brenda, Monica, and the model working in her room while she heads to Odile's room to see what she can edit of Collection. Richard is always a part of the editing process, and he sits slumped in a chair by the door. Along with Ornella, Kristina, and a production girl, he is watching Odile hang the red-and-white striped and red-and-white carnation print group on the armoire. After glancing at the armoire, Adrienne walks to the rack of clothes by the window and pulls out a skirt made of terrier-print fabric. "I love these little doggies," she says. "This is wonderful. I wish I had seen this yesterday. I would have felt much better."

Odile hangs up some more carnation pieces, and Adrienne starts deciding which should stay and which will be dropped. She hangs a red-and-white striped vest over a carnation-print pant but Richard says, "That's a tough call. Women aren't going to understand it. They need something that pulls it together."

"So we should have a carnation vest with a striped back," says Odile.

"No," says Adrienne. "I would wear this."

"But the average customer wouldn't," says Richard. "We're trying to edit, remember. We have to keep it tight. We have huge SKUs." What Richard means by this is that style is being offered in too many different colors. He wants to offer fewer color choices because, the fewer the choices, the larger the amount of units that will be made in each color. With too many SKUs, or stock-keeping units, the company may end up getting orders for just one hundred pieces of a color, and then the prices get high because the factory can't have the efficiency in production that it would with larger numbers.

"One thing that's good is that our liability is in the piece goods," he says now. The fabrics and yarns have not yet been made into garments, and, if necessary, the company can easily sell off what it doesn't use.

"Do we have hand knits for this group?" says Richard.

"We do," says Odile, "but they're not in yet." The hand knits are being made in China and will be delivered to Adrienne's production agent, who, in turn, will deliver them to the hotel.

"They'll be fabulous," he says.

Adrienne removes some of the tops and bottoms and drops them in a pile on the floor. After she is finished editing, she looks at what remains on the armoire and says to Richard, "Do you like it?"

"Yes."

"You like it?" she asks Ornella.

"Yes."

"You like it or you love it?"

"I love it."

They go on editing pieces of other groups. First they look at what's ready from a group that has blocks of navy, teal, and royal blue. "This is where we have to make sure they are shapes for the Collection, not sporty," says Adrienne. She steps back and stares at the pieces hanging on the armoire. "I'm trying to figure out how to make this more career. Maybe we need a solid blazer."

"Adrienne," says Richard, "you don't have to make this more career. In the stores, what sells best is stuff like this. Even in Saks. Sometimes the things stores tell you they don't want on the line are the things that sell best. Remember that there are customers out there who rely on Collection for their Active looks and buy their career clothes from people who are more expensive than we are. There are customers out there who will spend two hundred dollars on casual clothes."

They go on to another group and then another, and then on to four more print groups. With a lot of feedback from Richard, Adrienne decides which styles should be discarded and which should remain.

After the last group is edited, Richard says, "Let's forget the hearts and the stripes. We have too many prints."

He and Adrienne argue about it, and finally Adrienne says, "Then drop the hearts."

"We'll never be able to talk to the fabric company again," says Ornella.

"So buy it," says Richard. "We can do it as an exclusive for somebody."

Adrienne sits on a chair in the far corner.

"Why are you sitting in the corner?" Richard asks.

"I'm feeling major guilt." Her guilt stems from the fact that she had asked the factory to go through the work and expense of making the printing screen for this fabric. Although the company will be compensated for its effort, this compensation won't come close to the amount of money the factory would have gotten on a volume printing order.

"We should bottle Designer Guilt," says Richard. "Wear this and feel like your favorite designer today. Ralph Guilt. Calvin Guilt. Adrienne Guilt."

At one o'clock Adrienne, Richard, and I go to have lunch in the Regent's steak house. "Order the grilled chicken," says Adrienne. "We've eaten here so many times that we know what's good."

Over lunch, Adrienne was supposed to answer some questions I have about the procedures I've observed, but she prefers to talk about the problems she is having with some of the people who work for her.

Then Adrienne complains about how much she is expected to do in so little time. "I have to attend meetings, make personal appearances, and give interviews," she says. "I draw the line at being a party girl. I don't know how Carolyne Roehm does it."

"She only designs thirty-five or forty dresses each season," says Richard. "That's one dress a day for a month. Compare that to what we do."

Adrienne spends the late afternoon and early evening in Odile's room fitting the clothes that she and Richard edited that morning. With her are Odile, Kristina, Brenda, and Monica. Wearing black stockings and a short, full black slip, Adrienne tries on all the pieces from the carnation and red-and-white striped group.

"Is everything OK on the fabrics for this, Monica?" says Adrienne. "Are they coming in on time from Mr. Choy?"

"This we have to ask Ornella," says Monica.

"Kristina, make a list of things we have to ask," says Adrienne.

As she puts on the clothes, Adrienne dictates the changes that need to be made, and Kristina, Monica, and Brenda write them down.

Adrienne puts on a sundress. "This is a major redo," she says. "It needs a dart in front, and the skirt should be fuller, more gored. Do we really need this dress?"

"Yes," says Odile. "It has a lot of charm."

"It's the only dress you have in that pattern," says Brenda.

Adrienne tries on a red-and-white striped halter dress. It is also not right. "Who specced this?" says Adrienne.

"I did," says Brenda. Her high-pitched voice cracks.

"But I described it to her," says Odile, taking the blame.

"The armhole should be lower," says Adrienne. "There are so many things wrong." Odile draws the corrections directly on the dress, which Adrienne is still wearing.

"They didn't have a pattern for this," says Monica, referring to the factory.

"That should be the first priority for tonight's telex," says Adrienne. "She should make patterns for these two dresses and rush them." The telex will be sent to one of Adrienne's two pattern makers in New York.

Adrienne continues putting on skirts and tops and detailing corrections. When she gets to a long, wide, red-and-white striped circle skirt, Monica says, "The fabric is only thirty-six inches wide."

"This will be a fortune," says Adrienne. "They have to match the stripes."

"You'll need five yards just for the skirt," says Monica.

"We should price it now," says Adrienne. "It's silk broadcloth."

"Silk broadcloth is twelve fifty a yard," says Monica. "Let me call Benson. Maybe he can do it right away." Benson is the owner of one of Adrienne's factories. Monica calls him to ask how much the finished skirt will be.

"It's that expensive?" says Odile as Monica dials the phone.

"Yes," says Monica. "Last year it was twelve dollars a yard."

At 5:45 Adrienne puts on a red-and-white striped jacket. "What is this jacket based on?" she says.

"Our striped jacket from last year," says Odile. "The one Ornella had on today."

"The collar was double-stitched like that?" says Adrienne. "And it had this curving seam?"

"No," says Odile.

Adrienne slips on a pair of pants and throws her hands up in despair. "These pants were to follow my green pants," she says to Monica. "I left those pants with you forever. What happened?"

Monica shrugs, and Adrienne asks Kristina to go up to her room and get the jacket and pants that were to be copied. In the meantime she tries on a walking short. "I don't know what's the matter with me," she says. "I don't like anything."

Kristina returns with a mint green-and-white narrow striped blazer and solid dark green pants from Adrienne's closet. The first jacket has the same curved seam in the collar, but it is less obvious in the first fabric.

Monica hangs up the phone and says, "That skirt, Benson says, is fifty-seven dollars first cost for four and a half yards."

"Forget it," says Adrienne. "We have to come up with a new skirt."

Adrienne tries on the green pant that was to be followed as a model for the other pant. "That's a different pant," says Odile.

"It should be the same pant," says Adrienne angrily.

"But the green pant has four pleats," says Brenda. "The red-and-white has two. The green has more fullness; the red is tight."

"That's why the red is wrong," says Adrienne. She is very upset.

"But no holiday pants look like the green ones," says Brenda, her voice cracking again. "I don't know where we got two pleats, but all the pants have two pleats."

"The original had two pleats and then we made it four," says Adrienne.

"But all of holiday came in with two pleats," says Brenda. "We fitted with two pleats."

"I can't remember all these details," says Adrienne. "How many times do we have this in holiday?"

"Three," says Brenda.

"Call in all the pants," says Adrienne. "I want to see them. We used the green pants as something to follow." Next, Adrienne tries on a top, then a pair of pants, then another shirt and a pair of bicycle pants. She makes corrections on each of these items and says, "This is one hell of a big group."

At 7 P.M. Adrienne puts on a carnation T-shirt and red-and-white striped bicycle pants and says, "Odile, I'm losing my concentration. I'd rather edit. This is too hard. We should do this in the morning."

Just then David walks in. "Are we still going to edit tonight?" he says.

"Yes, we are," says Adrienne.

"Because there's *tons* in your room now," he says in a singsong voice.

Adrienne nods, and David says, "There's like six groups."

Adrienne nods again.

"When?" he says.

"Now," says Adrienne. "Get everybody down there."

"Don't you look cute with your little carnation," says David flirtatiously. Over lunch Adrienne had called her relationship with David "difficult," saying that it was like mother and son. "He charms everyone to get his way. But he'll take a line only so far and then I have to finish it for him."

Adrienne rolls her eyes at David but she is obviously flattered. He certainly does know how to charm her. "Sorry this was so hard, you guys," she says. "It was a hard group."

"It was a *big* group," says Brenda as Adrienne walks into the next room to put on her own clothes. When she returns, Monica says, "Some bad news. The tie-dye print? The factory said it can't do it."

"What do you mean they can't do it?" says Adrienne. "Why not?"

"They said they cannot do it," says Monica.

"Look, I'm not going to pressure," says Adrienne. "It should be Italy, but Italy screwed up. When Dianna comes tonight I will ask her to help us." Both the Italian and Canadian licensees are coming to Hong Kong to see how Adrienne has changed the collections. They will incorporate these changes into the lines they are producing for distribution in their countries.

A bellhop arrives with plastic bags addressed to Odile, who, along with Kristina, pulls black sweaters printed with stars and moons out of them. These are some of the Chinese hand knits. "These stars and moons are much too big," says Odile. "The swatch was much smaller. Monica, call in the original swatch."

"Poor Monica," says Adrienne. "She gets it from everybody."

At 7:30 Adrienne heads down to her room to begin editing Active, but her mind is still on the collection. She is obviously concerned when she says, "That's just the *first* Collection group out of thirty-four."

"Those green pants," she continues, "Monica really should have caught that. But I couldn't say anything. That poor girl is so overwhelmed. We had a wonderful girl, Jenny, working for us, but Jenny emigrated to Canada." (Because Hong Kong is reverting to Chinese rule in 1997, a flood of Hong Kong residents, fearful of the Communist regime, has already begun leaving the country.) "Now it's hard to find good people," she says.

In Adrienne's room the spotlight is shining on the armoire, and beginning with the multicolored striped group that was inspired by the beach towel Adrienne bought in Paris, Adrienne, Ornella, Richard, and David edit until 9 P.M. They break for dinner and then, exhausted, go to sleep.

Adrienne Vittadini *August 13*

In the Vittadini camp, tension is palpable and tempers are short. Neither Adrienne nor her staff have fully gotten over their jet lag, and with no time to rest properly they have been working from morning to night on a numbing array of details. My presence is adding to tension because everyone is trying to look and act well in front of me and my notebook. Unfortunately, or perhaps fortunately, much of the drama of this trip happens when I am not in the room.

Today Adrienne tells me that, wanting to cut down on the amount of work her factories have to do, she had told the dress designers to let the factories make the dresses in only four sizes rather than the six they had originally planned. (Unlike the sportswear, which is sized S,M,L, the dresses are sized with numbers.) But when Adrienne went to the factory yesterday she found that there were still six sizes. Back at the hotel last night, she asked Brenda why no one had listened to her, and Brenda's reply was, "You don't know what you're doing." I didn't ask, and Adrienne didn't volunteer, what her response to Brenda had been.

This morning, Adrienne asked David to hang some new groups from Active in her room while she took a break for lunch. When she came upstairs she found that all conceivable surfaces in her room were covered with clothing. She called David to ask why he hadn't hung anything and found that he was still sleeping. She yelled at him, called him lazy, and slammed down the phone.

All of this happened before 2:30, the time I arrive in Adrienne's room, having arranged to go with her to her main factory, Gloria. Brenda opens the door and, seeing me, snaps, "She's working now. Does she need to see you? Do you just want to be here?" Then I hear Adrienne yelling for me to come in.

Feeling very uncomfortable, I sit and watch as Adrienne finishes editing these Active groups, discarding the pieces that look like losers. The phone rings and David answers it. "No," he says. "Monica's not here. She went shopping. She needed to. She was depressed."

"She was depressed?" Adrienne says after he hangs up.

"When someone needs to go shopping like that they have to be depressed," David replies. "She looked depressed."

"She's so overwhelmed," says Adrienne.

"And overworked," says David.

A few minutes later Monica walks in with the fitting model. Breathing a sigh of relief, I leave with Adrienne as Monica, Brenda, and David start fitting the clothes on the model. In the lobby, Adrienne and I meet Odile, Richard, Ornella, and Kristina. I share a taxi with Adrienne and Odile, while the other three take another.

"I couldn't wait to get out of that room," Adrienne says as the taxi pulls away. "Everyone is so cranky and bitchy. I can't believe that Brenda told me I didn't know what I was doing."

"She's strong," says Odile.

But Adrienne is more concerned about Monica. "I think Monica is having a nervous breakdown," she says. "She's checked out. She doesn't care. She has too many details to follow. And she has no help," Adrienne says. "Both of Monica's two assistants quit. It's hard to find someone to do that work."

"Monica told me the line was too big," Odile says to me. "Even before we started working she said she didn't know how she was going to do it."

We arrive at Gloria at 3:50, taking a small, dingy elevator up one flight to a dingy fluorescent-lit room at the end of a long hallway. Richard, Ornella, and Kristina arrived before us, and in this room they have already hung up a group of red knit clothes with gold buttons. Fourteen tops, two skirts, and two pairs of pants are hanging on the wall.

"Adrienne, can I talk to you?" says Richard. His voice is serious, but he is smiling. He points at the clothing hanging on the wall, going piece by piece and counting from one to eighteen. He obviously means that the group is too big.

"And we already edited this," jokes Odile.

Richard walks over to the wall, and, pointing at six pieces, says, "These are the ones that I like."

Adrienne looks and looks. "I'm dumbfounded," she says finally. "I don't know what I love. I love these two jackets and that's it."

They pick the styles that will remain. A phone behind the partition rings and rings, and Adrienne says, "That phone!" Her jumpiness is a visible sign of frayed nerves.

Looking at different solid-colored swatches of yarn in which this group is being made, they decide to offer it in cream, dark blue, red, and black. Adrienne wants to include yellow and tangerine too. "It will look better in the fashion show," she says. "They are more airy colors."

"Fashion show!" says Richard. "You're gonna be a devil today. We'll have a nice fashion show this season and then we won't be able to afford one next season."

Adrienne fiddles with the yarn lab dips and says, "I am not happy."

"It's green," says Richard, referring to the color of money. This is his way of saying he thinks this group is very marketable.

Adrienne calls in Jimmy, a slight Chinese man who appears to be in his early fifties. She introduces him to me by saying, "This is Jimmy. He is a great technician. He taught me everything I know about knitwear." Adrienne has been working with him since 1969.

"Will you fit with me tomorrow?" she asks him.

"Yes," he says. "Tomorrow morning."

Jimmy leaves and Ornella and Kristina hang up a red-and-white horizontally striped group, and again Adrienne picks her favorite pieces. "I would love a pair of horizontally striped pants with this," Adrienne says, pointing to a cropped, horizontally striped jacket with gold buttons. "Do you think anyone would wear striped pants like this?"

"Yeah," says Richard. "I think about thirty people." He pauses. "On a runway."

After they finish with this group, Odile walks out of the room and into the sewing area. She finds pieces from their blue-and-white striped group and a solid-colored cream and brown group and returns carrying them. Adrienne feels one of the blue-and-white sweaters and says, "How come it's so mushy?"

"Because he shrinks it," says Odile. "The first time I saw it, it was this big." She stretches her arms all the way out.

"It has nice shoulder pads," says Adrienne.

"Not the first time we were here," says Richard. "The Dallas Cowboys could have used them. They were platters."

"I have a great idea," Richard continues. "Sit down for this. Go with the blue-and-white striped group and save the red-and-white stripes as an exclusive."

"No!" cries Adrienne. "Richie!"

"Think about it," he says. "We have two striped groups."

"But they're different moods," she says.

At 5 P.M. Adrienne says to Richard, "I was telling Ods in the taxi on the way here that I think Monica is cracking up. She can't stand the pressure."

"You know what we should do?" says Richard. "We should send someone over here two weeks before the samples are due in September."

"Jenny?" says Adrienne, referring to Monica's predecessor. Adrienne has hired the Canadian-based Jenny to scout production locations for her in Portugal and the United States. Without saying why, Adrienne's agent told Adrienne that he did not want Jenny in his factories here.

"You really want to start a fire," says Richard.

On the way back to the Regent, Adrienne takes a taxi with Richard and Ornella to discuss what to do about Monica. They disperse for a half hour, during which Adrienne picks up a pair of glasses for her husband at an optical store in the hotel and Richard picks up his suits from the tailor. By 6:30 everyone is in Suzie Welton's room reviewing the dress samples. Suzie is the vice-president of the dress division.

Adrienne and Ornella sit on the bed, Richard in a chair by a desk next to the window, and Odile helps Suzie hang the dresses. There's one group all of them love, and one group all of them hate. The latter consists of dresses made of horizontal bands of white cotton that alternate with horizontal bands of white lace.

"Oh, I'm so disappointed," says Adrienne. "I thought these would be so beautiful. Very Mexican. I would never wear these."

"The bottom line on this group is sayonara?" says Richard.

"Let's put it on hold," says Adrienne.

As the women hang up the next group, Richard picks up the *International Herald Tribune* and, looking at a cover story, says, "Wow! About twenty-five thousand people showed up to protest Martin Scorsese's *The Last Temptation of Christ*. He has Jesus Christ on the cross fantasizing about packing it in and being just an ordinary man. You know, the way you and I fantasize about packing it in and becoming cleaning people?"

They hang another group but quickly dismiss it because it lacks "hanger appeal." This means the dresses must be tried on in order to look flattering and don't look good simply hanging on a hanger.

From large plastic bags they unpack black dresses with big round gold bubble buttons. "These are beautiful," says Adrienne. "*Soooo* beautiful. Who made this?"

Suzie tells her the name of the factory.

"The Liz Claiborne factory," says Adrienne.

"I take back everything I said about this factory," says Ornella as they continue unpacking.

"Save that suit," says Richard, looking up from the newspaper and pointing at one of the two-piece dresses. "Nordstrom's has a half-yearly sale in May. We can use that. They love double-knit."

"I thought this was going to be so painful," says Adrienne as they finish up, "but it was wonderful. What a treat."

"Our next challenge is wovens," says Richard. "That's where we're getting killed."

"Does the market really need another woven dress division?" Adrienne asks.

"Yes. AJ Barry and St. Gillian have the whole business. We can go up against them for transitional," says Richard. Then, looking at the last group of dresses hanging on the armoire, he says, "What a great way to end the day."

Adrienne Vittadini *August 17*

Having finished editing and correcting the Active line, Adrienne starts the morning in her room, sitting on the bed with Richard and David, going through a book in which swatches from each of the groups have been posted on different pages. They flip through all the pages and give grades to the groups the swatches represent. Most of them get A and B+ but a couple do get C.

At eleven o'clock they go to Suzie Welton's room, where they evaluate each group and decide which dresses will actually make it into production. They keep an average of only three dresses per group.

At 11:20 they head for Odile's room to go through the same process—pick the styles that will remain in the navy and white group, which consists of stripes, polka dots, and the terrier print. Many of the other Collection groups are not yet finished, and it is these unfinished groups that Adrienne will edit, fit, and edit again, until she leaves on Friday. She throws the discards into a pile on the floor.

At one, as we break for lunch, Richard says, "By the end of this trip you're going to see a side of us you've never seen before. We're going to put all the clothes in one pile and jump on them. By the time I get home I'm on the same level as my daughter."

I can understand why. The amount of clothing that these people have had to review in less than a week is, literally, mind-numbing. When we say our goodbyes a few days later, Adrienne remarks, "I hope it wasn't too boring for you here. It was boring for me." She means it.

With a short layover in Tokyo, it took me twenty-four hours to get home—

from the moment I left the Regent to the blissful moment I opened the door of my apartment. Having experienced the ordeal of the twenty-one hour flight to Hong Kong, and the amazing amount of detail work that goes into fitting and editing one thousand pieces of clothing, I will never again envy a designer who must travel to faraway places for his or her work. As I put down my suitcase I remember Odile's comment on July 20 about her friends and family who wished they, too, could go to Hong Kong: "If only they knew what it was like." I do, and, like Adrienne, who must repeat this trip three times a year, I never, ever, want to do it again.

After she returns to New York, Adrienne will take three weeks off and vacation at her house in the Hamptons. Before she leaves New York, however, she will meet with her design staff and tell them what she "feels" for fall—the next season they have to design.

Although she will continue to ask her staff for ideas, she has learned that she must give them some direction. Therefore she will tell them she wants to design "rich, opulent, tweedy" looks. She also will tell them she wants to use fewer printed fabrics and to return to her original love—knitwear.

After she returns from vacation, Adrienne will make a few personal appearances and take the time to lunch with editors and retailers—two categories of relationships that must be perpetually nurtured.

In September, just before her samples are to be shipped to New York, Adrienne will send a woman from her New York production department to check them. Once the samples arrive in New York, Adrienne will review them and decide which will be shown in her show, on November 10.

Although her show is not until November, her lines will open for selling in the showroom on September 22. Since Adrienne is considered a "bridge" resource between the designer and better markets she sells her clothing during the bridge market week—the time when buyers from out of town come to New York to review and buy from vendors that fall into that category, vendors like Anne Klein II, Ellen Tracy, and Donna Karan's about-to-be-launched DKNY.

The high-end designers (who make many fewer pieces of each item in their collections and therefore can afford to open closer to the season) open at the end of October and the beginning of November. Liz Claiborne, which is part of the better market, opens in conjunction with other better firms. Its show will be on September 9.

Since the first set of samples arriving from Hong Kong will be used for showroom sales, they will look, as Adrienne puts it, "tired" by the time the show date rolls around. Therefore she will order a duplicate set of samples of those styles she has chosen for her show. It is this second set of samples that the models will wear.

On September 21, the day before her collection opens for selling, Adrienne will leave for Europe to look at fall fabrics.

We will return to Adrienne's company in October and November, when she, in maintaining her designer image, will preview her collection to magazine editors and hold her fashion show at the same time as the high-end designers. By the time the editors see Adrienne's line, it has already been completely sold to the stores.

Bill Blass *August 25*

Even though he was out late last night, having gone to a Sting concert (his first rock concert ever), by 9 A.M. Bill is behind his desk, as usual doing more than one thing at once.

He stops reviewing invoices to look at a pile of sketches that Laura brings in, and then, in the middle of his conversation with her, he yells, "Craig! Call Mrs. Buckley about that sweater. She needs it. She's home right now." And so, another day at Bill Blass goes into full swing.

Since we last saw Bill, he has designed and presented (on August 11) his resort collection in his showroom. This collection, which was crisp and sporty, was shown only to his largest accounts, and some of its most important groups will be incorporated into Bill's spring line.

His fall line, meanwhile, is on the road, being sold at trunk shows which his sales staff of three is overseeing across the country. (We will attend a personal appearance with Bill in Chicago in conjunction with a trunk show on September 8 and 9. This Chicago trunk show will be one of the last for the fall season. Any orders taken during this show will then be manufactured and delivered by October 30, the latest possible date stores will accept fall merchandise.)

Fall and even resort are just a memory now for Bill, as he turns his full attention to spring. Unlike his resort line, spring will be soft and draped, with a large concentration on chiffon—a fabric that most of the European textile mills pushed for spring.

With chiffon on his mind, Bill now walks to his fabric room and asks a worker there to show him swatches of all the different colored chiffons he has ordered. "I don't care who made them," Bill says. "I just want to see the colors."

"Gotcha," says the worker.

Barry, the man who is putting together the music for Bill's presentation for Saks Fifth Avenue's annual SFA-USA benefit evening, being held this year on September 19, arrives. In addition to Bill, Adolfo, Geoffrey Beene, Carolina Herrera, Mary McFadden, and Oscar de la Renta will be showing their clothing. Each designer will pick a benefit charity, and people will then buy tickets to sit at the table of the designer who is supporting their favorite charity. For years, Bill has supported Just One Break.

Bill has told Barry that he wants something "nightclubby," and Barry has brought over some appropriate selections of music. He puts an album on the stereo located behind Bill's secretary's desk. Patty Austin singing "They Can't Take That Away from Me" blasts loudly over the speakers throughout the entire floor. Harold Leigh Davis, executive vice-president of the company in charge of sales, rushes in looking very upset. "What are you doing?" he hisses. "I have customers in there. You've blasted them off their seats."

Barry lowers the volume and, as he turns off the showroom speakers, Tom Fallon, advertising and promotion director, closes the door to the showroom. The music is now coming only from the speaker in the hall outside Bill's office.

Bill is sitting behind his desk again, looking through some paperwork. Following Bill's earlier request, the fabric man carries in a large white sheet of poster board covered with multicolored chiffon swatches and lays it on the knee-high platform by the full-length mirror. As the fabric man leaves, Bill, taking his cue from the song's title, yells to Barry, "You can take that away. It's not right."

Barry puts on another song, "I Can Cook Too." Bill doesn't like that, either. Then Barry puts on a newly released album of relatively obscure Fred Astaire songs. As the music begins to play, Bill stands up and comes out into the hall.

"Now you've got him excited," says Tom.

"I love that," says Bill. He picks up the album cover from his secretary's desk and reads the back cover. "This is a wonderful way to start out," he says. Laura appears in the hallway eating a blueberry Dannon yogurt, and Craig comes out from his cubicle.

"I would love to use this album for us," says Bill.

"I'll keep it for you," says Barry.

"How many minutes per designer?" says Bill, referring to the amount of time each designer will have on the runway at the SFA-USA presentation.

"Eight," says Barry.

"I'd like to do another Fred Astaire song," says Bill.

Barry puts on another song called "You Worry Me."

"I like that," says Bill. "It's obscure but I like it."

Bill's secretary carries a stack of signed bills and other administrative paperwork out of Bill's office. Bill goes back to his desk, and, pulling a pink Magic Marker from the Lucite display case of Magic Markers that stands to his right, he sketches wide, flowing pink chiffon pants, a turtleneck, and a chiffon scarf. As he sketches, another song comes over the speaker, and Bill yells, "That's wonderful." He keeps sketching, and the Magic Marker makes a loud scraping sound as Bill guides it over the page with his wide, sure strokes.

Bill fills in the pants sketch with light pink Magic Marker and the turtleneck with a darker pink, and he carries the sketch out to Laura, who pins it onto a wall of her cubicle. On another wall hang miniature sketches of the spring collection. They hang in separate rows, each of which is dedicated to a separate category: coats, day dresses, suits, short evening, and long evening.

Laura returns to Bill's office with him and watches as he makes another sketch. Bill's secretary drops some more papers on Bill's desk and the fabric man brings in two fabrics, a navy chiffon and a georgette. Bill takes the fabrics, and he and Laura walk to the window where they hold the two fabrics next to each other and inspect them in the light of day. "This is great," Bill says. "Let's use this."

As Bill takes a phone call, an editor from *Lear's* magazine arrives. Under Tom's direction, a model puts on outfits from the resort collection and the editor takes Polaroid pictures. At 12:30 two editors from the *Washington Post* will come up to see the resort collection.

Oblivious to the editor in the showroom, Laura, from her cubicle, yells, "Bill, what about the pleated pants?" Bill, equally oblivious, yells back, "I'm on the phone." "Edith!" he says loudly into the telephone. "Are you in Tahoe?"

After he hangs up, Bill walks to Laura's cubicle with a new sketch. "Forget the turtleneck," he says of the sketch he had handed to her earlier. "It's too hot." His new sketch features the same pink chiffon pants, but now they are pictured with a crew-neck top.

Bill's barber arrives at noon, and, as Bill pulls a chair up to the full-length mirror in his office and sits down, his secretary answers her phone. The caller is someone who wants to apply for a job. The person talks on and on, and although Bill's secretary listens without interrupting, she rolls her eyes impatiently. Finally she says, "Write him a personal letter. But make it short. Don't go on and on."

Her advice is representative of how things work here: quickly and efficiently—
very different from the way things go on the two floors above him, where Donna
Karan is headquartered.

As I leave I hear the sound of drilling from the floor above. There Donna is
having a new showroom built for her about-to-be-launched lower-priced division
called DKNY. But more, much more, on that next month. For now let's turn
again to another extremely efficient company.

Liz Claiborne *August 31*

Two weeks ago, just as Adrienne was flying back from Hong Kong, the Liz
Claiborne principals, division heads, and sales vice-presidents sat down and,
item by item, priced the Spring I line. Here's how Jerry Chazen describes that
process: "We start with two obvious factors: how much it cost us to make the
item, and what kind of markup we need to stay in business. At the same time
we look at the retail situation. We ask ourselves if there's anything happening
out there that would cause us to look at the pricing of a garment differently. For
instance, have we gotten information from the stores that we can't sell cotton
shirts for over fifty dollars?

"Then we take into consideration inflationary pressures," he continues. "We
try not to have our prices jump too drastically from one season or year to the
next. If we had a gabardine pant on the line and it was eighty dollars, and
because of price increases that pant would have to sell now for one hundred
and ten dollars, we might decide not to make that move and just eat the margin
to maintain some credibility with our consumer. We take all of that into consideration as we look at every item."

This season, a major factor they considered was the fact that they had to re-
stimulate waning consumer interest in their collection. For this reason they,
unlike many of their competitors, decided to keep their prices flat and not pass
on increased raw-material costs.

As they were pricing the line, many of the actual garments had not yet arrived
from the factories. But, as scheduled, the samples have arrived in time for the
presentation that will be made of the Spring I line to the Liz Claiborne sales
force today.

As it is for each of these presentations, the showroom shared by Collection and Lizsport has been turned into a makeshift auditorium. Rows of folding chairs face a runway spanning the length of a wall that has been covered with a gridlike rack. These chairs are filling up with salespeople as well as all the individuals who were involved in one way or another with the design or production of the sportswear lines.

After this presentation the sales staff will take the line and will map out and write the orders for the purchases that their clients should, and usually do, make. "It's a very complicated kind of thing," says Jerry, in explaining the steps that will begin today. "The critical difference between us and typical designers is that we own all the merchandise we will show retailers before we show it. Most designers design samples, sell from their sample collections, and then make their commitments to buy the fabrics and manufacture the garments. In our case we own the whole thing in a particular way by size and color.

"That means our sales force is selling from a known quantity," he continues. "If we have a sweater on the line and we own ten thousand units of that sweater, and people want to buy fifty thousand units, we can't supply it. We're stuck. On the other hand, if everyone hates it we're in big trouble. If we don't get a reasonably good cross-section of all of the products we made into the stores, we're going to be in big trouble. The sales force is trained to get a good representation of our products out there.

"Our sales force has a different kind of role than the sales force of any other company. Rather than selling the line, they take our body of product and become its distributors. A very large percentage of our sales force used to be retailers, and they write orders as if they were store buyers. We have to do it that way because we've already put our money on the line.

"We plan the buy for the store," he says. "We try to put the thing together. We let them know how we assess the importance of the various groups. All the questioning you saw at the line and process meetings was done because those salespeople are the ones who are eventually going to write the order. As they looked at the line presented to them they were thinking about whether they will be able to distribute it to twenty-six branches."

Now, these salespeople/pseudobuyers are filing in. For women's sportswear there are close to fifty people who sell both Collection and Lizsport. The number of accounts each of them handles ranges from a low of two (in the case of a major account with many branches) to about one hundred to one hundred fifty smaller specialty stores.

I sit down in my designated chair, and a moment later, Ellen sits on my left and Liz on my right, with Art on her right. Jay walks to the front of the room and steps onto the runway. "I'd just like to say a few words before we show you the clothes," he says, "to let you know how we are doing. Large sizes is going great. We're working on the development of size ranges. Dresses has done a flyer for Bloomingdale's which is great for our image. Menswear and Dana Buchman are great, and we're seeing a major turnaround in petites, which was suffering during the short-skirt, cropped-top period.

"As for sportswear," he continues, "we're on a roll and it feels good. As you all know, Spring I this year was not that great for us." (He is referring to clothing that was in the stores this past spring.)

"That's an understatement," a male voice calls out from the audience.

"Yeah," says Jay, laughing, "but Lizwear is very hot right now. Actually, all three divisions are very close on SURF right now. We're doing great." (SURF, if you remember, is an acronym for Systematically Updated Retail Feedback, a report on how the company's current merchandise is selling in stores.)

Jay takes a breath and continues, "I'd like to thank a couple of groups before we go on. First, I'd like to thank the people who do marketing for both petite and missy. They do their thing compiling information and providing us with reports. They just kind of stay in the background. No one ever sees them but I'd like to ask the marketing people to stand up."

A small group of people stands and its members are applauded. After they sit down, he then asks the design director of petites to stand up. She does and is applauded.

"And," says Jay, "I'd like to thank the production people, who are responsible for getting everything made and shipped on time, which as we all know, is no easy thing. Mike Sciance? Walter Schneider? Please stand up and be recognized."

The two men stand up to receive their accolades.

"Our winter white group is seeing twenty-five percent sell throughs in one day," Jay continues, referring to a group of sportswear that is currently in the stores. "We're back to the old Liz Claiborne sell throughs.

"And we have aggressive plans. We went into this season saying we were going to lower our prices or keep them the same, and we've done that. People will love Liz because in this time of inflation she has thought of them. The price of fabrics has gone up and it will cost the company some money to keep prices down, but it's worth it. Although retail in general has not been great, we are performing out there. We've gone back to good basics, good fashion. And private label seems to be on the decline. We're hearing that stores are lowering their levels of private label merchandise. It's become a markdown business. One sign of this is their increased interest in items within our line.

"Remember that there is no one who competes with us as long as we understand our business. There's no one that does what we do, and now, let us show you what we've done in sportswear. Have fun, that's the most important thing."

With that, he relinquishes the floor to Richard Kramer, division head of Lizwear, who presents Lizwear's six groups. "Our first group, Claiborne Corps, is a December fifth delivery," says Richard, holding up a large board covered with sketches of the product. "December is the second most important denim month, with September being the first."

As he talks, four Lizwear designers and design assistants, all of them dressed in black, carry out clothes on hangers and hang them on the wall behind Richard as he talks. The audience claps enthusiastically.

"Look at this stuff," says Rob Bernard, senior vice-president of marketing, who is sitting behind me. "This stuff is going to blow out." Just as the girls finish hanging the clothes, four models walk onto the runway wearing the main outfits from this group, and Rob Bernard joins everyone in another round of applause.

Next, Richard describes the products, item by item, starting with what he calls "the narrow, directional jean, done into the Dirty Dancing short." He is referring to a long denim short whose legs are rolled up into cuffs.

Liz shakes her head no, and whispers something to Art. She and her husband will comment to each other throughout the presentation of all three divisions. When not whispering, they will take notes. From time to time Liz leans over and whispers to Ellen, too. She does so now. "He can't call it the Dirty Dancing short," Liz says. "That's what Calvin called his."

As Liz leans back into her seat, Ellen whispers to me, "Part of my job is to bring back styles that are doing really well. One of them was this short that Calvin Klein did. We reinterpreted it, but we can't be so obvious about it. We can't call it the same name."

"Isn't this fabulous?" Ellen says, turning around to Rob Bernard, as Richard continues explaining the styles.

"This is the way Lizwear should be," he says.

Richard presents the second group, a mix of solid blue denim and blue-and-white patterns. He holds up the concept boards, the designers and their assistants hang up the clothes, and the models walk out. This group, too, gets applause. Despite the clapping, Liz says, "Oy," and writes notes to herself about changes she wants to make. "I don't like that blue print shirt underneath that blue cardigan and with the jean," she says, looking at one of the models. "It's too blue. It'll look much better with a white T-shirt."

As the models walk up and down the runway, Liz makes a face and furiously writes on her show lineup. Seeing Liz's reaction, Richard says, "A lot of these samples came in last night, or the night before, so, if something doesn't look good, we apologize."

Turning to the clothes hanging on the wall, Richard describes each silhouette and explains why it is teamed with the piece it is with. "Jay loves black with denim, so here we have a black cardigan with the jean," he says.

As the third group is presented, Liz continues writing on her show lineup. Her notes say that she wants the models to wear tennis shoes instead of the black flats they now have on. "And," she whispers to Art, "these tall girls have got to go. The jeans are much too short on them."

As he holds up the sketches for the fourth group, Richard says, "The base of this group is the bottoms. This is our new volume short."

"Great short," Dennis Gay calls out from the third row.

After the assistants have finished hanging the pieces, a model comes out wearing a long beige khaki skirt and a matching khaki shirt. Liz and Ellen lean forward, look at each other, and smile. Liz gives Ellen the OK sign, making a circle with her thumb and index finger. This outfit was "inspired" by a khaki outfit from Ann Taylor that a Liz Claiborne employee had worn to work in April.

"The customer's really going to appreciate that outfit," Rob says. "She's going to love it."

"And this is our new pull-on pant," Richard says, pointing to another model. "Great!" calls Dennis.

The fifth group is centered on lightweight denim, and the sixth is "cotton suiting meant to be worn with sneakers." Richard finishes his presentation to great applause and then introduces the designers and their assistants, who come out to take a bow. "She's only been with us for two weeks," Liz whispers to me, pointing at one of the designers. Her predecessor was fired because, Liz says, "she didn't have follow-through in the fittings. She wasn't intimately involved with her product."

Jay announces a five-minute break, and Liz immediately gets up to talk to Richard. She talks and talks and Richard nods and nods, and afterward walks over to Dennis. "What did she say?" Dennis says.

"She liked it but hated . . ." Richard lowers his voice so that I can't hear him. He looks at me, rolls his eyes, and says, "details."

"Better get used to it," says Dennis. "That's what it's like all the time."

"I can understand it," says Richard, looking at me and the reporter's notebook in my hand. "After all, it's her name on the label."

After the break, Bob Abajian, division head of Lizsport, wearing a red-and-white paisley tie, red-and-white striped shirt, navy blue cardigan with a crest on the pocket, and khaki pants, takes the stage and asks for the runway spotlights to be turned off. He has prepared a slide show "of things that started us thinking."

The whole line is covered in this show. The presentation of each group opens with a close-up photo of its concept board and is followed by sketches, as well as pictures, taken at other designers' fashion shows. Most of them are from last spring's shows and many are from the Adrienne Vittadini, Daniel Hechter, and Joan Vass presentations.

After the show the lights are turned on again and Bob says, "Our first group is Manor Classics." A young male assistant designer walks out, wearing the same paisley tie as Bob. He holds a large concept board high above his head and walks back and forth with it on the runway. "The board will give you a point to begin from," says Bob of the Annie Hall-type menswear photos on the board.

The first model to walk out is wearing a long white raincoat over a blue-and-white striped shirt, the same tie as Bob and the assistant designer are wearing, an argyle vest and pants. "Oh!" Liz says, very loudly. "Terrific, Bob!" She claps and everyone follows suit.

Bob, assisted by this division's designers and assistants, all wearing the same ties, hangs the first group on the rack. "I guess you've noticed there are a few paisley ties around," Bob says, and everyone laughs.

As he hangs solid red and solid blue pieces printed with tiny white circles, he says, "If you were very observant and took a close look at the concept board as it went by, you noticed that this print came from one of the scarves in a photo of a model wearing a Gaultier garment. We are not proud. We look everywhere for our inspiration."

The second group is called City Prints. Again the male assistant walks out with this group's concept board, Bob and the other assistants hang up the clothes on the rack and the models come out. "It's a nice, relaxed, easy way to go to work," says Bob. "Each top can be worn with a matching bottom or they can be mixed."

"It's nice," Art whispers to Liz.

"Very nice," she whispers back. "This is the type of dressing, two-piece dressing, that Dennis hates so much."

"Those are nice buttons," whispers Ellen, as she looks at the group. "And that's a nice cardigan. We don't see this for so long, that we forget what it looks like. We didn't even have some of these actual garments for the pricing meeting."

As he presents the third group, which is made primarily of cotton sheeting but includes some sweatshirts, Bob says, "We have not forgotten the couch potatoes."

"I hate that word," Liz says to Art.

"What does it mean?" he whispers back.

"Someone who does nothing but stay at home and watch TV."

The third group is applauded and the fourth group is met with scattered comments like, "It's cute! Super!" As Bob presents the fifth group he says, "We have T-shirts in an amazing range of colors."

"Amazing," Art says sarcastically.

"That's great," says Liz. "I told Richard to do that, to add some drama. Some enthusiasm."

Again a five-minute break. Then Dennis and the Collection designers get up to show their designs. Although every single group is applauded, of all the presentations made, this is received the least enthusiastically. Judith looks absolutely miserable and Dennis makes snide comments throughout the whole thing.

He begins nicely enough by saying, "When the design team and I first sat down with Liz and began to philosophize, 'What do people want to wear for next spring?' we decided they primarily wanted career clothes, but we've also included some lifestyle clothes and what we hope is the beginning of a tradition— a group called Hot Item, which, we hope, will be just that. Last year we had four groups to show you and realized that was too narrow. This year we have seven."

Four models come out wearing the silk knit group that is a continuation of Naturally Neutral. "It's beautiful," says a saleswoman behind me. The audience applauds and Dennis says, "Notice how all the skirts are long and soft. However, we have the short version in the showroom, which is selling. No?" He wanted to design short skirts but the salespeople told him short skirts wouldn't sell. He is taking this opportunity to show that they were wrong.

Liz nods and some of the salespeople say yes. "But that's all right," says Dennis.

"Now that it's selling we're not making it anymore," Liz whispers to me.

The second group consists of the suits with patterned linings. "This is a simple, concise group," says Dennis. "We have three classic suits with classic patterns with a typical Liz Claiborne twist. We've added color in unexpected ways."

Three models walk out wearing the suits and the salespeople say, "Oooh" and "Aaah," and they applaud.

"The blouses are polyester," says Dennis, "so you can throw them in the washer and dryer and then go back to the office." The audience laughs.

"And the jacket is being shipped with the pocket square in the pocket." Here the audience mumbles approval.

"And, girls, if you will please take off your jackets, we have another surprise for you." Judith, standing in the hallway—wearing tight knee-length leggings and a black shirt roped in with a black belt—is stage-whispering to Dennis that one of the linings is not in yet. Liz tries to tell this to Dennis but he doesn't hear her, and the models take off their jackets.

"The pantsuits have red with black dot linings," he says. "The glen plaid has black on black and the other will have . . . Oh," he says, looking at the third suit, "it's not in yet."

"That's not right," says Liz, pointing to the black lining inside the glen plaid jacket.

"Yes it is," says Judith. "It became black on black."

"Oh," says Liz.

"And," says Dennis, hanging an array of blouses, "these are our item opportunity. We knew that these were career girl tops so they are all also one hundred percent polyester."

The third group, Classics by Liz, was to consist of the leftover linen, but, Dennis says, "We decided that Spring One was too early for linen." The models come out wearing brightly colored Honan silk jackets, and there is great applause. "These are all separates so there are lots of item opportunities in here," says Dennis.

"Great," says Art loudly, after the group is finished, and he leads the clapping.

"The fourth group is Tropic Mix," says Dennis. "This is the group you've been waiting for with bated breath: two-piece dressing. We saw a wonderful tropical print and loved it, and we showed it to Art and Liz and they loved it too, and you know how hard it is to get them to love any print, so when Art suggested we design a jacket in this fabric and base a group around it, we did."

"This is his way of disclaiming responsibility," says Art loudly, and everyone laughs.

"The tunic," says Dennis, as he hangs up the group, "covers a multitude of

. . . uh . . . flaws, but if you don't want a dumb tunic we also have this shirt you can wear."

"A tunic isn't dumb," Ellen says quietly. "I've seen women wearing them for evening over pants, and it looks very classic. I don't know why he calls them dumb."

"The fifth group is Stripe Out," says Dennis. "It comes in black-and-white or blue-and-black capsules. Notice all these easy long skirts you have. I don't know what the buyers are going to complain about this time.

"Next, we have Call of the Wild," he says as he goes on to the sixth group. The audience gasps and applauds as the animal prints come out. "Liz loves animal prints," says Dennis, "and I have to confess I am also very partial to them, so it was a combined effort to get this group on the line.

"We need to make some corrections in your books," he says, referring to the loose-leaf binder containing sketches and a description of every piece in the line that was received by each salesperson. "In your books there is a halter dress in the leopard print. Well—" he pauses for effect—"it died in the jungle. And the long skirt, believe me, be happy you don't have it. It looks better short."

Next, Dennis hands up six bright collarless jackets. "These are priced at one hundred and sixteen dollars retail," says Dennis as he hangs them on the wall.

"How can you do it at that price?" says Art sarcastically, imitating what seems to be a frequent retail question.

"Linen has gone up," says Dennis. He is used to being on the defensive and he thinks Art seriously thinks the jackets are too expensive. "Linen is more expensive than it's ever been. It's still good fashion and a good value. You can repeat that to the stores verbatim."

"It won't be a problem," Rob Bernard calls out. "That's a very good price for those jackets."

The seventh group is French Finesse. The models come out wearing the red and navy suits with gold buttons. "Oohhh," a saleswoman exclaims. "It's gorgeous!" and the audience breaks out into the most enthusiastic applause of the day.

"It's important for you to familiarize yourself with this fabric," says Dennis. "It's wonderful—soft and drapey."

"It feels great on," says one of the models.

"And we own more of this in navy than in red, everybody," says Dennis, "so don't get nervous."

As the models walk, Dennis describes each of their outfits individually. The first model is wearing a white cardigan, a white blouse with red dots, and navy pants. "Notice the size of the buttons," says Dennis. "They are very large gold buttons. Liz loves big buttons."

"What else is she wearing?" says Dennis. The model turns toward him and Dennis says, "Chains. She's wearing lots of chains, but we don't make those."

"Not yet," Liz whispers to Art.

And now the salespeople take the line to begin considering what Jerry calls "the enormous amount of factors involved in distributing this merchandise."

Meanwhile, in the more rarefied world of high fashion, most of the New York designers have not even designed their lines. True, they have made tentative fabric purchases and have put into work samples for some complicated pieces, such as the embroidery that both Bill Blass and Carolyne Roehm are having done in India.

But the Milan and Paris spring shows have not even taken place, and if a fashion direction should develop in those European cities, the New York designers, all of whom have sample rooms on their premises, can still change the slant of their entire collections.

As Carolyne Roehm, Bill Blass, Carolina Herrera, and Louis dell'Olio of Anne Klein begin the actual sample-making for their spring collections, they are still fulfilling part of their promotional responsibilities for the previous fall season and are flying to Chicago in a week to attend the opening of a renovated Marshall Field's. We will meet Bill there.

Bill Blass *September 8*

The first event Bill will be attending at Marshall Field's is a luncheon and fashion show benefiting the Medical Research Institute Council of Michael Reese Hospital and Medical Center.

The luncheon is scheduled to start at noon at the store's State Street branch. At 10:30 I take the escalator up to the Walnut Room, a restaurant on the seventh floor that has been closed to the public for the day. A cluster of curious customers stands outside the restaurant watching a group of waiters arrange silverware on the tables that have been set up on both sides of a long runway.

The runway cuts the room in half and ends in a circular platform on top of which a band is setting up its instruments. Neither the models nor Bill and his staff have arrived yet. With nothing to do here, I decide to take a walk around the store, where, I see as I head down through the various floors, almost all the summer merchandise is on sale.

Sales are great news for consumers but terrible news for both designers and retailers. Smaller companies that don't have much clout may be asked to take back merchandise that doesn't sell. Larger, more powerful companies tend to refuse to take back clothing, but they may provide the retailer with some money to cover losses. Some good sources have told me that this was how one major designer, whose clothing never sold very well, but who did a strong licensed business, managed to keep his main collection in the stores. Basically, the company that backed him paid off the retailers to allot space on their floors for his merchandise.

In the case of companies that will not take back their products, retailers continue marking down the items, believing that there is always a price that moves a garment. If the clothes still don't sell, then the retailers will most likely sell the clothes to off-price discount chains like Loehmann's.

As I walk through this massive old store, my heels clicking loudly on its wooden floors, none of the store's salespeople ask if they can help me. In fact, most of the departments seem to be without any salespeople at all. This lack of service is the largest complaint designers have about stores—no one is out there pushing their products, which, more often than not, are crammed into small spaces that they have to share with other designers.

I head back upstairs, stopping off on the sixth floor, and see that one of the few sales areas that is not unmanned is the most expensive one—the designer boutique, where two salesladies stand ready and willing to help anyone who enters the department. By the entrance to this boutique a small sign announces tomorrow's Bill Blass trunk show. (After they view Bill's collection on the runway today, women will be able to see it up close tomorrow in this department.)

I go back to the Walnut Room, where Hillary Rosenfeld, the store's young energetic public-relations person, tells me I won't be able to sit with Bill because "all the people who have donated a lot of money to the charity are being seated at his table," as are Phil Miller, chairman and chief executive officer of Marshall Field's and his wife, Anne.

No one from Bill Blass is here yet so I go out front where press photographers are photographing the women who are starting to arrive for the luncheon. If this were New York, these women would be wearing suits, and their suits would be black. Here, however, most of the women are wearing dresses, and black is the one color that is conspicuously absent except on women who are overweight. The favorite colors here are beige, red, and blue. I remember how Bill has said that much of his success is due to the fact that he travels around the country and sees how women in various cities dress. Now I am seeing firsthand that there really is a difference.

Hillary introduces me to Sal Ruggiero, the store's fashion director of ready-to-wear, who tells me that benefits like this are an integral part of the store's business. "A store has to have a high profile to become a vital part of the city, and these benefits help us get that profile," he says. "Once you're a vital part of the city you have a responsibility to raise money for its charities. Plus, it's a way for us to showcase our merchandise."

At 11:30 the photographers' strobes begin to go off repeatedly, signaling Bill's arrival. Sal goes to the side of the room to welcome Bill, who is accompanied by Tom, Gail Levenstein, director of licensing for Bill, and Harold Leigh Davis, his executive vice-president in charge of sales.

Phil Miller and his wife approach Bill, as do the two chairwomen of the event and Bill's buyer from Marshall Field's. I'm surprised to see that although many of the other women here glance over at Bill, almost no one goes over to talk to him, and Bill spends the bulk of the time before the luncheon talking to his own employees.

Bill notices my camera, and, in the same way that he used to sometimes give me instructions at parties I was covering for *Women's Wear Daily,* he says, "Make sure to get a picture of Phil Miller and his wife. That's him over there. Wait."

Bill calls the Millers over, introduces us, and then stands between them for a picture. Other photographers scurry over and photograph Bill between the Millers, then they pose him with a Chicago socialite, and then with the event's co-chairs.

For lunch I'm seated with eight other women across the runway from Bill. As dessert arrives, the band removes its instruments from the runway and Phil Miller walks out onto it. He welcomes Bill Blass, "a fellow midwesterner," and the fashion show begins. The main segment of the show, the one showcasing Marshall Field's fall selections from a wide variety of designers is surprisingly uneven. Most of the suits and dresses are nice, but the bulk of the evening wear is awful. "Women in Chicago would never wear this," says the woman next to me, as she watches a flashy, elaborate ball gown pass in front of us on the runway. "Women in Chicago wouldn't wear that," she says of an equally elaborate dress. "We're the Midwest. We are conservative." And they like being that way, I realize now. New Yorkers tend to look down their noses at the way midwestern women dress, but, looking around at this crowd of women here, I realize that they couldn't care less what New Yorkers think of them.

As the show progresses, one of the models—an attractive elderly woman with gray hair—comes out wearing a black dress that is meant for a much younger woman. It has a flounce on the bottom that flips up to reveal brightly colored layers underneath. She has to stand by herself on the runway for a long time, waiting for the models ahead of her to finish parading. She is obviously uncomfortable in this dress, and her discomfort makes the dress look bad.

"Do you think they're showing this stuff on purpose?" the woman next to me whispers. "To make Bill Blass look good?" It is obvious that the other women in the room don't like the merchandise either, since none of them are clapping.

The applause starts only when Bill Blass's work starts heading down the runway. Marshall Field's purchased only a few of the pieces that are being shown by Bill today. The rest are samples that have been shown by his representatives at trunk shows during the course of the fall retail selling season that started in July. These samples were flown here by Bill's company especially for this fashion show and for a trunk show that will be held in the store tomorrow. Most of his designs are classic and understated, and any woman in the room would feel comfortable wearing them. Sitting there I suddenly understand Bill's success. He knows exactly what middle-aged, wealthy women want to wear.

As Bill's presentation goes on, the gray-haired model who had been so terribly uncomfortable in her previous outfit comes out wearing a gray suit with a gray fox collar and cuffs. The suit's color perfectly complements her hair, and as she walks you can tell that she feels beautiful.

For the show's finale, all the models and Bill parade up and down the runway. Bill passes the gray-haired model in the fox-trimmed suit and says to her, "You look terrific in that." She beams. She knows.

Bill Blass *September 9*

Having had dinner last night with his staff and the Millers, Bill is up this morning at 10 A.M. After breakfast, he goes to the Chicago Historical Society, which is planning to mount a retrospective of his work in 1991. Then he has an interview with Genevieve Buck from the *Chicago Tribune* and meets a friend for a drink, and now he's on his way to Marshall Field's State Street store where he will be interviewed by the *Chicago Sun Times* as well as John Fairchild's *Daily News Record* and *Women's Wear Daily*. Bill may be busy, but the Marshall Field's designer department, where the Bill Blass trunk show is being held, is not. Only Jack, who is one of Bill's three staff salespeople, two models (one in a Bill Blass pantsuit and the other in a Bill Blass dress and jacket) and a few Marshall Field's salesladies are there. Bill's collection is hanging on a rack next to which a video of his fall show is playing.

The lack of customers isn't surprising, says Jack, since this is the last trunk show for the fall season. "Most of the designer customers have already bought their wardrobes."

"Overall," Jack says, these customers "buy their basics from the store (because it has their sizes) and then fill in for special evening wear from the trunk show." Unfortunately, only the stock size 10 is available at a trunk show, and, says Jack, these women know that often the dress they try on won't fit them. "There's a lot of guesswork and imagination involved. A lot of imagination.

"The garment will be shipped to the store and then alterations are made. There's a lot of work involved," he says. "Sometimes you have to rip out the entire shoulder and raise the whole dress. We do alterations in New York, too, when women order from us. They are altered, rather than made to order."

At 1:40 a male Marshall Field's executive walks in and says, "Where is everybody?"

Jack shrugs and goes into the back office to make a phone call. One of the models calls me over to the rack of Bill's clothes. "Isn't this great?" she says, holding up a gray wool chemise.

"It is," I reply, "but I should tell you that I'm not a customer."

"What are you?" she says.

"A spy," I say, laughing.

"For Saks?" she whispers, her eyes lighting up.

I shake my head no.

"Bloomingdale's?"

Again I tell her no and I explain to her what I'm doing.

"Who else are you writing about?" she asks.

I tell her.

She has some nasty things to say about one of these designers.

At first I am surprised at this model's cattiness but as I watch her working I come to understand why she is so bitter. Modeling is supposed to be glamorous, but almost every model I have ever come in contact with hates her job and does it only for the money. This poor beautiful girl, for instance, is spending her day standing around in high heels, bored in a windowless store, listening to music from the video and the hissing sound of the air-conditioning coming through the vents. It's neither an easy job nor a stimulating one. If one has to stand in high-heeled shoes all day, one can easily come to envy fashion designers, pressure packed lives and all. While this young woman spends her day modeling his clothes, Bill finishes his interviews, has lunch, and then rests up for tonight's party.

Even from the outside, it is immediately apparent that this Water Tower benefit—a gala coming-out party showcasing the recent renovation of Marshall Field's at Chicago's Water Tower Place—is a big deal. A red carpet has been rolled out onto the sidewalk, and crowds of spectators are jammed behind police barricades watching the 1,150 guests, each of whom paid $150 a ticket, walk into the party.

Inside, like it or not, every party-goer makes an entrance by stepping onto, and then immediately off, a stage erected just inside the front door. The idea behind this is to make everyone feel like a star, at least for a few minutes.

Then, from 7 P.M. to 8 P.M., on the ground floor, guests mingle and drink among the cosmetics and accessories counters as tuxedoed waiters bearing such goodies as seashells filled with caviar circle the room.

At 8 P.M. everyone heads upstairs to the sit-down dinners being served on the third, fourth, and fifth floors. On the way, they pass a seemingly naked former Miss Indiana who is sitting in a bathtub set up for the night in the Esprit sportswear department. The girl is holding a glass of champagne and resting her feet on the edge of the tub. I walk over to take a closer look and see that there's no water in the tub and that she is actually wearing a flesh-colored bodysuit and stockings. "How long do you have to sit here?" I ask.

"Until nine-thirty. What time is it?" she replies.

On the third floor, among racks of designer sportswear, are candle-lit tables covered with gold foil, a three-piece orchestra, and a buffet table loaded down with crown roasts of veal, crescents of gnocchi with asparagus, a tiered montage of red salmon, a rondelle of warm fresh vegetables, and a basket of fruit-shaped breads.

Many of the guests immediately start eating, but not the designers. They, along with store executives and members of the opera board, stand at the far right end of the floor, making themselves available to any and every photographer present. They are all standing around a raised circular platform on which display mannequins are dressed in Bill Blass gowns. Bill's work is getting special attention because of his earlier personal appearance but the other designers' clothes are prominently displayed on racks nearby.

Just as I am about to say hello to Sal Ruggiero, who is talking to one of the store's buyers, a photographer comes up to Sal and says, "Get a designer between you two."

Sal looks around, spots Louis dell'Olio, the creative force behind Anne Klein, and says, "There's one."

Sal grabs Louis and Jac Dubelle, who is both his girlfriend and fitting model, and the three pose for a picture. Bill, meanwhile, is talking to Carolina Herrera, while the exuberant Carolyne Roehm waves to a passerby and calls out, "I look a lot different than the last time you saw me, don't I?"

She turns back to me and says, "She saw me two hours ago when I just got in. I was green, and my hair was drooping."

Then, lowering her voice, she says, "So, when does this start? When do we eat? I'm starving."

Although everyone else is eating, there is no sign of food for the designers, who will be served their meals at tables that have been reserved for them here on this side of the floor. I ask Carolyne how her spring collection is coming along. She crosses her eyes and says, "I just crossed my eyes. Did you see?" She rolls her eyes toward the ceiling and says, "I'm under pressure with it. I have two dresses started. I have an idea in my head for what I want to do but it changes as I go along.

"But now I have the press after me." She jerks her head toward Patrick McCarthy, executive editor of *Women's Wear Daily*, who is sitting next to Carolina Herrera on a raised platform holding the mannequins dressed in Bill's gowns.

"*Women's Wear* wants to photograph the collection," Carolyne says. "What collection? But I guess it's good that they're after me because that gives me the impetus to get going. Designing has got to be the hardest job in the whole world," she says sincerely. "Even Henry says that being a designer is the hardest job in the world." She is referring to Henry Kravis, her mega-rich husband who is a partner in the leveraged-buyout firm of Kohlberg, Kravis and Roberts.

Just then a newly slim Oprah Winfrey arrives and Carolina brings Bill Blass over to her. "Excuse me, Oprah," she says. "Someone wants to meet you. This is Bill Blass."

Oprah stands at attention and sticks her hand out to shake his. "Hello, Mr. Blass," she says.

"It's a pleasure to meet you," he says. Then he gives her a sly smile, looks at her outfit and says, "That's Carolina, isn't it?"

For a moment Oprah looks uncomfortable. She looks at Bill uncertainly. It is only after he winks that she realizes he is teasing her and she laughs, as does Carolina. "Yes," she says, exchanging a glance with Carolina.

"Do we have any of his stuff?" says Oprah to Jennifer Jacobs, her personal wardrobe consultant and stylist, as Bill and Carolina walk away.

Jennifer thinks and thinks, says, "I don't think so," but then remembers, "Yes, there's that suit."

"Right," says Oprah.

"I buy all of Oprah's clothes," Jennifer tells me. "I always go to Louis's show, and to the other New York showrooms. American designers are so open and wonderful. Some of them send me videotapes of their collections. I went to Bill Blass and met with the head of sales, who showed me everything. That type of service is wonderful."

The designers' meals are served to them at 9 P.M., and by 9:25 they are finished and heading up the escalator to the higher floors, where the evening's entertainment is being presented.

On the sixth floor Buster Poindexter and his Banshees of Blue are performing *very loudly* in the men's shoe department. In front of the band, people are sitting at small tables loaded down with silver bowls of Cajun popcorn. Carolyne Roehm is in a hallway talking to a woman by leaning forward and yelling into the woman's ear.

Louis and Jac are standing off to the side, listening to the music, as anonymous as the bulk of the other people here. In fact, all the designers have simply blended into the party.

On the seventh floor, Bobby Short is performing behind the women's lingerie department. A sign saying "Bobby Short, courtesy of Carolina Herrera fragrances and Bill Blass fragrances," heralds his appearance. Carolina is standing by the sign talking to Gail and Jack; Bill Blass, himself, is nowhere to be seen. Rows of chairs are lined up around Short, and the small space is very crowded; even so, more people are trying to get into the room. Finally, at ten o'clock, a guard says, "Sorry, the room is full. It's a fire hazard. The next show is at eleven."

Carolyne is on this floor now, talking to two men, one of whom is photographer Victor Skrebneski, her escort for the evening. Victor photographs Carolyne's ad campaigns.

On the eighth floor, in front of the luggage department, party-goers are dancing to music by Vince Giordano and the Nighthawks. On the way downstairs, I see that dancing has started on seven, too, as people dance to the tunes of Buster Poindexter, holding their elbows against their waists to avoid bumping into racks of men's suits. Although the designers aren't dancing, they are talking, laughing, and eating and seem to be having as much fun as anybody else. Designing may be a hard job, as Carolyne put it earlier, but it certainly has its enjoyable moments.

Liz Claiborne *September 14*

The Liz Claiborne sportswear show was held on September 9, while we were in Chicago with Bill. The show, handled just as the holiday show was, went off without a hitch. Today, in its review, *Women's Wear Daily* writes: "Liz scores with her terrific sporty looks and signature career styles. . . . Spiffy jumpsuits; shorts in every category; a smart mix-and-match black and white graphic group; denim in every conceivable shape, including "boyfriend" shorts, highlighted with bright sweatshirts; a great white safari pantsuit; career looks featuring both skirts and pants worn with silk blouses; animal-print suits and sportswear; a pretty ode to Chanel."

Liz Claiborne *September 15*

This whole week has been "Liz Week" at Macy's, with various promotions held at stores throughout the tri-state area. Today's Liz Claiborne fashion show on the third floor of Macy's Herald Square is being held to publicize the newly renovated 5,500-square-foot Liz Claiborne department, housing all three sportswear lines, at the rear of the third floor. Liz Claiborne has gotten this much floor space because the store does an excellent business with the merchandise. Liz Claiborne and Macy's are sharing the cost of this promotion.

A raised runway has been set up on this floor, running between racks of sportswear by other designers. About two hundred folding chairs surround the runway. All of them are occupied by customers ranging in age from about sixteen to seventy. Still more shoppers, as well as executives from Liz Claiborne and Macy's, crowd around the runway to get a glimpse of the models and of Liz herself. She is at the foot of the runway, giving the models a final once-over before they step out beneath the spotlights.

Art, Jerry, Jay, Ellen, and Dennis are stationed throughout the crowd watching the thirty-minute show, which focuses on sportswear, dresses, menswear, and accessories. I stand next to Dennis, and, as the show ends and Liz comes out to take a bow, he says, "Oh, Liz is wearing black. Oh, good."

Some of the customers in the audience stand up and wave at her. She looks surprised for a moment, squints to see if she knows them, seems to realize she doesn't, and waves back uncertainly. She walks to the end of the floor and into the department where the Liz Claiborne merchandise is hanging, surrounded by video screens showing the fall fashion show and large photographs of models in the clothes.

She stands in the middle of the department near the racks of Lizsport clothing. As the customers form a circle around her, she seems relaxed, although some of the customers are staring at her as if they were watching a TV screen rather than a real person. They stare with absolutely no expression on their faces.

A few women look Liz up and down in the competitive way that some women size each other up. And then, of course, there are the ones that go up to talk to Liz.

"How do you stay so thin?" says an older woman.

"*Uuuuuh*," she says, drawing the word out. "I work at it." Then she lowers her voice and talks to the woman some more. Liz treats every customer as an individual, and she certainly doesn't put on any airs. Each woman who went up to talk to her will go home feeling as if she has really met Liz Claiborne, the person.

Behind me are two young girls who are both students at Toby Colburne, a fashion school. "This is your chance," says one to the other. "You've got to do it. You admire her so much. Hurry up before it's too late."

As the girl goes up to Liz, and her friend sees that Liz is talking to her, the friend quickly darts up to Liz as well, just as a photographer from *Women's Wear Daily* takes Liz's picture.

Later, I ask the fashion students what they said to Liz. "We just said that we really loved her and we loved her work. She's so unique. My hands were shaking. It was like meeting a star."

"She is a star," says the other girl.

Arnold Scaasi *September 19*

Figuring it's about time we contacted Arnold, whose fall made-to-order show is in a week, and whose spring ready-to-wear is debuting in six weeks and has yet to be designed, I give him a call. Made-to-order collections are always shown closer to the time that women will actually be wearing the clothes. Unlike the ready-to-wear, which is manufactured in bulk, and therefore needs more leeway, the made-to-order is, as its name suggests, ordered and then manufactured item by item, according to need. That need becomes more apparent to the customers as the start of the spring or, in this case, fall social season nears.

"How are you?" I say when Arnold gets on the phone.

"Harassed," he replies. "Can you hold? There's a call on the other line."

I do, and when he gets back on, he says he's going to be working on this collection "up to the last minute. Some embroideries are still coming in. It just never stops. That's how I feel this morning. It builds up until it opens and then you start all over again."

When I point out that I still haven't seen Arnold design a single dress, he says, "I don't like having people around me when I work. I work alone." Finally, after I insist, he says, "OK. Come by the salon at three-thirty."

I arrive at the appointed time to find Arnold, wearing gray flannels, a white shirt, and a red tie with large yellow, blue, and white polka dots, making changes on some muslin samples that have been placed on dressmaker dummies.

"This has too much shirring," he says, standing in the rear fitting room and picking at one of the muslins, as a seamstress listens and his assistant, Timothy, takes notes. "I want pleats. And this is longer than this. It shouldn't be."

Connie, the model, arrives and Arnold tells her, "I'm not going to fit till later."

"Then I'll come back tomorrow," says Connie. "I don't want to work all night again."

"I've been trying to call you," he says. "Something happened." He pulls her into his office, where racks of dresses stand pushed against the walls, and closes the door. "I'm very excited," I hear him say to Connie. Then he says, "I can fit this and this on you. And this. We should be finished by six-thirty. You can lie down while you wait or you can use the phone."

"OK," she says.

Arnold opens the door, walks out, and goes back to work, reviewing the muslins. He looks at a sleeveless sample for a short dress. "Maybe you need another drape here," he says to the seamstress, Suheyla, who has her brown hair back in a bun and is wearing a housedress. "It's too broad. This dress should be in the same feeling as the black dress with little white flowers that we made for Mrs. Scripps and Mrs. Steinberg. It's not a big dress. It's a restaurant dress."

He finishes this muslin, makes corrections on another, and, when he is done, a seamstress drags both dummies into the workroom, which is actually divided into two separate rooms. The first is the fabric room, filled with floor-to-ceiling shelves stacked high with folded fabrics. Inside the entrance to the fabric room, to the right, is another door leading to the other workroom, where the samples and the made-to-order dresses are sewn. In the fabric room Arnold looks at a dummy that has been draped with a long dress.

"The drape should come up higher," he says of the dress.

Connie is now sitting behind one of the desks in the fabric room, talking on the telephone. Every time I've seen models, either in a photographer's or a designer's studio, they have spent much of their free time on the phone. They have to check in with their agencies to see what other bookings may have come up, call in to their personal answering machines, and then return phone calls from friends and relatives. Unlike professionals with desk jobs, models generally cannot be reached during the day.

Seeing Connie on the phone, Arnold says, "Maybe we can have our meeting now." With his staff, he wants to review which dresses are ready for the show and what still needs to be either sewed or designed.

Arnold walks into the salon's large waiting area where his assistant has pushed aside the four little coffee tables and, in straight rows on the floor, has lined up seventy-three 8½- by 11-inch pieces of paper, each of which features one large sketch and one fabric swatch. The sketches are arranged in the order that they will be appearing in the fall made-to-order show. The style number of each dress is written on the bottom of both the sketch and the swatch.

"Where are you, Jerry?" Arnold calls, sitting down on a banquette in front of the window. "Where are you, Timothy?" Jerry Solovei, who has worked for Arnold for two years as the general managing director of all Scaasi enterprises, Timothy, and three of Arnold's main fitters walk in. Suheyla is still in her housedress, and the other two women, Margaret and Anita, are in very plain blouses and skirts. Margaret has worked for Arnold for twenty-five years and is head of his workroom. The women sit on the banquette and the men pull up chairs.

"We have a list of the dresses," says Arnold as Timothy passes out three-page-long, stapled copies of the typewritten list. The heading on the first page says, "Arnold Scaasi, Fall Made-to-Order Collection, Monday, September 26, 1988." The style numbers of the dresses are in a column on the left side of the page and a description of the dresses is on the right.

"The first one is done," says Arnold, looking at the list and referring to number 3501, a crimson-red double-face wool capecoat. "And the second one is done" (number 3502, a crimson-red pebble crepe twist draped short afternoon dress). "Let's put checks next to the ones that are finished and write down who's working on the ones that aren't."

Anita, whom Arnold has just reassigned from ready-to-wear sample-making to made-to-order work, reads the list through a magnifying glass and makes her checks in pen. "Anita, we always write in pencil," Arnold tells her, "so that we can erase. Timothy, get her a pencil." Timothy stands up and goes to one of the back rooms to get one.

"OK," says Arnold. "The first two are done. The third is what you're working on now. Who's doing that?"

"Elsa," says Margaret.

"All right. So write that down. Write the initials." They all write "E."

"The fourth is the coat," says Arnold. "That's going to Suheyla."

"And 3505?" (This is a red wool chesterfield coat with a black velvet collar.) "The collar's not cut yet. Give that to Elsa. And 3506 (a black wool crepe basket weave tucked afternoon dress). What's happening with it?"

"It's upstairs," says Margaret. "She's working on it."

"Where's Michael?" says Arnold, referring to the young man who is responsible for the made-to-order fabrics.

"He's on the phone right at this moment," says Timothy.

"Jerry, tell him to get off the phone and get on in here," says Arnold. Jerry jumps up and does as he's told. Michael, a young man with blond hair, comes in, looking very serious.

"I need some brown velvet and brown chiffon," Arnold says to Michael. Arnold is planning to design a group of dresses with sheer yokes and he wants to see if these two brown fabrics will work well together. "Could you hurry with it?"

Michael returns and hands the fabrics to Timothy, who walks toward Arnold, who barks, "Don't come in the room. Stand by the swan." He is referring to a silk flower-filled swan that stands on an end table just inside the room's entrance. Timothy backs up and holds up the fabrics so that they fall off their long bolts and hang to the floor.

"I don't have too many dresses with a sheer yoke, do I?" says Arnold, studying the juxtaposition of the sheer chiffon against the velvet. "Maybe I should do that."

He then goes down the show lineup (very few of the seventy-three outfits are done, and many still need to be sketched) until he comes to a short black dress and asks Jerry to get it from the workroom. "This is wrong," says Arnold peevishly, looking at the dress. "They were supposed to leave the top sheer." Timothy and the seamstresses write this down.

Arnold asks Timothy to get him two bolts of "wine" and "rouge" chiffon. While he waits, Arnold looks at the sheets of paper on the floor and says, "Margaret, do you like the short purple dresses?"

Margaret stands up, looks at the sketches, and says, "Which one?"

"All of them. Do you like those dresses in purple?"

"Yes," she says. "I do."

"You don't think the purple is too old?"

"No," she says. "I don't. I like them."

Then he yells, "Timothy!" No answer. "What's he doing?" Arnold says to me. I shrug. "Go see," he tells me. "Tell him I need him."

I go to look for Timothy and find him carrying the purple and red chiffon. We return but Arnold is still looking at the sketches. "I'm not crazy about the purple," he says. "Don't you think it looks old?"

"It depends on the style," says Margaret.

"No it doesn't," Arnold snaps at her. "It doesn't depend on the style. It just looks old." I wonder why he asked her for her opinion if he doesn't want to hear it.

"Timothy," says Arnold, "count how many short cocktail and how many long evening dresses I have, please, while we're doing this." Timothy stands up and walks among the sketches, counting.

"I would take the whole violet group out," says Arnold. He calls Michael in and asks him to "bring the pansy prints."

Arnold looks at one of the fabrics, a red-and-purple print, and says, "It looks springy to me. What do you think?" he says to everyone. No one answers, and I can't say I blame them. "I like the brown," says Arnold, referring to a more toned-down version of the print. "I'll show it under a fur coat."

"I need a good basic dress," says Arnold. "Want to do the one with the pleats? I think people like it." Again, no one answers.

Timothy brings in a gold dress that has flowers appliquéd onto it and holds it for Arnold to review. "I hate it," Arnold says. "They've put the flowers on all wrong. They've flattened them out."

"Maybe the finisher did it," says Margaret.

"I don't care who did it," Arnold yells. "I just care that it wasn't done right. This is unbelievable to me."

The meeting ends at 4:50, and Connie walks into the first fitting room on the right side of the hall, undresses down to a pink teddy and nude hose, and then puts on a jacket that Arnold wants to fit.

I take a break to go to the bathroom, which is in a hallway behind the fabric room. I pass a door that says "Gentlemen," then a water fountain, and then an open door that says "Ladies." Inside, the stale air reeks of cigarette smoke, and the large full plastic garbage can doesn't have a cover. The two beige stall doors open in the center like old saloon doors, and they don't have locks. A paper sign taped to the mirror says, "Your Mother Doesn't Work Here. Please Pick Up After Yourself." After seeing Arnold's apartment and his showroom I am surprised that the bathroom isn't somewhat nicer. True, it's behind the scenes, but what happens if his clients have to go to the bathroom?

When I return, Arnold, along with a tailor and Margaret, is fitting the jacket as Timothy stands in the doorway and writes down all the changes Arnold wants done.

And now finally, *finally*, I see Arnold Scaasi create a dress. He does so by draping the brown velvet and chiffon he'd inspected earlier over Connie's body. First, maneuvering the long bolt of fabric, Arnold places the sheer chiffon over the very top of her chest area. Then, so that it forms a vertical line, he places the velvet, starting just above her breasts and falling all the way to the floor. Connie holds the fabrics against herself and Arnold picks up the bottom so that it resembles a short dress.

"What do you think?" he says, inspecting the dress in the mirror.

"It's nice," says Connie, also looking in the mirror.

"Do I need a dress like that?"

"I'm not really sure what you have at this point," she says.

"Timothy, call Suheyla." The seamstress arrives quickly and Arnold tells her, "We're going to use this velvet." He quickly makes a sketch of the dress.

Next, Arnold asks Timothy to bring him a long bolt of brown satin. Connie holds the bolt of fabric horizontally in front of her, and Arnold leaves her standing there while he goes into the fabric room searching for black tulle. He comes back with a piece of the stiff fabric, and, with Suheyla's help, Arnold pins the black tulle so that it stands away from Connie's shoulders. Next he pins the satin on her and then he holds a very sheer gold metallic print fabric on top of the satin and pins that, too. From where I am standing, behind Connie, I can see all the pins, but in the mirror it looks like a finished dress.

While Timothy unpins Connie, Suheyla leaves. Arnold goes into the fabric room and comes back carrying a beautiful pink floral fabric with a green-and-black background. "What am I going to do with this fabric?" he says. "I haven't a clue."

Arnold puts a sheer black net fabric across Connie's chest and then holds up the floral fabric so that again there is a straight line across her chest and a sheer yoke. "Now I'm crazy about this yoke thing," he says. "I don't know why." He looks in the mirror and picks up some fabric in the back. "It should be draped at the bottom," he says.

"That's beautiful," says Connie.

"Call Suheyla, Margaret, and Elsa," Arnold says to Timothy. As he waits, he extends the floral fabric so that it covers Connie's upper arms and looks in the mirror. "I like it like that," he says. "With three-quarter sleeves."

When Suheyla and Margaret arrive, Arnold explains how he wants this dress to be made. "It needs a three-quarter sleeve," he says. "There should be a seam down to the drape and then the drape should start. Now look, I don't want any seams in these yokes. None. All you have to do is work it. Work with the fabric. It can be worked out."

Elsa wanders in and Arnold snaps, "Come here, Elsa. I'm doing this for your benefit, not mine. I know how to do it."

Then he says to Connie, "OK. Just hold it like that if you can." He picks up his sketch pad and, as he draws, says in a deadpan voice, "So we have another dress."

Donna Karan *September 23*

"Trying to catch Donna is like trying to catch water in your hands," one of Donna's design assistants once told me. I'm beginning to see what she meant. I had an interview with Donna for this book back in March, and since then she has rescheduled meetings and put me off until today, when finally I will get to see her at work.

Although I haven't seen Donna since March, her secretary kept me informed of Donna's doings and mental state, succinctly summing up the latter with comments like "She's crazed" or "She's frantic" or "She's out of her mind." The reason for Donna's perpetually unnerved state was this: Besides designing her signature Donna Karan spring collection (which will be shown on November 4) she is launching, also for spring, an ancillary business. The show for this line, which is called DKNY and consists of man-tailored casual clothes priced one-half to one-third lower than her designer collection, is in three days.

The idea for DKNY stemmed from the fact that Donna, for comfort's sake, had taken to wearing her husband's shirts, sweaters, and jackets on the weekends. Then one day she decided to make the same type of oversized, comfortable clothes for women.

After just five years of designing under her own name, this energetic, brash, exuberant woman is considered a world-class designer, and wholesale volume for her business is approaching $80 million. DKNY has been previewed to stores and the press, and based on their reactions, Donna already knows the line will be a huge success and expects it to catapult her company's total volume to $130 million in 1989.

How does she feel about all of this? "I wish I could tell you that I'm excited," Donna—who is wearing a neck brace thanks to a herniated disk that has been aggravated by stress—tells me today. Donna has covered the ugly white brace with fabric cut from a pair of black Donna Karan opaque tights, which she manufactures under license. "I have such mixed feelings. DKNY is bigger than I ever thought it would be. I'm elated one day and crying the next. When my daughter calls me at seven P.M. and says, 'Mommy where are you?' it's not so exciting. Until the day I die, I will be a guilty mother."

When asked to describe herself, the first word Donna utters, without hesitation, is "confused." And who can blame her? She is a top designer who hates her job yet is obsessive about doing it, and doing it well. "It's the worst job in the world," she says. "There's so much pressure. You're only as good as your last collection and you're always working against a deadline." Fear of missing a deadline has permeated her subconscious, and her recurring nightmare of frantically designing as she tries to beat the clock, often wrenches her and, in turn, her husband out of a deep sleep.

She keeps the hours of a workaholic, frequently toiling until 9 P.M. and often later, and has clothing-in-progress shipped to her when she is on vacation—yet she says working is one of her least favorite things. Then why does she continue churning out hugely successful collections and launching new businesses? "I don't know," she says. "That's why I'm in therapy. To figure it out."

Donna's fixation with design and her conflicted, guilt-ridden relationship with her teenage daughter both seem to revolve around her own relationship with her mother—a former showroom model who, Donna says, did not give her the attention she craved as a child. Born on October 2, 1948, Donna grew up in Lawrence, Long Island. Her father, a tailor, died when she was three and her mother went to work as a saleswoman at the design firm of the late Chester Weinberg. That summer Donna's mother shipped her off to summer camp at the age of three and a half.

From an early age, Donna, who was a shy and gawky child, was not accepted by her peers. "I was a social misfit," she says. "I had to find something I was good at doing." Not surprisingly for the daughter of a tailor and a mother whom she remembers as "always looking so impeccable, dressed in the blazers my father had made for her," that something turned out to be designing clothes.

When she was fourteen, Donna lied about her age and got a sales position at a dress shop. She hated school, frequently played hooky, and did not get good grades, but with Weinberg's help she was accepted into the prestigious Parsons School of Design. In 1968 she got a job with the late Anne Klein as a summer intern. Klein persuaded Donna that she could learn more by working full time for her than by going to school, and Donna dropped out of Parsons. Nine months later Klein fired her because, Donna says, "I couldn't do anything right."

Donna worked for nine months for another firm, called Addenda, and in 1970 she married Mark Karan, who ran a small boutique in Brooklyn. Donna asked Anne Klein for a second chance and was rehired as a nondesigning assistant— she picked up pins, got coffee, and made charts. This time she did things right, and, as she kept proving herself, Donna was given more responsibilities and was soon promoted to assistant designer. In 1971 she was named associate designer.

When Anne Klein died of cancer in 1974, twenty-six-year-old Donna, who two days before had given birth to a daughter, Gabrielle, took over as chief designer, signing a twelve-year contract with Takihyo, Inc., Anne Klein's parent company. The contract gave her almost complete creative control.

Donna asked Louis Dell'Olio, whom she'd befriended at Parsons, to join her at Anne Klein. From their very first collection, the team was a smashing success. In 1974 sales at Anne Klein were about $10 million, and as the Anne Klein business began a steady climb upward, Donna's marriage simultaneously began a decline that eventually ended in divorce.

In 1983 Donna did two important things. She was remarried, this time to Stephan Weiss, a sculptor and father of two, whom she had dated as a teenager and whom she began dating again when her first marriage dissolved. She also oversaw the launch of Anne Klein II, a less expensive spinoff line that was introduced in 1983 and was aimed at women who have designer-level taste but cannot afford designer prices.

Once Anne Klein II was launched, Donna, secure in a happy marriage, began to explore her feelings about work and admitted that she wasn't happy. She decided she'd gone about as far as she could go with Anne Klein and that it wasn't far enough for her. She wanted her own business.

In 1984 Donna began talking to Tomio Taki, chairman of Takihyo, Inc., and to Frank Mori, the president of Anne Klein, about designing a collection under her own name. Donna told them that although she wanted her own label she was afraid to let go of her secure position at Anne Klein. Taki and Mori told her she had to make a complete break. She was afraid to do so, and, in the end, Frank Mori made Donna's decision for her. He fired her.

Forced to finish what she'd started, Donna formed a partnership with Tomio Taki; his company; Frank Mori; and her husband, Stephan. Takihyo, Inc., provided the initial $3 million needed for start-up costs. Ownership of the company was segmented among its principals, with Donna (who was named chief executive officer) and her husband owning 50 percent; Takihyo, Inc., 30 percent; and Taki and Mori each, 10 percent.

Her first collection, launched in May 1985, centered around a bodysuit worn with dark opaque tights, and, usually, a formfitting, knit wrap skirt. The models all wore turbans on their heads, just like Donna's chic mother used to wear. The collection made Donna a superstar. By the end of 1985, *Women's Wear Daily* was calling her "the hottest designer on Seventh Avenue" and *The New York Times* was reporting that "in less than one year, Miss Karan has catapulted to the first rank of American designers."

Soon Donna launched shoes, handbags, belts, gloves, scarves, and jewelry, all of which she oversaw in-house. After six months in business, a licensing division was formed and her name was stamped on hosiery made by Hanes and furs by Birger Christensen.

With one business creatively churning along and another about to be launched, Donna says she is depressed, mainly because she has been working at a pace "that is not normal." She feels as if everyone is pulling at her all the time, and, in describing her workdays, says they are much like those of a doctor. "I feel like everyone should have a chart hanging outside of their doors and I should look at their charts before I go in and say, 'How can I help you?' or 'What is wrong today?' "

Besides the pressure of producing four collections a year, and overseeing her licensed products, now that she is a partner in her company Donna has to worry about things like budgets, overhead costs, and whom to hire for what position. Luckily, she says, she has found wonderful assistants.

Also, she raves about the assistance of Peter Arnell, the twenty-nine-year-old co-founder of the Soho-based advertising agency Arnell/Bickford Associates, which handles all of Donna's advertising.

Right now Peter and his staff are hidden behind closed doors in an office just behind the reception area where I am waiting for Donna. The door opens, and Peter, wearing a red shirt and faded jeans, sends out Patti Cohen, a pretty woman with a mop of curly red hair, who is one of Donna's best friends and fashion director of the company, to call Donna in.

The cherubic Peter, whose intelligence is obvious and whose enthusiasm is infectious, is about to show Donna the tiny dollhouse-size model he and his staff have designed as a prototype for DKNY departments in various stores. Each of these departments will feature black-and-white photographs depicting a New York of years gone by. The photos will hang suspended from the ceiling at various levels,

This concept was inspired by photographs and articles about Edward Steichen's three-dimensional 1955 "Family of Man" exhibit at the Museum of Modern Art in which the photographs were placed at odd angles to reflect where the photographer was standing when he took the picture. If the photographer looked up to take the photograph, the image was suspended above eye level; if he looked down, it was placed below eye level.

Donna, wearing her neck brace, a black T-shirt, and navy pants, walks in and stares at the dollhouse-size store replica. She looks and looks at it for a full thirty seconds without saying a word. Everyone in the office had been very excited, but now they start exchanging looks, wondering why Donna isn't saying anything. "Doesn't she like it?" is the unspoken message behind their glances.

Finally, Donna says, "It's absolutely unbelievable. It's fabulous." The sense of relief in the room is practically palpable. Everyone smiles, and Donna walks over to Peter, who is standing by the window, to give him a hug and a kiss. "It's fabulous," she says in her deep, loud, New York-accented voice as she walks back to the prototype. "Look at these tiny hangers (she pronounces it 'hangus')!"

Peter picks up his 35-mm camera and starts taking picture after picture of Donna looking at the model. Many of his ads feature his photos of his clients, and he is rarely without his camera.

Jane Chung, Donna's chief assistant on DKNY, rushes into the office. "Let me see! Let me see! . . . Oh," says the young Chinese woman who worked with Donna at Anne Klein and has been with her since Donna started her own company. "It's wonderful. And there's a mother and a baby! Donna, did you see the mother and the baby?"

"What are we missing in here?" Donna says, squinting into the prototype without answering Jane.

"The belts and accessories," says Peter.

"Where's the video?" she says, and Peter points it out.

"And we have to do the floor," says Donna. "How about having black-and-white tiling?" Peter tells two of his male employees that they have to install this tiling.

"Or a cement floor?" says Donna.

"Does she want these changes for Monday?" says a girl in the reception area in the tone of voice that makes her question sound more like "Is she out of her mind?" Today is Friday, and Monday is the day Donna will be launching DKNY for the spring season. This prototype will be displayed at the entrance to the show.

"How about chairs?" says Donna.

"I saw this more as people shopping quick," says Peter. "Chairs to me implied more of a salon."

"How about benches?" says Donna. "Gallery benches."

"OK," says Peter.

"And how about the lighting situation? Do we want spotlights?"

"Let's make a list of what we have to do for Monday," says Peter to his staff. "I have to do belts and put some benches in and we need lights."

"Yes," says Donna. "Don't you love the idea of spotlighting the clothes?"

"Is that possible, guys?" says Peter to two of his employees. "Can you do lights up here over the weekend? Do you have your tools?"

"Are you gonna make it?" Donna says to the workers. "Are you exhausted?" They smile at her without answering. Their silence clearly implies that they are.

After they are done inspecting the model, Donna, Patti, and Peter walk down one flight of steps to the fourteenth floor to check on the progress of the room where the DKNY fashion show will be held. Rather than walking down a runway, the models will stand in groups on raised platforms so that the fashion editors can closely inspect the DKNY clothes and jewelry.

"What is this light?" says Donna as she walks into the very long white room that smells like fresh paint. "It's disgusting. This light has got to go." She is referring to the lights erected by the crew that will be videotaping her show.

"This light's killing the whole thing, the whole space," says Peter. "Look at him," he says pointing at one of the workmen. "He's green. And people are going to be falling all over this shit," he says, kicking a tripod.

"How to kill a room in one easy step. It's amazing how important lighting is to life. Can you imagine walking around and looking up at that," says Donna, squinting into the glare of a light. "You won't even see the models. You're blinded."

"We said he could fix it or mount it," says Peter.

"There's no place to mount it," says a workman.

"Why did you need such large lights?" says Donna.

"Because you're fighting sunlight."

"Can't you just use sunlight?" says Donna.

"The windows are brilliantly blue. The video will look blue."

"Put our lights on," says Donna. Someone does. The overhead lights cut some of the glare. "Why not this?" says Donna.

"Because they are a different lighting temperature."

"Let's see it during daylight," says Patti, as a group of young kids pulls white cloth off of a large bolt and cover one of the platforms with it. "It's so unfair to do this now. Tomorrow's supposed to be a beautiful day and so is Monday. Let's see how it looks tomorrow."

"And maybe we can mount lights somehow," says Peter.

"The fixtures don't bother me," says Donna. "They look real. That's what our showroom is all about. We'll have the black-and-white photographs mounted. It's supposed to look like a gallery. What bothers me is the lights."

Donna walks to the room's entrance and notices that large black letters spelling DKNY have been painted on the wall next to it. "I hate it," says Donna, pointing to the letters. "This goes. I don't want people to say, 'What happened to Donna Karan New York?'" This is the name of her collection. After the show, this room will be converted into a showroom for her collection and accessories lines, not just for DKNY. It is because of this that she doesn't want to give the lower-priced line exclusive billing.

Donna sits down on the platform by the door and tells Denise Seegal, a thin young woman who was executive vice-president of sales and marketing at Ralph Lauren Womenswear and has just joined DKNY in the same capacity, to sit down next to her. "Denise," she says, "short skirts look wrong. I wish you could get everyone into pants. The short skirts are old and dowdy. The skirt looks great alone but the minute you put it with a jacket it looks wrong. I wouldn't offer it because if you give it to the customers they'll wear it." Denise nods.

Just then Jane, the assistant responsible for designing DKNY, who has walked downstairs to show Donna the navy blue blazer that the in-house sample room has just completed, stops by the huge DKNY letters painted on the wall and says, "I love it."

Walking behind Jane is Edward Wilkerson, a tall young swooshy black man who is one of Donna's two main assistants for her collection. He has worked with her here for one year but had previously worked with her at Anne Klein, part time for three years and full time for another two. "He's gonna hate it," Donna whispers, looking at Edward.

"Is this always going to be here?" says Edward, wrinkling his nose as he looks at the huge DKNY letters.

"Do I know my people?" says Donna. "It's like when you bring a newborn baby home from the hospital and everybody makes a big deal over the infant and forgets about the other child standing in the doorway crying, 'Look at me. Look at me.'" Lately DKNY has been getting all the attention.

It is now 6:25, and Robert Lee Morris, the jewelry designer, walks in carrying a small shopping bag filled with jewelry. He dumps the contents of the bag next to Donna on the platform.

"Oh, I love these," says Donna, scooping up the pins, earrings, and bracelets. "Look at these." The jewelry was inspired by the streets of New York and features miniature replicas of such things as pothole covers, garbage cans, subway tokens, and the Empire State Building. Donna picks up a miniature mailbox and says, "This is such chic jewelry. Oh, it's to die." She kisses Robert on both cheeks.

She goes back to inspecting the jewelry and then says, "Are we gonna have enough jewelry for Monday? We need thirty-five girls decked." She sounds frantic, and Robert calmly answers, "You'll have it."

Robert points to Donna's neck brace and says, "You look good in that thing. You could start a national trend—wearing a neck brace with no sweater. A turtleneck with no sweater attached."

Donna turns to Denise again and says, "Denise, do we have enough without the washed silks for April? Can we save the washed silks for May? We have navy, rainwear, jeans, and the whole natural thing." These are the four groups that will be delivered for April. While Denise thinks, Donna says, "What's our C buy?" Designers rank stores from A+ to C according to the size of their purchases, with A+ being the largest and C the smallest.

"A minimum is twenty-five thousand dollars at wholesale for five months," says Denise. "That's what they must buy."

"No way," says Donna. "Three months."

"We know everybody's gonna buy the navy jacket, crepe pant, raincoat, jean, and denim shirt," says Donna, listing the base items in DKNY. "That is what everyone—A to C—will buy. On top of that we have plenty more for the A stores to buy. I think if we show the washed silks now it will be asking them to digest too much at once. We want to make sure we don't give them too much so they don't drop anything."

Denise agrees. "We're going to say thirty-day delivery?" she says. This means the company will promise to deliver the clothes within thirty days of receiving orders.

"Yes," says Donna.

"What if you have a problem? The last thing you want to do is ask for an extension. [Stores can cancel their orders if merchandise is delivered late.] Why not tell them forty-five days?"

"So we'll have two delivery periods instead of three," says Donna. "Two periods of forty-five days each."

At 7 P.M., Donna walks back up to the fifteenth floor to go to the design room for her higher-priced collection, where Edward, Katie O'Brien, a soft spoken British girl who is knitwear designer for Collection, and Istvan Francer, a ponytailed young man whom Donna hired right out of school, are waiting for her. Edward peels off the small DKNY sticker Donna has attached to her T-shirt and says, "You're in couture now."

"We heard what you told Frank Mori, Edward," says Donna, referring to the president of Anne Klein and one of Donna's partners in this business. "He asked where I was and you said—here Donna makes her tone very snobby—'She's working on the less expensive line.'"

Indeed, Donna has been working on "the less expensive line" almost exclusively for weeks. Right now, however, she has to change her mindset to focus on her higher-priced collection, Donna Karan, which, although it is opening November 4, will not even be designed until next month.

Fabrics for that collection have been purchased, but just a few have been delivered, and only a few prototypical silhouettes have been created. This, however, is true for most of the high-end American designers, all of whom are officially opening their collections around the first week of November. Although Donna hasn't made the actual bodies, she has a strong idea of what she wants to do.

By Tuesday she has to put the sweaters for her collection into work, since, as we saw with Adrienne Vittadini, it takes longer for knitwear to be properly manufactured and approved. Tonight she is reviewing the sweater program that, under her initial instruction, her assistants have developed.

She turns to a chart covered with tiny sketches of sweaters that is hanging on the wall. "I love that sweatuh," Donna says, her accent becoming more pronounced as she begins editing. "This one I'm discarding [discahding]. . . . What is this? You don't need both. . . . I see it right here. . . . Which one, darling? . . . Is it the same . . . Is this the one I love? . . . I think we need a basic black cardigan in here. . . . Oh, so you have all the cardigans. Sorry, I didn't understand it. . . . I still think our black group looks too big. . . . That V-neck would look divine here. Let's do a shaped boat and a deep V. I'd love some fitted, divine black sweaters. . . . How many different bodies are there? Has anyone counted? . . . We have to discard [discahd].

"I think this looks terrific, darlings," says Donna. "I couldn't do any better."

"We'll do this tomorrow," says Katie. What she means by "do" is draw up extremely detailed sketches for their Hong Kong contractors to follow.

"Tomorrow?" says Donna. "These are due Tuesday. Why don't you do them on Monday?" She is trying to give her assistants Saturday off. Katie doesn't answer, and Donna says, "Now we have to pick out the pale sweaters. I should go over the yarn with you. You're not going to see me all next week. I'll be too busy with DKNY. Tuesday I have to educate the whole sales staff; they start showing Wednesday." She doesn't detail her other obligations, but she will be also merchandising and meeting with retailers and giving press interviews.

Donna has spent many precious weeks, which would normally have been spent thinking about her Collection, working on DKNY, previewing it, and hiring people to staff that division. As soon as DKNY is launched Donna will try to devote herself full time to her Collection with an unfortunate week-long break that she must take in a week and a half so that she can attend the fabric fairs in Europe, where she will choose her fabrics for fall. Here is another instance of how every designer has to stop midstream, just as her or his creativity is going into high gear, to conceptualize her or his next season.

Remembering that she has to go to Europe, Donna asks Istvan if he would like to go with her to the Première Vision fabric fair in Paris, or to Ideacomo, another fabric fair being held in Italy a week later. "The first will give you a first indication for fall but Ideacomo is where we really work. Where do you want to go?" Aware that her assistants work extremely hard, Donna tries to do what she can to keep them happy.

"Wherever you think is best," says Istvan.

"But which would you prefer?" she says.

"It doesn't matter," he says. "Whichever one you think is better."

"Istvan, if I told you you had to pick one, which one would you pick?"

"If I had to pick," he says, looking down at the ground, "I would pick Paris."

"OK," says Donna. Edward has walked out of the room for a minute, and when he returns, Donna says, "Edward, you'll come to Ideacomo. Istvan will go to Première Vision." Then, sarcastically, she says, "And for the trip you love so much—to the mills—I'll take Istvan."

This last trip will take place after spring opens, when Donna goes to the factories to work with them on fabric development. She later tells me that her assistants hate going to the mills "because it's hard work. You work from nine A.M. to two A.M. And you're not sitting in a hotel. You're into the nitty-gritty technical things, going into the archives, into the technical aspects of making fabrics."

She, however, loves the trip because "I'm out of here and really concentrating. I'm totally focused on design. I don't have to do interviews or talk on the phone or worry about production, stores, or advertising. There, I don't have to talk to *The New York Times*. I mean, nurturing relationships with the press is very important but it takes you away from your work."

"OK," says Edward, looking down at his desk. "But I was going to go to Paris

Thursday." He had made his own arrangements to go to Première Vision. "Not even a consideration," says Donna. "We have a line due in four weeks." To Istvan she says, "We leave October fourth." To Edward she says, "We'll go to Ideacomo and then you're going to want to go to Paris, right, darling? I'll go to [a textile manufacturer] then because they don't show at Ideacomo and I'll work with them while you're in Paris. All right? Now everyone has a piece of what they want."

Donna leaves the room and Katie makes a phone call, saying, "Hi, honey. It's eight-fifteen. I'm still at work. I'd love to do something with you tonight."

She hangs up and pouts at Istvan saying, "All my friends have gone out." She sits down and she and Istvan patiently wait for Donna to return, while Edward leaves. "At least you have your priorities straight," Katie says to Edward's departing back.

"You become obsessive working here because Donna is," Katie tells me. "But then you leave and you think, 'My God, what am I doing? It's nine o'clock and I'm just getting out of work.'

"You can't set up a meeting with Donna," she continues. "You can't say, 'I need to see you Tuesday.' It just doesn't work that way. Donna is very chaotic. You just have to grab her when you can. You say, 'I have to see you,' and then you do something else as you wait for her."

At 8 P.M., tired of waiting for Donna, who is sitting behind the desk in her office, reviewing some DKNY pieces, Katie knocks and asks if she can show Donna some of the yarns they will be using for the spring knitwear.

"The ones for Hong Kong," says Donna, "because that program has to be done by Tuesday."

"This will take two weeks to dye," says Katie, showing Donna some small skeins of yarn.

There is a knock on the door, and Donna's favorite fitting model, Doreen Ericksen, with whom she works almost exclusively, comes in wearing an unfinished denim coat from DKNY. With her is the assistant designer who created it. "This is Josh's coat," says Doreen.

"I love it," says Donna. "It's fabulous."

"Really?" says the assistant.

"Who did this?" says Donna.

"I did," he says.

"You fit the muslin yourself and sewed it?"

"Yeah," he says. "No one else was around to help me. I had to do it myself."

"You did a great job. It looks great."

"Oh," he says, looking as though he's about to swoon, "I'm so happy." Doreen and the assistant leave, and Donna and Katie talk about where to place their knitwear production.

"Give it to Gracie," says Donna. Katie says this factory is overbooked with DKNY and won't be able to handle everything.

"Dye the yarn," says Donna, "and then we'll see. We have to find another knitter."

At 8:30 an assistant sticks her head in the door and says to Donna, "You have to leave in ten minutes."

"Oh, shit," says Donna. "Can you get Jane?"

Katie meanwhile tries to get Donna to plan some fall production with her. But when Jane comes in, Donna cuts Katie off and starts discussing personnel problems with Jane. One of the assistant designers is trying his best, but his work is not up to par. "Be hard," says Donna.

"I am," says Jane.

Katie brings up the fall production twice, whenever there is a lull in the conversation Donna is having with Jane, but Donna ignores her. I leave with Katie, who says Donna will never plan ahead. "She's focused and only sees one thing at a time. Did you see how I was trying to talk to her about production? She couldn't deal with it and she just completely shut me out. I have to start working on fall in October, and she's not even going to start thinking about fall until January, which means I'm on my own till then.

"Oh, well," she sighs as we walk toward the elevators. "Goodnight," she says to the DKNY employees who are staying behind. "I'm glad I don't have to stay, but it'll be my turn soon enough."

Donna Karan *September 24*

The conflict between Donna's two roles, as a designer and as a mother, is blatantly apparent this afternoon as, with her daughter, Gabby, present, she works in the DKNY design room, a room that is about half the size of the design room for Collection and is crammed full of racks of finished clothes. She is deciding which of these clothes will be worn by which models during the DKNY show on Monday, and which clothes and accessories should be worn together. The fitting model, Doreen, and Donna's twenty-three-year-old stepdaughter, Lisa, are both

trying on clothes for Donna. Each time Donna finishes coordinating and accessorizing an outfit Jane takes a Polaroid picture of it. These Polaroids will be
attached to the outfits on the day of the show so that the models will know
exactly how they should look.

Gabby, a slim girl with long dark wavy hair and braces on her teeth, sits in
a chair watching as her mother works in front of a mirrored wall, surrounded
by racks of clothes. Gabby thinks nothing of frequently interrupting Donna. "I
can't believe you won't let me come to the opening of DKNY," Gabby whines
as her mother ties a sweater around Lisa's hips.

"You have to go to school," says Donna, who, in addition to her black neck
brace, is wearing black knee-length leggings, a long fuchsia sweater over a white
T-shirt, and Keds-like sneakers with no socks.

"It's Spanish 101," says Gabby. "I can skip it. I've taken it before."

"You failed it," says Donna. "That's why you have to go." Donna approves
Lisa's outfit: a denim bodysuit, white shorts, white anklets, and brown loafers,
then walks out of the room in search of some food. Looking at her stepsister's
outfit, Gabby says, "Lisa, that is so not you."

"But I would wear this in a minute," says Lisa, who is tiny and looks much
younger than her age. She kicks off the loafers. "Except for maybe the shoes.
The shoes I couldn't see."

Donna comes back carrying an Italian hero sandwich and some salad on two
separate plates. She puts the plates down on one of the desks, and she, Gabby,
and Lisa look at the Polaroids of the DKNY outfits that have already been
accessorized.

"Mom, can we have some money?" says Gabby.

"For what?" says Donna, as she shuffles through the Polaroids.

"We want to buy the baby some clothes," says Gabby. Lisa, who has just
separated from her husband and moved in with Donna and Stephan, has a one-
year-old daughter. This is the baby who appears in Donna's current ads, which
portray a glamorous female executive juggling the demands of a job and a baby.

"I'll give Lisa the card," says Donna. Then she tells both Doreen and Lisa
to put on different outfits. As Donna finishes accessorizing the clothes, Gabby
noticeably shifts in her chair and both Donna and Jane look at her. "Gabby
thinks these clothes are too grown up," says Jane.

"Come on," says Gabby to Lisa as Donna goes back to inspecting the Polaroids.
"It's nice out."

"She might still want me in something," says Lisa. They both look at Donna,
who is obviously in deep thought, trying to figure out the best way to present

her collection. "Mom," says Gabby, "what else do you want Lisa in?"

Donna looks up, says, "Are you directing again? Are you her agent?" and goes back to the Polaroids.

Lisa, who is wearing a bodysuit, looks in the mirror and shakes her right leg. Although she is skinny, her leg is slightly flabby. "This is what happens when you lose fifty pounds and you don't exercise," she says. "I want to start exercising."

"I loved it when you were pregnant," says Gabby, while her mother inspects a pile of belts lying on the floor. "That was the only time I was skinnier than you. You want to go to a gym? Mom and Dad can get us into a gym."

"No," says Lisa. "I'd never go." The two girls pick at Donna's sandwich while Donna wraps one of the belts around her waist and stares at it in the mirror.

"Mom," says Gabby, "can you pass me the Sprite?" An open can of Sprite is on the desk to Donna's left. Donna hands her the can and then gives her a look that is full of love, but also of concern at Gabby's obviously spoiled ways. "You can get up and get it yourself," she says, but her voice is gentle and teasing. "Exercise is integral to your health."

Donna hands Lisa a slouchy denim jumpsuit to try on. "I love the jumpsuit," says Donna, looking at Lisa. She turns around to look for a white sweater to wrap around Lisa's waist and notices Gabby is still picking at the hero. "Are you full, Gabby?" she says.

"Yes," says Gabby, taking her hand away from the plate. "I'm not eating for the rest of the day."

"Well, you've already eaten about three breakfasts," says Donna.

"Do you like the jumpsuit?" Donna asks everyone.

"I love it," says Lisa.

"I love the pants," says Gabby, referring to slacks that Lisa had tried on earlier.

"Will you forget the pants?" says Donna. "We're doing a whole line here. Not just pants." She hands Lisa a white cotton bodysuit and a short denim jacket.

"Mom," says Gabby, "when does this go into the warehouse?"

"It depends on your behavior," says Donna. "Why? You want some?"

"Is Gabby finally admitting that she'd wear some of this?" says Jane.

"You want some?" Donna asks her daughter again.

"It would mean so much to you if I said yes," says Gabby, and then she laughs nervously.

"You don't?" says Donna.

Gabby laughs, for real this time. "I do. I'd wear some of it. But this is for summer."

"It's a February delivery," says Donna.

"This goes into the stores in February?" says Gabby. "Why? You wouldn't wear this in February."

"Keep asking questions and you're gonna get it," says Donna. "It's seasonless."

"Seasonless?" says Gabby. "So you only have to make one collection for the year?"

"Gabby!" says Lisa, exasperated. "You wouldn't throw this on tomorrow and wear it to school?"

"Yes," says Gabby.

"And you wouldn't throw a jacket over it and wear it in January?"

Gabby hesitates but then says yes.

"So that's what she means by seasonless," says Lisa. "You can wear it in any season. It doesn't mean she's only making one collection."

One of Donna's tailors carries in another pile of clothes and drops them on the carpeted floor. "God, this is a beauty," says Donna, picking up a khaki dress. "One after another. It's all beautiful. How are we going to do it all?" She knows her collection is too big but loves everything so much that she doesn't want to edit anything out.

Lisa puts on a short black dress with spaghetti straps and a flounced bottom. "I like that a lot," says Gabby.

"Well, well, well," says Donna. "Finally."

As Lisa puts a white cardigan sweater over the dress, Gabby says, "That's great." Doreen, meanwhile, puts on the khaki dress Donna loved and a pair of sunglasses.

Edward and Istvan, the main assistants for Donna's higher-priced collection, walk in, and Jane says, "Are you going to steal my ideas?"

"We have a slight interoffice war going on here," says Donna. "They used to get along until Jane . . ."

"Me?" says Jane.

"It's the boys," says Doreen.

"Doreen!" says Istvan.

"Don't worry. When I'm in your room I'll say it's Jane," says Doreen.

"Just remember you're working with us in two weeks," says Istvan.

Doreen waves the pendant on her necklace at him. "Begone," she says teasingly. "You have no power here."

The two men leave and Gabby says, "I'm skipping school Monday."

"No you're not," says Donna.

"Yes I am."

"You show up, Gabby, and you're in trouble."

"I'm showing up."

Just then Donna overhears Jane saying something to Doreen about Ideacomo, the Italian fabric fair she says she'll be attending with Edward. "Are you going to Ideacomo?" says Donna.

"Yes," says Jane.

"And where are we getting the money from?" says Donna.

"Are you saying I can't go now that I'm designing the (she drags out these next words) less . . . expeennsiive . . . liiiinnnne?"

"That's right," says Donna. "You can't afford those fabrics."

"But I need inspiration," says Jane.

"Yeah," says Donna, fiddling with the shoulder on Doreen's dress. "I'll inspire you."

Donna sits down on a stool by the mirrored wall and looks at a pile of Polaroids on the desk in front of her. "We have thirty-five outfits here already," she says. "How are we going to do this? Maybe we can have the models change their clothes onstage. They can go from a pant to a skirt and that will get across the idea that it's all based on one shirt. That says the shirt is pretty important. For the finale they can all undress to their shirts."

"I think it'll be too confusing," says Jane.

"Me too," says Doreen. "It's so clean having them just stand there."

"But each girl can have just one bottom change," says Donna. "That way, instead of thirty-five looks you have seventy."

"Mommy," says Gabby, who is now sitting in the back of the room with Lisa.

"She's talking," says Lisa.

"What?" says Donna to Gabby.

"Can we have some money? We're gonna go."

Donna gives Gabby an American Express card. "There's a limit on this card," she says. "We discussed it. And it's not for you. It's for the baby."

"But, Mom, we're going to the stores on Madison. It's going to be expensive."

"We are *not* going to the stores on Madison," says Lisa. "What, are you hallucinating? You know what you did to me the last time we went to Madison? And that was on my card. It wasn't even on hers."

The girls leave at 2:30, just as an assistant from DKNY comes in and says, "Who's free? We have to cut a thousand Hanes labels out of the T-shirts we're giving away on Monday." No one volunteers.

Next, an older woman named Rita, who is a friend of Donna's, comes in with a small dog named Honey. "How do you feel?" Rita asks Donna.

"I can't move my arm forward, or up," says Donna.

"Because it's swollen back here," says Rita, pointing to a spot on Donna's back. "You should get a hydraulic chair."

"What, are you kidding?" says Donna. "And lift myself up and down while I'm doing fittings?"

"You can lift me up and down," says Doreen. "I'll stand on it. You should get one. I've never worked for anyone who works so hard. That arm is always in motion."

"I hope I don't end up like that in ten years," says Jane, looking at Donna very seriously.

At 3:05 Edward comes in and says, "Jane, how many looks do you have?"

"More than enough, thank you," says Jane. "What's it to you?"

"I'm not really concerned," he says, immediately returning to the joking, upper-crust-inflected tone of their daily banter. "I'm just making conversation."

At 3:10 a DKNY design assistant carries in a denim coat and asks Doreen to try it on. "Have you recut this yet?" says Donna, looking at it.

"No," he says. "You'll have it by tomorrow if I have to stay all night. I swear."

"That's inhuman," says Donna. "It's three o'clock."

"That's OK," he says, slipping the coat off Doreen's shoulders. "I got eight hours' sleep last night. That's more than I got all week."

Rita is looking at the racks of clothes. "These are really beautiful," she says to Donna. "You want a denim jacket?" she says to the dog. "What do you want for evening?"

The tailor brings in some clothes that are still in progress. Doreen tries them on one by one and Donna corrects them. "There's something funny happening down here," says Donna, of a long navy blue skirt. She makes a lot of adjustments to it and adds a pleat. "Two dollars, three dollars, four dollars, five," says Donna in a singsong voice. "They said we're getting too expensive."

"I know," says Jane. "I put a stitch on something and it's another two cents."

"We have too many clothes," says Donna. "Can we get more models? We can't afford any more girls. Anyone have any gorgeous friends who would want to be in the show?"

At 4 P.M. Doreen says, "All I want to do now is eat, but I'll wait until you guys are finished. You're quick compared to others. Are we having dinner?"

"Yeah," says Jane. "Should we have both workrooms stay, Peter?"

"Not too late," he says. "Till eight, eight-thirty, especially since they're coming in tomorrow."

"But we should feed them," says Jane.

"They deserve it," he says.

"OK," says Jane. "So we'll eat at seven. Is First Wok OK?" It is, and she calls the restaurant to place an order.

Saying, "Excuse me for a minute," Donna leaves. When she doesn't return in ten minutes I go out to look for her and find her sitting at the round table in an office behind the reception area. With her are Peter Arnell, a writer from Peter's ad agency, Patti Cohen, and Rita, whose dog, dressed in a DKNY T-shirt, has curled up under the table.

The writer has completed a press release explaining the concept behind DKNY, and as Donna sits and reads it Peter photographs her repeatedly.

"I love what's being said in here," says Donna.

"So it's close?" says Peter, putting down his camera.

"I think what's missing is quotes," says Patti. "Things the press can pick up."

"I think what's not said is that it's ageless," says Donna. "Donna Karan [the higher-priced collection] is for me and my friends, but DKNY is for everyone. And we have to say that it's about an item. I have to compare it to my first collection. That was about black jersey. *Basta*. That was it. This is about your undershirt—your undershirt packed in threes—and your white shirt. If you ask a woman what she never has enough of, it's the white shirt. Then there's a navy jacket that goes with jeans, a long chino or gabardine skirt, a trench coat, a sweater, and a dress. That's it. That's all you need in life, and from there you buy inspirationally."

"But I see it written like a telegram," says Patti. "You know how a telegram is written? You go, 'Stop. Stop.' And we have to give the press something to pick up. You know that last release when we said, 'I get up in the morning and grab my glasses and my coffee mug and go.' That was picked up by everybody. Every paper I saw started their stories that way. We don't give them anything like that here. This is too wordy."

"DKNY is about the streets," says Peter. "It's about playing in the streets of New York."

"Peter, I do not play in the streets of New York," says Donna. "That is not my scene. I sit in a car and view New York. New York to me is dressed and polished. For me these clothes are for another side of me. They are street-inspired, but I don't play in the streets here. When *Women's Wear* shoots the Collection in the street it looks weird. But when we took DKNY out there it looked terrific."

"Something else that's important is fit," says Donna. "I cannot stand it if a woman looks fat in something."

"Think of the Midwest," says the writer.

"I don't care how big she is," says Donna. "Most women have big asses but I've learned how to make them look thinner. I always use shoulders and a plunging neckline. It's almost like a prism, bringing your clothes to the center, but that has nothing to do with this press release."

At 4:30 Peter says, "Why don't you give us another half hour to make another pass at it."

"Let me cross out what I don't like," says Donna. She does so as Peter continues photographing her.

At 4:40 Donna goes back to the DKNY design room, where her assistants are flipping through the new issue of *W*. "Do we have any ads in there?" says Donna.

"I don't know," says one of her assistants. Then he says, "Oh Donna. Here you are. There's a picture of you at that Bloomingdale's dinner."

He keeps flipping the pages and then says, "Did you see Kitty Dukakis wearing Donna Karan?"

"*Nooooo*," says Donna in a disbelieving voice. The editors of *W* have taken a picture of Kitty Dukakis's face and pasted it over the bodies of various models wearing clothes by different top designers. Donna walks over to look and says, "She looks a lot better than she does normally."

Marie Lavallo, who oversees Far Eastern production for Donna's Collection, comes in with her two little kids, a girl and a boy. Although Donna is concentrating exclusively on DKNY today, Marie is working on Collection's knitwear. Her son, who is about five years old, says, "Mommy, I saw a piece of fabric and buttons that would make a great belt. I'll show you." He goes out into the hall and comes back with a narrow swatch of bright pink silk. He lays it flat on the table and places three gold buttons in a horizontal row on it. It actually does look quite nice.

"So that's how a designer is born," I say, seriously.

Peter walks in and photographs Donna as she fits more pieces on Doreen. Everyone is eating Oreo cookies that belong to Marie's children. "During collection time your eating habits go to pot," says Donna. "All the good food you normally eat? Forget it."

"I have to go back to my charts and tell them what's on and off," says Donna, referring to the sales department, which is currently pricing the DKNY collection. It will wholesale for between $15 and $250, which means it will retail for between $30 and $500.

Donna goes into the sales office, where a woman is reviewing a chart labeled "February, March and April." Under each month are tiny sketches of the clothes that will be delivered then. "I want to make sure the right dress is the right price because everything gets changed so many times," says Donna. "I want to make sure you're pricing the right yardage. I'm not going to ship the skirts as long as they are now. I'm going to take as much as six inches from some. Is that taken into account in the pricing? I mean, I'm fitting on someone who's five feet eleven."

Donna reviews the prices and then goes back to the design room. She and her staff stay until midnight tonight, until 2 A.M. on Sunday, and then, finally, the day of DKNY's premiere arrives.

Donna Karan *September 26*

"I've never seen so many girls in one room in my life," says Patti Cohen, at 9:30 A.M., looking more than a little overwhelmed as she stares at the thirty-four models crammed into Collection's design room and Donna's office. (Since Collection's design team has a design room that is not only larger than DKNY's but also has a door leading directly into Donna's office, DKNY has taken it over for the day.) The door between the design room and the office is propped open, and, following Patti's instructions, the models are going first to the design room to have their hair done and then to Donna's office, where they are getting dressed.

Peter Arnell is taking pictures, and a video crew is filming the preparations, but despite the crush of people, the noise level is relatively low. There is the hum of a hair dryer and the buzz of models' conversation as they greet one another with kisses on the cheek and wait for their outfits—freshly pressed and brushed clean of lint—to be brought into Donna's office.

Donna's conference table, covered with accessories, stands pushed against one wall, and her desk, holding a coffee urn, milk containers, and Styrofoam cups, stands against the opposite wall.

At 9:31 a pressed outfit is carried into Donna's office and Patti yells for the model who will be wearing it. At the same time, she heads toward the phone in the corner to talk to Donna, who is calling from her car telephone. "Donna's on her way," Patti yells after she hangs up. "She'll be here in five minutes."

"Let's go," says Peter, leading his assistant and the video crew into the elevator and down into the street. "The press is gonna freak when they see this," Peter says to me, referring to DKNY. "It's instant fame and fortune. She did it right. All those teeny-boppers. In fashion you've got one businessman, Ralph, one promotion whiz, Calvin, and then you've got Donna. Listen to what I'm saying because it's major. And it gets deeper and deeper. There's licensing and everything."

We wait outside for Donna, and at 9:45 her chauffeured black Lincoln Continental pulls up in front of the building. Wielding their cameras high, Peter and the video crew surround the rear passenger door and a crowd immediately gathers. "Who's in there?" a man asks me. The car has black windows so that you can't see inside.

"Donna Karan," I say. He nods but looks slightly puzzled, seeming not to recognize the name. For a long minute no one gets out of the car, and the crowd and the cameras wait patiently. Finally the rear door opens, and, as the video camera rolls, Donna gets out carrying the black mug, filled with hot water and lemon, which she takes with her from home every morning. She is wearing a long white sweater, black leggings, Keds, and dark sunglasses. She walks slowly, leaving her husband, Stephan, and stepdaughter, Lisa, in the car. Looking straight ahead, Donna doesn't acknowledge either the cameras or the crowd. The cameras follow her inside the building and into the elevator. There, after the cameras are lowered, Donna turns to Peter and says, "After I calm down about this, I'm going to kill you." She sounds as if she means it.

"But think about it," says Peter. "It'll be great. Three hundred people staring at you. It'll be like an old Steichen photo."

"Ah," says one of the video men. "Inspiration revealed."

"This is no time for anyone to see me," says Donna. She gets off the elevator and goes directly into the design room. "Oh, my God," she says. "Look at all these girls." Some of the models come over to say hello to her and the video crew goes back to filming the models getting dressed.

At 9:50 Patti says, "Did anyone look up into the sky?" The company has retained five skywriting planes to write the letters DKNY in the sky for two hours.

"Not yet," says Stephan, who is dressed in a blue blazer, jeans, and a DKNY T-shirt. He and Lisa followed Donna upstairs in another elevator. "It's not due to start until eleven.

"I like this," he says, pointing to Patti's blouse.

"It's couture," she says, referring to Donna's Collection. "We have to get into couture now." (Collection is opening in six weeks.)

At 9:53 Donna says exactly the same words Patti had uttered earlier: "I've never seen so many girls in one room in my life. I don't know how to deal with this. I'm trying to be real cool."

The model Iman is sitting in Donna's office applying makeup. Istvan comes up to her and says, "You look great in French *Vogue*. Perfect."

"Thank you," she says.

At 9:55, as Donna's stepdaughter puts on a denim jumpsuit and wraps a white sweater around her hips, one of the other models asks Donna to tell the video crew to leave. "Don't worry," says the cameraman. "We're not filming anything we shouldn't be filming." The model ignores him and Donna tells him to go. He does.

Donna tells this same model, "There is one girl in every group that has to undress. You get to be the lucky one. There are five changes, but, this (she points to the denim bodysuit the model is wearing) always stays on.

"This is about real clothes," Donna continues. "This has nothing to do with . . . fashion." She pauses for effect before the word "fashion." "The F-word," she says, laughing. "You can forget about the F-word. You start out like this." She indicates the outfit the model is wearing—a long denim skirt belted with a man's tie, a denim bodysuit and a long navy blazer with a lot of jewelry pinned to the lapel. "You put on a khaki skirt second. You just keep undressing and dressing."

"At any time?" says the model.

"Whenever you feel like it."

"So what is this for?" Iman, who is still putting on her makeup, says to Edward. "Donna Karan New York? What is that?"

"It's DKNY," says Edward. "Just the initials."

"How is it different from the other one?"

"It's a long story," says Edward. "It's different." Donna walks over and asks Iman how she wants to wear her hair.

"However you want," says Iman.

"How would you wear it normally?" says Donna.

"Like this," says Iman. Her long hair is pulled away from her face with pins.

"OK," says Donna. "Then we'll leave it like that. I want you to feel comfortable. This is not about fashion. It's about comfort."

At 10:05 Donna inspects a model's outfit and says, "You're missing a shoulder pad." She turns around to find one and bumps into her husband, who has walked behind her and is waiting to give her a kiss.

They kiss and smile at each other and then Donna leaves her office and walks down the hall to the smaller DKNY design room to check on the three male models dressing in there. "What's your name?" she says to one of them.

"Scott."

"You're married," says Donna.

"Yes."

"See how fast I figure that out?"

"My wife is here," he says.

"Who's your wife?" says Donna. He names one of the models.

"You're kidding," Donna shrieks. Then, without skipping a beat, she says to the other two models, "Who wants to meet my daughter?" They both shrug and Donna says, "She's twenty-three years old."

"Too old," says one of the men.

"But she looks like a little girl," says Donna. "She's adorable. She's in the show. She's wearing a blue jumpsuit." Then, lowering her voice, she says, "She has a baby."

The models don't react. "And then there's my other daughter who's sixteen," says Donna.

"Now you're talkin'," says one of the models.

Getting back to business, Donna says, "We need a trench coat for the group." She searches the racks until she finds one. She hands it to one of the men and tells another to exchange his black T-shirt for a white one. He takes his shirt off and Donna sighs, "Ah. I don't want you to wear anything at all."

She raises her voice and, as if she were making a pronouncement at a press conference, says, "I believe in no men's fashion." She means men should be naked. Then, with a grin, says, "I better be careful. I'll be divorced in ten seconds." The model gets dressed, Donna approves his outfit, and says, "I could stay here and look at you all day but I've got to get back to the girls."

Donna is wearing one sneaker and her other foot is barefoot. "She's out of control," says Peter, taking a picture of Donna's feet as she runs around her office, checking what the models look like.

"I'm too old for this," grumbles Patti as she turns to a model and says, "Go straight through there where it says 'Exit.' Get your Polaroid taken and then go downstairs."

At 10:25 Donna changes into a jumpsuit from the DKNY line and Patti says, "There's no way we'll be ready on time."

At 10:30 Donna sits in a chair in the design room to get her makeup done. Once that's finished, she goes downstairs to the showroom, where the models are having their pictures taken by the press photographers. These photographers have been admitted early so that they wouldn't have to shoot around people later. Some of the models stand on the large platforms that have been specially erected for today's show, while others pose languidly on the windowsills. Donna's business partners, Tomio Taki and Frank Mori, are silently watching the models while Peter Arnell's partner, Ted Bickford, stands by a window looking for the skywriting.

At 10:50 Donna gives last-minute instructions to the models while Peter takes picture after picture of her. Doreen, holding Rita's dog, climbs onto a platform. The dog is dressed in a DKNY T-shirt, and, holding the leash, Doreen places the dog down on the platform. "OK," Donna yells. "Turn on the song." "You Belong to the City, You Belong to the Night" has been playing over the speakers, but now it changes to "I've Got a New Attitude."

Right on time, at eleven o'clock, as Donna holds her black mug freshly filled with hot water and lemon, and pets the dog, the doors open.

Gene Pressman, executive vice-president of merchandising and marketing at Barneys New York, is the first one through the door, followed closely by Polly Mellen, creative director of *Vogue*, who gasps and says, "Fabulous." She quickly darts through the room. "Fabulous!" she says to Gene as she passes him. He laughs and nods.

"Are these trash cans?" says Polly, darting up to a model and fingering her necklace. The model nods, and Polly snaps her fingers, a signal for the photographer with her to take a picture of the necklace. "That's marvelous," she says.

All the heavy-hitting magazine editors and retailers are here. As the magazine editors take Polaroid pictures and the retailers inspect the clothes, Donna, holding her black mug, circulates around the room, trying to talk to everybody. Peter takes a picture of Donna explaining the concept behind a group of clothing to a senior executive from Bergdorf Goodman.

At 11:10 Peter walks over to Ted, and both crane their necks and look out the window. "Nothing," says Ted. "I'm waiting. They might not let the plane go up because the President's in town. But maybe they're on the other side of the building." The plane did go up as scheduled, and the letters DKNY did indeed fill the sky.

At 11:15, Donna starts giving a long series of interviews. "This isn't fashion," she says to Bernadine Morris of *The New York Times*. "It's environment. It's a place to have fun."

At 11:16 Gabby walks in. "You're not supposed to be here," I say, grinning. "I am," she says, grinning back.

Donna's daughter was just one of the many who witnessed her triumph. Not normally given to positive hyperbole, *Women's Wear Daily,* in the following day's issue, started its review of DKNY by saying no less than "A sportswear star is born." Indeed it was. DKNY turned into one of the strongest-selling collections of the Spring 1989 season.

Donna enjoyed one afternoon of glory, and then, the next day, did all the production fittings for DKNY. That done, she turned her thoughts (and her heart and her soul) to her Collection.

For her, she says, design always comes from the past, from what was right and what was wrong in previous collections. When approaching her Donna Karan collection last spring, she says now, "I didn't want to hear anything more about working women. I felt that, like me, my customer had had it with work. She was exhausted and she wanted to go out and have some fun. I was going out a little bit and I missed dressy clothes, so I did them and abandoned what my customer wears to work. The lack of professional clothes was where the collection was weak.

"After I designed it there was a big explosion over why is my collection so dressy?" Donna continues. "Because last spring was dressy, that will take me to a sportier spring this time, because there needs to be a balance. I had filled a woman's need for dressy clothes last year and knew I had to give her something new to wear to the office."

Donna already knew this last March when, while just beginning to fully execute her fall collection, she, as always, had to stop and go to Europe to attend the fabric fairs. Nothing she saw there sparked any ideas for spring. What was catching her eye, though, were, as she puts it, "the drapery colors that look like minerals." She would leaf through interior design magazines and notice that "the pale pinks and greens that weren't pastels, but were more mineral-oriented colorings, kept popping out at me. I kept on tearing pictures of rooms from magazines." Having shown fall and presented it to retailers, she called her collection designers, Edward and Istvan, into her office and said, "OK, fellas, this is where we're coming from, this is what we did last year, and this is what we have to do here."

What she told them was: "I want a feminized but suity feeling. I want clothes to glide, to be really relaxed. I don't want them to have short skirts and be tarty."

With this general sense of what they were doing, Donna went to Italy in May with Edward and Cristina Azario, who handles fabric development for Collection, to work with about a dozen mills in developing fabrics for spring.

During that trip, Donna was in a car with Edward and Cristina, on the way to a mill, when the car pulled into a gas station and Donna saw two camel-and-black rattan chairs standing behind the gas pumps and said, "That's it! Bamboo and black! That looks fabulous!" And that's how bamboo (or beige) and black, accented with muted pastels—namely celadon and pink—became the basis of her spring collection.

In Italy, Donna ordered sample fabrics and colors. These were then sent to the company in New York in their raw, uncolored state during June and July along with lab dips—pieces of fabrics dyed in Donna's requested colors. Once the construction of the fabrics and their shade lots were approved, the fabrics were dyed and sent again to New York for approval. This was the tricky part because Donna, planning to do many monotone looks, wanted the different fabrics (chiffon, crepe, wool, etc.), all of which were being made by different mills, to match one another within their respective colors. They didn't. Figuring out what to do with the odd unmatching pinks, beiges, and celadons will be a problem Donna will work on until the day she opens her collection.

Donna, knowing that Italian mills always close in August for vacation, approved most of her spring fabrics at the end of July. The fabrics went into production in September and are currently being delivered to her in New York.

"Coming from DKNY," she says, "I was still feeling for relaxed clothes." After the DKNY show, and before her trip to Europe to attend the fall fabric fairs, she designed a few items for spring Collection. Most notable was a pair of pants whose front was made to look as if a sweater was tied around the waist, and her signature bodysuit blouses. But she had a real tough time deciding how to design the jackets and the skirts. While she was in Europe, wrapped in a bathrobe in her hotel room, the idea for the jackets came to her—she would design them to look like bathrobes.

In Europe all the mills were showing paisleys and beautiful, rich velvets for fall. Donna decided to get a head start on the paisley trend and offer them for summer—a smaller collection, which she designs and presents separately from, but right after, spring. She decided that for fall she would to do a luxurious collection centered on velvet.

She returned to New York with her summer and fall collections germinating in the back of her mind. But she still had only a nebulous idea of how to design the jackets for her spring collection and absolutely no idea of how she was going to design skirts. Panic gripped her as she thought about the fact that her collection was opening in less than a month.

We'll pick up with Donna again in two weeks to see how her collection is progressing. Know only that from now until November 4, the day of her show, she will be working day and night on the collection. In the meantime let's return to September 26, the day of the DKNY launch and see how Arnold Scaasi made out with the launch of his fall made-to-order collection. He, like Donna, is designing two collections at once. After his made-to-order opens today, he must start designing his spring ready-to-wear, which opens during the same week-long show period as Donna's.

Arnold Scaasi *September 26*

Arnold's made-to-order show was scheduled to start at 2:30 P.M., but, at 2:45, he is still backstage at his fifth floor salon telling the models, one by one, which shoes to wear with which dresses. They haven't even started getting into the clothes.

"How close are we to being ready?" asks Jerry Solovei, coming backstage at 2:45 as I go out into the showroom to have a seat.

On my way I pass Joan Rivers, whose tiny Pekinese dog is seated under her chair, Blaine and Ivana Trump, Anne Bass, and Georgette Mosbacher. I sit near Michael Gross of *New York* magazine, who is chatting with Saks Fifth Avenue's Ellin Saltzman, who is seated to his left. Etta Froio, the editor of *Women's Wear Daily,* walks in with a junior fashion reporter and a photographer. They sit in the front row between Michael Gross and Bernadine Morris from *The New York Times.* "Power seats," says Michael to Etta, by way of greeting. Etta gives him a small, tight smile.

The show starts at 2:50. As the models come out a woman's voice calls out the style numbers of the dresses. As the models walk, Michael points out the many empty seats behind him and Ellin says, "Maybe some of the ladies died." Michael chortles, and he and Ellin continue talking throughout the whole show.

One by one, the models walk to the end of the runway, stop long enough for the *Women's Wear Daily* and *New York Times* photographers to take their pictures, and then they turn and slowly walk away. Michael blows a kiss at Carrie Donovan, assistant editor of *The New York Times Magazine.* Ellin says to Etta, "Now is it your turn to go to Milan?" The spring Italian ready-to-wear collections will be shown next month.

"No," says Etta. She is clearly not comfortable with talking throughout the show.

"Then who?" asks Ellin. "Mr. Coady?" She is referring to Michael Coady, the group publisher, editor, and senior vice-president of Fairchild Publications, of which *Women's Wear Daily* is one.

Etta nods.

"And?" says Ellin.

"Mr. Coady and . . ." Etta says.

"Aha," says Ellin, giving a big nod. "Patrick?"

"No," says Etta. "Our people in Europe."

"Ah yes," says Ellin. "They're scared of me."

"Not in Milan," says Etta. "Paris is scared of you."

"Dennis?" says Michael, referring to one of the newspaper's Paris-based writers. "I didn't think Dennis was scared of anyone." And all the while the clothes keep coming out and, with one eye, the editors and retailers notice them.

As yet, there has been no applause but when a model in a shocking pink satin coat comes out, one of the customers, wearing a pink dress herself, says, "Wow!" She claps and two other women clap with her.

"Oh," says Ellin, trying not to laugh. The model stops in front of the cameras, expecting the photographers to take her picture. They take a few obligatory shots but they are obviously not excited. Etta and Ellin exchange looks. "You woke up for that one," says Ellin. The dichotomy between what fashion editors and retailers like and what the customers will most likely buy is amazing.

As one of the models removes a fur to reveal a sequin dress, Ellin says, "*Yeechhh,*" but she does join Austine Hearst in clapping for a brown gown with a sheer chiffon bottom.

"These chairs are so hard," says Etta.

"Just stretch," says Michael, lifting his hands up over his head.

"We've gotten so thin we feel it," says Ellin.

The press and retailers look almost as bored as Joan Rivers's little dog. At beginning of the show, the dog had lifted its tiny head and watched the models walking back and forth. Now, however, it is sleeping.

After the show, I meet Austine Hearst by the elevator and she tells me "everything" she wears is by Arnold. "I'm a frustrated designer," she says, "and I like his made-to-order because I can choose the colors, materials, and everything. This was pink," she says of her lime green tartan plaid suit. "I picked this fabric." Just then she sees Arnold and yells out, "I want the chinchilla coat."

"You've got it," mutters Jody Donague under her breath. The press and retailers may enjoy laughing at Arnold's work but he's the one who will be laughing all the way to the bank.

· · ·

Two days later, without saying whether the show was good or bad, *The New York Times* "reviews" Arnold Scaasi's made-to-order collection by simply reporting on the types of styles he had shown. "His strongest direction is to slender evening dresses that show off the body," the newspaper says. "Yet the reduced sweep does not mean the clothes are quiet or unassuming. Elaborate embroideries, metallic stitching and even rounded appliques of feather puffs give the narrower clothes the same extravagant look as the more bouffant styles. Mr. Scaasi, the head of his own made-to-order fashion house for 25 years, said he was ready to try something different from the big dresses for which he is best known. . . . Scaasi dresses, which start at $5,500 are rarely unobtrusive. The biggest applause was for a long hot-pink satin coat reversing to white mink. . . ."

You've got to give the *Times* reporter credit. No matter what she or her colleagues may have thought of this hot pink coat she reported the facts.

Bill Blass *October 6*

Bill, who has been busy previewing his spring line to publications, as well as planning a video, a press kit, an advertising campaign, and music and lighting for the show, has designed three-quarters of the collection. Many of these samples are finished and the rest are busily being produced by his workrooms.

At 9:30 A.M. Bill is out of the office, introducing his line of home furnishings to the press. One of the salesmen has taken the resort collection to Martha's for a trunk show, and therefore the showroom has been cleared of all racks and merchandise.

The mood here is quiet and calm. The only sounds are the low chattering coming from the workrooms and the distant sound of traffic filtering in through the open windows in the showroom. Then Bill strides in, and immediately the energy level is heightened.

"Get Mrs. Kellogg," he says to his secretary, Chauncey, by way of greeting. He talks to Mrs. Kellogg on the phone in his office, and after he hangs up, Laura walks in wearing a navy halter dress with a white starburst top, and the day's fittings begin. With Laura is a seamstress, a middle-aged Chinese woman wearing brown pants and a brown tweed jacket. Sitting behind his desk, Bill verbally describes the changes he wants made on this dress but, when the seamstress doesn't understand him, he stands up and shows her what he means. Then he sits back behind his desk, smokes, and sketches a pattern for a scarf. He glances up from time to time, checking the progress of the dress: "On her left," he says to the seamstress. "*Her* left. That should be longer."

His door, as usual, is open, and Chauncey brings in a paper for him to sign, and the woman who mans the kitchen brings him a cup of coffee. Tom walks in carrying a spring ad and reviews it with him. Just watching all this, I feel my adrenaline level start to rise.

Tom leaves and Bill goes back to sketching. As Laura and the seamstress fit the dress, the sound of Bill's Magic Marker scratching the paper's surface is very audible. He seems not to be paying any attention at all to the fitting, but when the seamstress says, "Should the straps go into the white area?" Bill says yes, and goes back to sketching.

He finishes, and, as Laura changes into another long dress, he tells her, "I have a scarf idea I want you to give to the scarf lady." Then he stands up to correct Laura's dress. From the hall outside Bill's office Tom's conversations are clearly audible as he conducts other aspects of Bill's business.

"I have a feeling if we had a crepe de chine stole with this it wouldn't just be a boring dress," says Bill. He grabs a bolt of sheer maroon chiffon standing in the corner by the mirror. The bolt rolls across the floor as Bill holds on to the end and drapes a long piece of the fabric over Laura's shoulder. "There," he says, standing back. "That's good."

He sits down behind his desk again and looks at the front cover of *Women's Wear Daily*. "Armani made everything long," he says to Laura, "and they say that everything in Paris will be long."

"What?" says Laura. "Skirts?"

Skirts are indeed what Bill was referring to, but he doesn't answer Laura. He reads *Women's Wear Daily*'s cover story, headlined "Giorgio [Armani] Goes Long," while Laura continues telling the seamstress what changes should be made on the dress.

Finished with the dress, Laura takes it off and puts on a long, slim navy gown and Bill looks at the dress without really seeing it. "I was thinking," he says, referring to an outfit they had worked on yesterday. "You were right. With that lace blazer we should have crepe pants."

"All right," says Laura.

"Is this too tight?" says the seamstress about the navy dress.

"That's all right," says Laura. "There are a lot of skinny girls in the show. We're going to have to change the shoulders, too."

"Let's just keep going like this until we know who's going to wear what," Bill says. Then, going back to the *Women's Wear Daily* story, he says, "I don't think going with long skirts is the answer."

"No," says Laura. "Jeez."

Bill gets up to look at the back of the gown, which has straps meeting in a starburst, and walks out. He comes back with a round brooch, which he pins on the back of the dress.

"Won't that be a bump under the jacket?" says Laura.

"The jacket's not that tight," says Bill.

Bill's phone rings and he answers it. "Let's see," he says. "Oh, God. This week has been awful and next week is awful. I have a dinner Monday, Tuesday, Wednesday, and Thursday, and I'm trying to run a business, you know? . . . Lunch? . . . OK. . . . I'll see you next week." He hangs up.

Laura puts on another outfit and Bill goes back to sketching. He draws a navy-and-white long dress.

It's a good thing Bill finds interruptions stimulating to his creativity because now Sheila Marks, who oversees all of Bill's Japanese licensing, walks in carrying poster-size sketches of seven outfits from Blassport, Bill's lower-priced licensed line of ready-to-wear. A Japanese department store wants to hang these sketches in its Bill Blass department, and Sheila asks Bill to sign the sketches.

Bill signs them and then says, "The Japanese will be very pleased that everything went long in Italy."

Sheila hands Bill snapshots of his departments in several Japanese stores. "Who has the best?" he says, looking at the pictures.

"Isetan," she says, naming one of the stores.

Tom walks in and Bill shows him the snapshots. As Tom looks at them, Sheila says to Bill, "I have a story for you. I can tell you a really long version of this, but I'll tell it to you the short way."

Bill's employees are obviously used to not getting his full attention. As Sheila tells Bill of how he was praised by a top kimono designer in Japan, Bill both listens to her and skims *Women's Wear Daily*. "He wrote you a letter," says Sheila, placing a sheet of thick paper covered with Japanese calligraphy on Bill's desk.

"Do you have his address so I can write to him?" says Bill without looking up from the newspaper. As Sheila says, "No, but I can get it," Laura walks in wearing a navy jacket and steps onto the round wooden platform in front of the mirror. Bill looks at Laura and says, "Do we want a fuchsia chiffon dress under that?" Having finished her business, Sheila leaves without a goodbye.

Before Laura can answer, Chauncey appears in the doorway and says, "Chessy's having a copy of your table made for someone and the guy who's doing it is right up near your apartment, and she was wondering if it would be all right if they went over and took a look at your table so he could see it firsthand." Chessy is Chessy Rayner, the interior decorator who wrote the *Vogue* article about the New York Public Library's Ten Treasures Dinner in May.

"Yes," says Bill. "Of course."

Laura unravels some fuchsia fabric from a bolt and holds it against her waist. Bill leaves the room and comes back with a couple of fuchsia buttons. He holds them against Laura's navy jacket.

"Nice," says Laura.

"You look expensive," says Bill.

"Very rich," Laura agrees.

"They can buy it short or long or in one color," says Bill. "However they want it. Should we do the halter dress? I'm afraid it's worn by a woman of, uh, a certain age. Then we'd have to put a sleeve on the dress, although she does have the jacket to cover herself up."

Changing the subject, Bill says, "Maybe we should have a girl in different colored chiffon be the last girl down the runway instead of a bride. I was thinking last night—do I really want a bride? It's so traditional, so . . ."

"Corn–ola," says Tom.

Bill sits down and sketches a long dress that he colors in with the fuchsia Magic Marker as Tom and Laura watch. "Of course they are going to scream bloody murder because all these dresses are naked," he says, referring to his customers. "But then, they are covered up with a jacket."

He finishes the sketch and hands it to Laura, along with an invoice with a check attached. "Give this to Chauncey," he says of the latter.

"Maybe it's more effective if we never bring in blues and greens," says Bill, referring to the chiffon dress. "Let's do peach, pink, and red."

Chauncey comes to the door. "A guy from *Vanity Fair* is on the phone," she says. "He wants to talk to you about tartan and plaid. Your use of plaid in relation to the FIT show, in which you have a piece."

"I have to call him back," Bill says.

"Maybe I can help him," Tom says.

Laura goes through Xeroxes of photos from a hardcover book of vintage fashion. "I need one other dress like fall for the line," says Bill. "A big, voluminous finale dress."

"How about the one you did of the one with all the multicolored chiffon coming out at the neck?" says Laura.

"Where's that sketch?" says Bill. "I had it here yesterday."

Laura clears off his desk and Bill sketches one of the dresses in the book. "The arms would be covered," says Bill as he works. "This is for someone who doesn't want her arms uncovered." The top of the dress looks like a chiffon cape, and he colors it in with orange, red, and yellow Magic Marker.

Bill's phone rings and he answers it. "How are you?" he says. "I wondered what happened to you. You disappeared. . . . Fine. OK. We didn't do extraordinarily well. They were delighted. We did $180,000. But it's only one-third. . . . Let me tell you, that store is a gem. I was in the Beverly Hills store. Don't you think it's a gem? Ah, my lord. I've never seen such a luxurious way to shop. . . . According to *The Wall Street Journal*, if California was a country, it would have the sixth largest gross national product in the world. I'm afraid we underestimate them. The potential is huge." He goes back to sketching as he continues, "How's Myra? . . . Nancy's the chairman of an antique show in the country in a few weeks. . . . I thought you were going to lose twenty pounds for the wedding. . . . I'm desperate. I went to a party every night last week. It's just impossible. . . . I'm going to the country, kid."

He hangs up, and Tom walks in, looking for an answer to the *Vanity Fair* reporter's questions. "Bill," he says, "talk to me about how you feel about tartan and why you used it this year."

"Tartan is not a phenomenon this year," says Bill. "I always use tartan in one way or another."

"But why do you like it?" says Tom.

"Tartan has always been synonymous with the holidays. It's a classic. It evokes spirit. But it's like the Prince of Wales plaid. I like all plaid."

"So it's Anglophile," says Tom, writing down Bill's comments.

"Tartans are Scottish," says Bill.

"But as part of the British Isles," says Tom.

He is about to leave when Bill asks, "What do you think of the long skirt?" Judging by the number of times he has raised the subject, he is obviously considering whether or not he should include long skirts in his collection.

"I don't think the market's ready to react that fast," says Tom.

"One has to stick to one's guns," says Bill. "It's a great look for Armani, but I don't think it's for everyone."

Laura walks in and tells him they are out of fabric for a dress Bill wanted to design.

"Reorder immediately," he says.

"Can't. We'll never get it in time."

"Well, then substitute."

"Domestically?" she asks.

"God, the things you have to think of," Bill says to me. "When it comes to fabric you either have too much or you run out. It's so difficult to anticipate."

Bill gets another phone call, this one from Pat Buckley. "Good morning, dear," he says. "Do it on a night that's convenient for you. . . . How many people does she propose inviting? . . . Where does she get the information that this is needed? . . . I met with her last night and I said I couldn't do it. I have too much on my plate right now. But I have the impression that it's very well funded. I don't think it's needed."

Bill asks me to step out for a moment so that he can continue his phone conversation privately. I walk out into the hall and stand by Tom's cubicle. Tom is on the phone saying, "I have to ask Bill." He puts his caller on hold and waits for Bill to hang up. As soon as Bill does, Tom heads for Bill's office, but Bill gets right back on with another call. "Oh, for Christ's sake," Tom says. He walks to his phone and says into the receiver, "He hangs up and he gets right back on."

Bill hangs up from his second call and yells, "Chauncey, get Mrs. Buckley back on the phone."

Chauncey dials and yells back, "It's busy."

"Yes," Bill says. "I figured." He walks out of his office and into the rear sewing room where they make the dresses. Just then Chauncey calls out, "She's on the phone." Bill didn't hear her, and I walk back into the sewing room to tell him. He walks back into his office. I wait outside his door and hear Tom giving the *Vanity Fair* reporter a quote. "Tartans are spirit," he says, speaking for Bill. "They evoke the spiritedness of the Scots. I use tartan every year, in one form or another. They're used by the Scots for festive occasions so it's appropriate."

"Put her through," Bill calls. But Chauncey is on another line. "Chauncey!" he bellows.

"Just a minute," she bellows back.

"Well, I can't wait," he says, and stalks back to the sewing room. He chooses red and orange chiffons and then goes back to talk to Pat Buckley. "You see what it's like to do three or four things at once?" he says to me.

Again I wait in the hallway, and again I hear Tom on the phone: "Well, Helen isn't expecting Bill to appear in the store, is she?" he says, referring to Helen O'Hagen, director of publicity for Saks Fifth Avenue. "She is?... Well, how is that possible?"

Bill ends his conversation with Pat Buckley and walks to a wall-length closet behind Tom, Craig, and Chauncey's cubicles. The closet, which holds Bill's spring collection, is covered with curtains onto which someone has pinned a sign saying, "Please keep closed." Bill opens the curtains and looks through the various navy daytime separates, long chiffon dresses, sequined tops, and sweaters that have large fake pearl necklaces sewn onto them. "Laura," he yells, "I want you to try this on. I don't think the shoulders are big enough."

Bill pulls out a navy coat, white pants, and a white blouse and hands them to Laura. They both walk to his office, and, as Laura gets dressed, Chauncey walks in and says, "Bill, the Clurmans can't do that dinner. It's the one night they can't. Everyone else can, but you need another woman."

"Ask Marilyn Evans," Bill says, referring to the society publicist.

Bill looks at me and says, "I don't have a Bergé [Pierre Bergé is the chairman of Yves Saint Laurent] or a Giancarlo [Giancarlo Giammetti is the chief executive officer at Valentino] or a Barry Schwartz [vice-chairman, with Calvin, of Calvin Klein]. Every detail depends on me. Every shoe, all the jewelry. And in addition to running my personal life. That's why, so often, I'm on the verge of a nervous breakdown."

"Well, now," he continues, pausing and looking up at his doorway. "What is this?" A young man is holding a five-month-old golden retriever in his arms. "It's my neighbor's," says the man in a British accent. "I took it to get its shots. It's the same as yours."

"I wish mine was that calm," Bill says and goes back to sketching. "Now we still haven't got a blouse for this suit," he says.

Laura gets on the phone and calls the fabric department to see what blouse fabrics are available for them to use. "The line's busy," she says.

"It's easier if I go back there," Bill says. We walk down the hallway and around the corner to the fabric room. As we walk in, the man in charge of fabrics says into his phone, "Yes, Laura. He's right here." He hangs up, saying, "Yes, Bill?"

"Have we got any navy-and-white striped jersey?" Bill says. Without waiting for an answer, he pulls a bolt of navy fabric with very thin white stripes off a shelf. "What is this?" he says.

"The navy-and-white raincoat fabric," the man replies.

"This just came in?" Bill says.

"Yes."

Bill takes it with him to the tailoring sample room and puts the bolt of fabric on the head tailor's table. "This just came in and no one told me," Bill says. "That's why you have to keep going back there." The puppy walks into the sample room and nuzzles Bill's ankle. "Craig," Bill yells to Tom's assistant. "Get this pup out of the sample room. We cannot have a pup in the sample room."

As Craig takes the dog away, Bill pulls a wide blue-and-white striped swatch off a sketch lying on the tailor's worktable and, placing the bolt of striped fabric on the worktable, says, "I want this in place of this." He replaces it with the fabric he's just discovered.

We go back to his office. He seems very tense and I ask if he minds my following him so closely. "You don't bother me," he says. "It's my staff that is driving me crazy."

Craig comes in and tells Bill, "Some daytime-accessories people are here to see you for a minute."

"The last thing in the world I need are more day earrings," says Bill. "We've overjeweled ourselves once and for all." But he goes out and spends thirty seconds glancing at the line.

At noon Chauncey says, "Mohammed is on the phone. He wants to know what time you'll be ready to leave." Mohammed is Bill's driver.

"A quarter to one," says Bill.

Tom comes in and shows Bill two magazine tear sheets of the same model. "I don't like that girl," Bill says. Tom leaves, taking the tear sheets with him.

At 12:05 Chauncey says, "Bill, I have Chessy on the phone." Bill, who is coughing heavily into a tissue, yells, "Chauncey, could I have a box of Kleenex, please?" He talks to Chessy and then Tom comes back with another model portfolio. "Do you like the looks of this one?" he says.

"No," Bill says. "It has to be a man who has the appearance of youth. This man does not."

Bill is sketching again. "Laura!" he yells. She comes in. "Can I have a folder so I can put in all the things I'm going to do for Martha?" She brings him one. He sketches. "We'll have the Christmas windows at Martha," he says to me, referring to the Park Avenue specialty store.

He goes back to sketching, using long, sure strokes. The sound of Craig talking to the jewelry designer in the showroom and the sound of traffic on Seventh

Avenue outside are the only sounds to be heard outside Bill's office. The relative silence is palpable because it is so rare. But, here, at Bill's desk, is the most important sound of all—that of a Magic Marker being steered swiftly and surely over a piece of paper.

Previews

Regardless of when they started designing, all the top designers must have their collections ready at the same time. Just as designers have deadlines, so do magazine editors, and in order to meet their deadlines they have to be shown the major thrust of the collections even before show week starts on October 31. Although the fashion press attends the shows to see the final version of the collections, these shows are timed around retailers' schedules, not those of magazines.

Since the clothes will be shipped to the stores in January, fashion magazines want to have their coverage of the spring collections in their issues that same month. Thus, to meet printing and distribution deadlines, *Harper's Bazaar* will be photographing the clothes two weeks before the shows begin.

From October 11 to October 17, five editors from *Harper's Bazaar*, myself included since I was working at *Bazaar* at the time, will visit the showrooms of the top designers to see what they are designing for spring and to look for trends that carry through the various collections. (Since Liz Claiborne's show is so much earlier than the high-end designers, it is not necessary for her to preview her collection. Arnold also will not hold a preview this year simply because he's just starting to design his Scaasi Boutique line and does not yet have anything to show the editors. Other designers not featured in this book also missed the preview deadlines. This simply means that they will not be covered in the January issue but will most likely be featured in February.)

If you pay close attention to the captions on a *Bazaar* fashion layout, you will notice that, besides identifying the designer of various garments, they will also tell you the color, fabric, and price. The fashion guide in the back of the magazine will name the stores where the clothes can be purchased. In rare instances, however, the caption will give you only the designer's identity and omit the other information. What this means is that the editors chose this garment during a preview, before the designers knew which clothes would be popular among retailers, and therefore, before they knew which items would actually be manufactured. In short, even though it was photographed by a major fashion magazine, that garment went into the scrap heap.

Let's watch now as the editors, led by June Weir (who was at that time executive fashion editor but would leave the magazine during the following year), go to see Bill Blass.

Bill Blass *October 11*

Although Bill is present and comes out to say hello, Tom handles the entire preview. First he shows us the sketches hanging in Laura's cubicle. "Oh," says June. "Look at the use of color for evening."

"Yes," says Tom. "Thank God the black-and-white dress is dead."

"Look at this," says Marilyn Kirschner, one of the fashion editors, very excited. "These chiffon capes. These are wonderful." (These are the dresses Bill sketched on October 6.)

"Are these all made?" says June.

"No," says Tom. "We're three-quarters done, but some are just ideas. Who knows? Everything can still change. We're still three weeks away from the show, you know."

"Where are you showing?" Marilyn asks.

"At the Pierre."

"Did you hear Calvin is showing at the Plaza?" says Marilyn. "I was shocked when I saw my invitation."

"It will be interesting to see how that affects how we see his clothes," says June. "We're so used to sitting squeezed into his showroom on those bleachers."

"I see you're not doing any long for day," says June, inspecting the sketches.

"No," says Tom. "Short."

"Did you ship your fall lengths as long as you showed?" says Marilyn.

"No," says Tom. "We shipped them mid-knee."

Tom leads the editors to a spread of breads, crackers, pâté, ham, turkey, and wedges of cheese by the kitchen. Everyone fills their plates and, as we walk by Bill's office, I peek in and see him sitting behind his desk sketching. The editors eat while, following Tom's instructions, two models show them the clothes.

The first outfit is a sequined T-shirt, beige skirt, and a short navy coat. At the editors' request, Craig is taking Polaroid pictures of every outfit.

"This is our national ad," says Tom, holding up a sequined tennis sweater, cream pants, and a yellow scarf on a hanger.

"Oh, that's wonderful," says June.

"What month is your ad?" Marilyn inquires. "We'd like to scoop you on it."

"February," says Tom.

"Oh, that's fine. This would be for the January issue."

A model comes out wearing a long tangerine, peach, and yellow chiffon dress. "I love the use of color on color," says June.

Connie Cook, Arnold Scaasi's favorite fitting model, comes out in the sequined tennis sweater. "We've seen the idea before," says June, "but putting it into sequins is what is so new."

The other model comes out in a sequined T-shirt, cardigan, and long cream-colored pleated skirt. Her neck is bare, and June says, "I like it better with the scarf. The neck is a little bare. And can we see the sweater with the pants? I think it looks better with the pants than with the skirt. Add the scarf and change the earrings too."

"Can we see this on?" says Marilyn, about a blue-and-white striped jacket with yellow piping. Connie puts it on over the tennis sweater.

The other model comes out in a short sheer navy dress with roses at the cuffs. "So no black for evening," says Marilyn.

"Navy is it," says Tom.

"And this is Blass's definitive simplicity," says Craig as Connie comes out in a beige wrap blouse with beige pants and high-heeled pumps.

"So Bill likes high-heeled shoes," says June.

"We're not sure," says Tom. "We're still arguing about it."

The other model walks out in a red jacket with gold buttons, a short red skirt, and a red chiffon scarf wrapped around her neck. "I love that chiffon scarf as a key accessory," says Sheila Sullivan, another of the editors. "For day and night."

Connie comes out in a short navy blue chiffon dress with white cuffs, white roses on these. "And the cuffs," says Sheila. "The important cuffs."

"And what about the five-layer chiffon dress that I saw in the sketch?" says Marilyn. "The capes."

"Those are just the ending dresses," says Tom, referring to the ending of the show. "Those are birthday cakes. They are not directional."

"Here's a suit we just sold six of at Martha's," says Tom. The model comes out in a navy jacket with round gold buttons, a sheer wrapped blouse, and a skirt with pleats on the bottom.

" 'We just sold six.' " June laughs. "And you haven't even opened yet." The suit is one of the resort outfits that Bill will incorporate into spring.

"How much does that suit retail for?" asks Marilyn.

"It's three thousand three hundred retail," says Tom.

"Any other evening pants besides the navy and white?" asks June.

The editors tell Tom they would like to photograph one of the sequined T-shirts. This shirt, which retails for about five thousand dollars, has a fake pearl necklace attached to it in such a fluid way that the pearls look like a real necklace. They also want to shoot the tennis sweater.

Tom agrees, saying, "We're shooting ads on Monday. The photographer is flying in from Paris. W is shooting Tuesday and then we're shooting the video Wednesday. You can have them after that."

Adrienne Vittadini *October 13*

Without calling to explain their delay (they stopped to get something to eat after another preview) June Weir and another fashion editor, the only *Bazaar* editors who, besides me, will be previewing Adrienne's collection, arrive an hour late.

Adrienne, who is busily conceptualizing fall, has asked one of Donna's assistants in the public relations department to handle the preview. As I wait for my colleagues, Donna, who is once again overseeing the photography for Adrienne's ad campaign—this time for the spring clothes—brings art director Benita into the room where I am waiting and shows her a group of clothes (the Scottish terrier prints Adrienne loved so much) that are displayed on the racklike wall fixture.

If you remember, one of the first meetings we watched Adrienne conduct (back in June) was the advertising meeting for her holiday collection. This was done after holiday was completely finished and spring was just beginning to be designed. In the same way, the spring ads are being conceived while Adrienne begins to work on her next season—fall. Similarly, the production samples for spring are returning now, just as the production samples for holiday were coming in while she was beginning spring.

This, then, is an example of how these designers come full circle in the fashion cycle. The steps that we watched being done for spring will now once again be repeated, from conception to execution, for fall and then for the next season and the next.

I finally get tired of waiting for my colleagues and ask Donna's assistant to show me the line. She does, and soon after she's finished, my colleagues arrive. Adrienne, however, does not. She has already selected the clothing that will be featured in her fashion show next month, and, although she will approve the models who will appear in it, she will leave the show's execution to Donna and a free-lance stylist Donna will hire for that purpose. Except for double-checking the appearance of the models and the clothes backstage during the fashion show, Adrienne is done with spring and is on to the next season.

Donna Karan *October 14*

At 2 P.M. six of us go over to see Donna Karan. Patti leads us to Donna's office and seats us around the conference table, which is buried under piles of sketches and fabric swatches.

Donna comes in wearing a DKNY T-shirt and her neck brace. The other editors ask her what happened to her neck, and, after she tells them, she says, "I was in Bergdorf Goodman [in June] making a personal appearance trying to sell thousand-dollar alligator bags, and this woman comes in and says, 'I love your jewelry but I can't wear any because I wear a neck brace.'

"She opens her bag and shows me her neck brace in there. She wasn't wearing it because of vanity, the same reason I wasn't wearing mine. She said, 'It's just so ugly,' and I said to her, 'Go into the hosiery department and get a pair of my matte black jersey stockings and come back here with them.' She did, and I started cutting up the stockings and putting them over her neck brace. I'm designing this neck brace and then I think, 'I'm supposed to be selling jewelry here,' so I take this two hundred and fifty-dollar gold-and-jade pin and I put it up against her neck brace and say, 'I think this looks fabulous.' It did, but she said, 'No, I don't think so,' and then she came back and said, 'You're right. It did look fabulous. I'm going to buy that pin.'"

Everyone laughs, and then Donna begins presenting her collection, something she has to do since she wants coverage in the fashion magazines, but is not very prepared to do since last month's launch of DKNY cut so significantly into the time she had to spend on her collection. It's understandable why Donna begins her presentation with a reference back to DKNY: "For DKNY I was in a relaxed mood," she says. "There's a tailoredness to the clothes, but it's a soft tailoredness. The bare minimum needed.

"As I left that behind and started working on the collection I was still in the same frame of mind. I wanted the clothes to be undressed. I want the clothes to feel as if you just threw them on. I'm doing a lot in the golden family, the decorator colors. You know how when you look in magazines a lot of those home colors are golden and sage with black and with quartz lighting. They're very environmental and comforting. There are two places where I feel relaxed—my living room, which to me is golden, and the beach, which is softly colored stones."

Doreen, the fitting model, comes in wearing a white cotton bodysuit and black pants with a gold chain at the pocket. "I don't know how anyone can wear a shirt now that isn't a bodysuit," says Donna. "To me it's inconceivable. I like to wear my shirts open, and unless it's a bodysuit you really can't, because when you lean forward or sit down, then the shirt slips and moves and you fall out of it."

June comments on the fact that, unlike Donna, many designers didn't include black in their spring collections, and Donna says, "I always start with black and white."

As we wait for Doreen to come back in her next outfit, Donna says, "I must tell you, we just came back from Como, and I am exhausted. I didn't realize how much DKNY took out of me. I loved doing DKNY. It came so easily. I've already done fall for DKNY and I haven't done spring for collection.

"I didn't realize that by doing DKNY we were basically doubling our company. Now I have to do accessories—bags, belts, and jewelry—for two different lines. That's twice as much work."

"I don't know how you do it," says June.

"I'm getting some excellent clones of me," she says. "Like my assistant Jane. She's terrific. God bless my assistants. They understand me so well."

Doreen comes in wearing pants that tie in the front, simulating the look of a sweater tied around them at the waist. "The idea here," says Donna, "is to look like you just threw on the clothes."

Next Doreen comes in wearing a jacket that ties at the side, and Donna says, "My new jacket is like a bathrobe jacket that just ties to keep it feminine. It's a fine line that you tread when you approach menswear. To me, I want it to be in the feeling of the woman, not to be hard. And I'll have chiffon scarves with chiffon T-shirts with the big trench coats."

"And what about skirts, Donna?" says June.

"Long," she says. "Long and short. I love them both."

"Long looked so good in DKNY," says one of the junior fashion editors.

"The short coat and the short skirt look right," says Donna. "The key word for the season is 'relaxed.' And quality.

"My knits you can't see because they aren't here yet," she continues. "I put an enormous sweater program into work. They're being made in Hong Kong, but here are the swatches." She shows them fourteen small knit swatches pasted on a board. "I feel very strongly for knits," she says. "Knits, to me, are comfort."

"Will you be doing shirts?" says June.

"In chiffon and georgette," says Donna. "Almost every fabric is on its way in. We are a little late."

"How about coats?" says June.

"I love long and I love short coats," says Donna. "Both, as long as they look free, relaxed, and easy. Sometimes I wonder about what we do here. Like this whole sheer thing. That's strictly editorial. It's to keep us stimulated. But who wears it? Sometimes I wonder. We sit here in our wonderful atmosphere creating our own stimulations, but who gets it? Like the whole short thing. If women didn't go out and buy short last year, the whole thing passed them by, and now long is back again. They have to realize that they no longer have to buy what we tell them to. It all happens so fast. All they have to do is sit tight and their old clothes will be back in style."

"Don't let them hear you say that," says one of the editors.

Donna Karan *October 21*

There is a general rule in business: The more positive editorial coverage you and your products get, the better your products sell. It is for that reason that Donna has agreed to let *Self* magazine spend the day photographing her, even though the day would be much better spent designing. This story will run in the February issue of *Self*, the same month that DKNY will be delivered to the stores. The more exposure Donna's name, face, and products get that month, the better.

This morning the magazine photographed her at work in her design room. At noon they went into her office to photograph her working out with her personal trainer. Donna usually works out at home three mornings a week, but the magazine photographed her at the office for expediency's sake. Now, at 1:45, they are about to head out to Central Park for some pictures of Donna at play. For all these pictures, she is wearing different outfits from DKNY.

In the corner of the design room, Doreen is getting a haircut, while *Self*'s fashion editor, Anne Kampmann, who had been an editor at *Vogue* and had just joined *Self* last week, is trying to find a model release for Donna to sign. Anne's assistant is speaking, very loudly, on the phone to her office, while Istvan, Edward, Patti Cohen, Rex, a prominent makeup artist, and a photographer and his assistant all watch Donna, who, with shrieks of dismay, is looking at some washed silk fabrics that were delivered last night. They are a completely different shade of pink from what she'd expected them to be. She needed them to match the pink wool she is using, and the two colors aren't even close.

Handing Donna the release, Anne suggests a style that Donna could design with the washed silk, but Donna ignores her. She signs the release and decides to deal with the silk when she returns from the photo session. This is not the first time a fabric has come in miscolored.

"The light is different in Europe," she says. "It sounds really strange until you see it for yourself, but you can look at two colors in Europe and then come back to New York and those two colors will look completely different. If they matched in Europe they won't match here. This season the color palette is so unusual, so particular, that it matters."

Donna grabs her black mug filled with hot water and lemon and we head outside, where it is raining. A hired car is waiting for us and we pile in. Anne and the photographer's assistant sit in the front, while Donna and I, with the photographer wedged between us, sit in the back. We stop to buy umbrellas, and then, once we're on our way to Central Park again, the photographer points his camera sideways at Donna and asks me to look through the viewfinder. "Is it in focus?" he says. It is, and he starts taking pictures of Donna, who talks fast and furiously, jumping from topic to topic and taking intermittent sips from her black mug.

"I have so much to do but I have to get away," says Donna. "I'm going to Canyon Ranch for Thanksgiving. I can't do aerobics because of my neck, but I'm going to go anyway. I haven't exercised in a month. I've gained seven pounds and it's all water bloat from tension. I know what it is and I know I have to move to get rid of it. At least I can do the hiking out there."

Then she says, slapping her knee, "These are the new jeans. I'm wearing a twelve. Aren't they a fabulous fit? The most important thing is to have a great fit. That means now I can get into the jeans business too."

Jumping to another topic, Donna says, "I worked with John Fairchild yesterday. He called me up and said he wanted to come in and see the collection, and I said, 'Sure, but nothing's ready.' He never comes to see the collection. I don't know what's going on. It was the first time I'd ever worked with him, and, I've gotta tell you, I was impressed. That man is so smart. He really knows a shoulder and an armhole.

"But I could kill him for killing the fashion industry," she says, referring to a series of articles *Women's Wear Daily* has printed about how poorly the business is doing. "He's saying fashion is dead. You want to know what's killing the fashion industry? The press is killing the fashion industry."

Except for *Vogue*. "I love the new *Vogue*," Donna says. "I mean, it's supporting fashion. It's making fashion fun. I love the cover. The only story I didn't like was the one with the black girl. She looked like a nymphet."

"You'll see more of a change as Anna's [Anna Wintour, editor in chief of *Vogue*] stamp is felt," says Anne. Then she asks, "Did you go to the Ralph Lauren thing?" She is referring to the recent Museum of American Folk Art's tribute to Ralph Lauren, held in conjunction with a preview of the annual Fall Antiques Show on Pier 92.

"No," says Donna. "No more going out. But I read in the paper about how he said that now he is going to run for President." (In response to a standing ovation Ralph Lauren received at the event, the embarrassed designer joked, "After all that, it's as good a time as any to announce my candidacy for President of the United States.")

"That was hysterical," Donna continues. "He *should* run for President. It would be a lot more interesting than the campaign we're watching now. Ralph or Calvin should run."

"I don't know about Calvin," says Anne.

"Yes," says Donna. "Absolutely. Kelly would make a great First Lady."

The driver, who doesn't seem to know his way around New York, misses the turnoff into Central Park and keeps driving up Central Park West. "Where are you going?" Donna yelps. "Stop. Back up." The driver backs up into a parking space near the park roadway where the pictures will be taken. It is pouring rain, and Anne and I wait in the car while Donna goes out and poses for the photographers. "Just think," says Anne, as Donna gets back into the car. "Elle MacPherson gets one hundred thousand dollars for doing this."

Donna gives the driver specific instructions on how to get back to the office, and, as we go, Anne asks if Donna is going to any social events this week. "No," she says. "Gabby's had to deal with a lot of separation this week so I'm staying home and playing mom." (Donna's stepdaughter, Lisa, who had moved in with Donna and her husband, reconciled with her husband; and Donna's housekeeper, who had worked for her for fifteen years, quit. These are the two "separations" Gabby has had to deal with. "I want to be home with her even though she doesn't ever sit and talk to me. Just so that I'm there.

"I miss having the baby around," she continues, referring to Lisa's child. "That really grounded me. You could come home all tense and see this little mushkette and everything would be put back into perspective. The baby was great. It was the daughter that was difficult, with the smoking and the no smoking. I can see now why Stephan said no." Before deciding definitely to launch DKNY, Donna had told her husband that she wanted to have another baby, but he told her it was either a new business or a new baby. Donna picked the business.

"I want to do maternity clothes," she says. "The ones out there are so ugly. People told me to do menswear next, but I'm doing maternity clothes."

By 3 P.M. we are upstairs in the DKNY showroom. This is the same room where the show was held but I hardly recognize it. No longer the sparse, art gallery-like space it was for the DKNY show, the room has been subdivided into three smaller rooms which serve as showrooms for the collections and accessories divisions as well as DKNY. In the DKNY showroom huge photographs of old New York line the walls. Clothes are hanging on racks, and a retailer sits at one of the tables drinking iced tea and placing orders. Donna stands by a rack of clothes and the photographer takes her picture.

Suddenly Donna realizes that no one has eaten lunch yet. "Let's order something," she says. I walk upstairs with Donna and as we climb she says, "I took Fairchild down to DKNY along these steps and he said, 'The least you could have done is swept if you knew that I was coming.'" She laughs. She is obviously very excited that finally the all-powerful John Fairchild had come to pay her a visit.

By five o'clock the sandwiches Donna ordered have not yet arrived and the editors from *Self* have left. Donna sits at one of the desks in the design room and, with an Aretha Franklin tape from the overhead speakers, she reviews shoe sketches with the woman she employs to oversee her shoe designs. Donna is wearing the same DKNY jeans she wore to the park, an untucked white blouse and white Keds-like sneakers. Suddenly Donna says to me, "Come here. I want to show you something." She takes me into her office and shows me two pieces of fabric. The colors are two completely different shades of beige. "In Europe these colors matched," says Donna. "And if you saw these now in daylight the colors would look even more different. So now I own the fabric and I don't know what to do with it. I have to design a whole new group, a whole new feeling."

We walk back into her design room and Donna says to Edward, "I need a rainwear story. One jacket does not a rainwear story make." She wraps a piece of the beige fabric around his neck and pretends to pull it.

"Do you see how she treats her assistants?" says Edward. "Write it down."

Julie Stern, president of the Collection division, sticks his head in the door and says, "Gabby's on the phone." Donna goes into her office to take the call. As she closes the door behind her, Doreen says to Steve, "Is she leaving early today?"

"At eight-thirty."

"Good," says Doreen. Here, at this time of year, 8:30 P.M. is considered early.

Donna comes back and edits a group of silk sweaters, reviewing the sketches that Marie Lavallo shows her and asking Doreen to try on some of the samples. After Donna corrects the samples, Marie writes down the changes that need to be made.

At 5 P.M. the phone rings. It is the receptionist at the front desk saying that the sandwiches Donna ordered for the *Self* contingent have just arrived. Edward gets them, and both he and Donna take a sandwich. "I'm going on a diet after the show," says Edward. "I eat when I'm nervous."

"Me too," says Donna, sitting at the desk behind Edward and taking a bite from her sandwich. "When I'm relaxed I never have to eat."

As she eats, Donna reviews a list of possible models for her show, crossing out the ones she doesn't want. She writes "Go see" next to three of the names, meaning that she wants to see them in person before she makes a decision.

Doreen puts on a pair of sheer chiffon pants, and, as Donna hems them, Edward says to her, "Didn't I put you together well today? I think I'm going to leave and be a stylist."

"Trade places with Anne," says Donna.

"I will," says Edward. "She said today that she wants to be a designer."

"Really?" says Donna. "Let her come in and do our washed silk group. Let her see what it's really like."

"Everyone wants to be a designer," says Edward. "And if you can't be a designer, be a critic."

Doreen tries on another outfit—a long print skirt with tiny pleats, a white blouse, and a black jacket. The shoe designer carries over two pairs of shoes. Doreen puts one style on one foot and the other on the other foot. Donna stares at the outfit and says, "Why does this look so wrong? Maybe it's the hose. The nude hose. I think it needs the ivory hose."

Doreen pulls on a pair of ivory pantyhose, and then Donna tells her to put on a black jacket over the outfit. Doreen does so and Donna sits and squints at the model. "Pull the skirt up," she says. Doreen hikes up the skirt. Holding one hand up in front of one eye, Donna squints at the model again. Without saying whether she likes what she sees, Donna lowers her hand and, turning to Edward, says, "Last Friday at this time we finished all the jackets. Last Friday and Saturday. Now we must put all the skirts into work. The skirts and rainwear. It really concerns me that we don't have skirts to go with these jackets."

Still wearing the outfit that Donna thought looked wrong, Doreen says she has to go to the bathroom. "Go to the bathroom like that and come back," says Donna. "I want to take a fresh look at you."

As Doreen leaves, Donna sits on floor and reviews the corrections Marie has made on the sweater sketches. "This I want in blue," Donna says, "this in blue, this in pink . . . pink . . . pink. And now I need some white, right?"

When Doreen comes back, Donna tells her to take off her jacket and put on a short sleeveless sweater with a very deep V-neck. While Doreen changes her top, Marie takes a phone call and says, "I'll be home as soon as I can."

"While your kids are still young," says Edward, but Marie ignores him.

"I'm depressed," says Donna, lying down on the floor and staring at the ceiling. "I've been going at a pace that is not normalized. I'm tired." She looks at Doreen and says, "That looks great from here." She jumps up, all evidence of fatigue disappearing, and wraps a cardigan around Doreen's hips. "We'll give it a cardigan to give it some attitude.

"I like this V-neck sweater," she continues. "I've been wanting a V-neck sweater for a long time. I am a nut for V-necklines. I just think that it opens up a person so much.

"Do we need more cutters for tomorrow?" says Donna, thinking of the pieces that still have to be cut and sewn.

"We have four cutters for tomorrow," says Josh.

"I think we'll finish everything in time for the show," says Donna.

"Yeah," said Edward, in a tone implying "I'll believe it when I see it."

"Oh, shut up," says Istvan.

"You know what we have to do, Istvan?" says Donna.

"I know," he answers. "Rainwear."

"Be inspired," says Donna. "It's raining out."

"I want to do the blue dress," says Donna, pulling a light blue dress off the rack and looking at it. "It looks like a coat, not a dress."

"We can always use it as a coat," says Edward.

"Oh, shut up," says Istvan.

"Istvan, if I were you, I would be on my side for this one," says Edward.

Doreen puts on the dress and pulls on a pair of white stockings. "Legs are such a problem," says Donna. "I think that's why I hate spring. I hate legs." Her fall designs are featured with very heavy opaque tights.

"I love this color," says Donna. "I'm insane for this color, but I don't know if you are a dress or a coat." She turns up the hem and pulls some fabric back in her hands to narrow the dress. "This is it," she says and calls in a tailor to show him what she's done. "This is the new dress," she says. "You know the look I'm looking for, right?" The tailor nods.

Doreen puts on a few other blue pieces, but Donna says, "I'm going to do this tomorrow. This is too much. I have to think this out."

Just then her husband calls and Donna tells him Gabby is going to an Elton John concert with a friend and the friend's parents. "I'm on my way home," she says. She hangs up and absentmindedly walks over to the rack of clothes and removes a pink jacket and a long beige skirt. "So we have this color and this color." She holds the pink jacket and the beige skirt against herself and looks into the mirror. "Actually," Donna says, "these two colors go great together.

"Oh, my God, this could solve a major problem. Look how beautiful this looks. They could wear the pink silk with the beige silk and the pink wool with the beige wool. We could separate the color and the fabrication. So first delivery goes wool, then comes the silk group. And this washed silk is great for the South."

"Any idea for dresses?" says Edward. "Since you are on a roll?"

"I always get my solution on Friday."

"At midnight," says the shoe designer.

"You have no idea how happy this makes me," says Donna. "Accidents do happen. We've got to work on this. Now I'm excited again."

"I think the all-pink look is so chic," Edward whines. He doesn't want to mix the colors.

"You'll get it," says Donna. "They will still get a monotone look with the other fabrics.

"So we deliver the pink washed silk with the beige, and the blue with the white," Donna continues. "If you happen to have a green wool blazer, and you wanted to wear it with a beige silk skirt, you could. It becomes an alternative bottom, which is what we wanted from the beginning. It's very sportswear, which makes sense. I really should remember where I came from." (The whole point behind sportswear is that it gives a woman the ability to mix fabrics and colors.)

"Oh!" says Donna. "I'm happy as a pig in shit!"

Bill Blass *October 29*

Up and down Seventh Avenue, the tension and excitement of show week is building. Most of the models who will be working in the shows returned from the Paris collections just yesterday, and many of them immediately began making the rounds of the designers' studios to be fitted with the clothes. There are few excellent runway models, therefore the designers tend to use the same girls.

Arnold Scaasi and Donna Karan are still busily designing their collections; Adrienne Vittadini is deciding which models will wear which clothes. Only Liz Claiborne is completely finished with Spring I.

Since Bill will be the first major designer to open his collection next week, the models came to him first. By two o'clock today, all the models have been fitted, and by early afternoon, he is sitting behind his desk attending to personal business while his staff works in the showroom, packing up the collection and the accessories for the truckers to move to the Pierre Hotel tomorrow.

Tom, Craig, Laura, Gail, Chauncey, Sheila Marks, and two young men who design Bill's licensed products are in the showroom surrounded by racks of dresses, black trunks, and huge round black boxes. Sitting by the windows, Gail, Chauncey, and Sheila pick up pair after pair of shoes from a pile on the floor in front of them and, using scissors, scrape the shoe bottoms. This makes the new shoes less slippery and insures that the models will not slip on the runway.

As Laura, reading from the show's lineup, calls out the names of the models, along with the accessories they will need for their outfits, Tom and Craig place the accessories (pantyhose, jewelry, gloves) in plastic bags and then attach these bags to their respective hangers.

Two salespeople are at the far end of the showroom pasting fabric swatches into black loose-leafs that will be used as reference by the sales force. Bill, wearing brown corduroys, a blue oxford shirt, and a navy scarf, comes out every so often to check on how the packing of his collection is going. When I comment on how calmly and efficiently everything is progressing, he says, "I couldn't work the way Oscar or Scaasi do—up to the last minute. There was a model in here this morning who said Scaasi was fitting last night until one-thirty in the morning. And Scaasi shows Wednesday."

"Tuesday," I say.

"And Oscar's Wednesday," Bill says. "I don't know how they do it. We're done, all except for one jacket. We tried on a dress this morning and realized we needed something with it. So a tailor who insists he needs a week to make a jacket can now make one overnight. We're done. I don't know if it's done right, but it's done."

He'll find out soon enough if it was "done right," I think, as I leave Bill's showroom and head up to Arnold's salon, where the action is substantially more heated.

Arnold Scaasi *October 29*

Arnold, wearing blue wool pin-striped pants, a white shirt, and a gray tie printed with a yellow diamond pattern, is in his Fifth Avenue salon fitting ready-to-wear samples on Connie. He is showing his collection the day after Bill, but unlike the methodical Bill, Arnold only started designing his ready-to-wear collection three weeks ago—sketching and matching each sketch to the appropriate fabric. Two hours after he presented his fall made-to-order collection on September 26, he was at his bridal licensee's showroom fitting his premiere bridal collection, which he launched at the Plaza Hotel on September 28.

Arnold "had a few quiet days" and then spent the week of October 3 to 7 helping his made-to-order customers pick their dresses for the fall season. (It takes anywhere from two to five weeks for a made-to-order dress to be ready.) On Saturday, October 8, he sat down at his weekend house in Quogue, Long Island, and, finally, began sketching the spring ready-to-wear clothes. He already knew, however, what approach he would be taking. He wanted his ready-to-wear, like the couture collection he just showed, to have slim, close-to-the body shapes. The two collections would be very similar, but the ready-to-wear would not use the lush embroidered fabrics of the couture. During the next three weeks, his sample makers sewed like mad, and today both they and Arnold still have a huge amount of work to do.

As I come in I hear Arnold yelling in the fitting room: "I don't think we should change it now. It's gonna sell or it isn't going to sell, whether or not we open the seam." Then I hear him tell Timothy to call Margaret, the head of his workroom, and Maria, a seamstress, into the fitting room. The tall, skinny Timothy, dressed in jeans, rushes out of the fitting room and across the hall into the workroom. In the fitting room, Connie is standing in front of the three-way full-length mirror, wearing a navy dress that falls just below the knee.

Timothy returns with the two women and Arnold says, "Is the navy dress cut yet? Tell her we need it now." He is referring to one of his seamstresses.

In the hallway, Timothy picks up the phone and calls the workroom saying, "Is the navy dress cut yet? We need it now."

He hangs up and says, "It's cut. They're doing the draping now."

"How do you like the length?" Arnold says to Margaret, who has just returned from a stay in the hospital. "You haven't seen any of these new lengths yet. Do you like it? Do you hate it?"

"It's nice" she says.

"What do you think?" he says to me.

"It's nice on Connie," I say.

"I'm not making anything short," he says. "It looks old to me. I saw so many of them the other night that it was scary. Women just shortened their dresses with no idea of the proportion of the dress."

Arnold explains to Maria what to do with the next dress that she will be working on. Maria leaves, but Margaret remains behind.

"This is our day to fit everything," Arnold says to me as Connie puts on another navy dress, one with a very large white collar.

"Pretty," says Arnold. "Do you like it?" Connie nods. "Do you think the neckline should be lower?" he says.

"A quarter of an inch," says Margaret. Arnold picks up an artificial red flower from the table in the fitting room and holds it against the white collar. He puts it back down and then pins a narrow piece of white paper to the bottom of the right sleeve.

"Do you like it?" he says. "Or do you think it's too nursey?"

"I don't like it," says Connie, referring to the sleeve border.

He asks me what I think. I don't like it either, I say. I am surprised that he is asking so many people for their opinions, but I notice that he never asks Timothy for his.

"OK," he says. "Forget it. But I want something else on it. Maybe on the pockets." He holds a piece of fabric up to the pocket. "I want a flange put onto the pocket," he says.

"I'm sorry. I didn't hear you," says Timothy, who, as usual, is standing in the entrance, writing down all the changes that Arnold wants done.

"I want a flange put onto the pocket," he says, raising his voice.

"I like it a lot," says Arnold. "Do you?"

Connie nods yes.

"I do, too," he says.

They fit another navy blue dress, and, while Arnold goes into the fabric room to hunt for something, Connie says she was here until midnight four nights this week. "And," she says, sitting down, taking off her high heels and rubbing her feet, "I had all my regular bookings during the day. I am exhausted and my feet are killing me.

"Modeling is a cyclical business," she continues, as she massages her feet. "Now I'm turning down work, and in December I hardly work at all."

Arnold comes back with Margaret, and, as they go on fitting, Connie tells Margaret to sit down. "She doesn't want to sit down," says Arnold.

"Yes she does," says Connie, losing her temper.

"Believe me, when she wants to sit down she'll sit down," says Arnold. I'm surprised at his lack of sympathy for the woman.

Next Connie puts on a dress with a sheer white chiffon top and a blue sequined bottom. "Do we like it?" says Arnold.

"Yes," says Connie.

"Sure?"

"Positive."

" 'Cause if we don't we should take it out." He means take it out of the collection.

He asks Connie to do a big twirl. The sequined fabric is very lightweight and it lifts up in a huge circle as she spins. "You're gonna hit somebody in the face," he says.

"Tell me who you want me to get," says Connie, laughing.

Arnold lengthens the skirt and says, "I like it longer. It works."

The window behind the mirror is open and the sound of buses driving down Fifth Avenue filters into the salon as Arnold pins a white flower onto the center front of the dress. "Margaret," he says, "I want someone working on the red-and-white dress so Connie can try it on." The woman leaves.

They adjust the chiffon-and-sequined dress, and when they are finished, Arnold says to Connie, "I'm going to try to put this on you in the show."

"I love it," she says.

It is 5 P.M. and Arnold says to Timothy, "Can you call Lazare and ask if we can have the sequined pajama?"

Timothy calls the workroom and tells Arnold, "It will be ready in forty-five minutes."

"That's too long," says Arnold. "Get Margaret in here."

Margaret comes in and Arnold says, "Look over the list and see what we still have to do."

She names a dress. "That's finished," says Arnold. "Isn't there a dot next to it?"

"Oh," she says. "Yes."

"Timothy, you're going to have to make your dots larger," says Arnold. "And write them on the other side of the page. They're hard to see."

Arnold tells Margaret to "stick around in the workroom to see that nobody goes home." The two of them go into the workroom and Connie sits down, moaning, "Oh, my feet." She's been standing since this morning when she was at Bill's showroom being fitted with the clothes she will be wearing in his show. "And we're going to be here for hours," she says. "There are dresses I haven't even seen yet."

I ask if Connie does fittings with anyone besides Arnold and she says, "No. It's too time-consuming."

"I can't believe Arnold's done his whole collection in two weeks," I say.

"It is unbelievable," she says. "No one else works the way he does."

I say Oscar is late too. "He used to be normal," she says.

"We should try the green crepe dresses on Monday," says Arnold. "To see if they need tacking or pressing.

"Is Margaret still upstairs?" says Arnold.

"I haven't seen her go by. Would you like me to call up to her?" says Timothy, speaking in a very precise, controlled tone, as if he is reining in his anger. I can't say I blame him for being fed up with Arnold. I couldn't stand being so subservient to someone either.

Arnold orders Timothy to tell another seamstress to "get in here. I've got to explain something to her." As he pins Connie's dress, Arnold talks in a soft mumble, but when the seamstress comes in, he raises his voice as if by speaking louder he can help her understand him better.

"Are you getting anything today?" says Arnold to me.

"I'm writing everything down," I say. "How boring," he says, and I must say I agree. Although fittings are a very important part of the design process, they are extremely tedious.

Margaret pokes her head in to say, "The pajama will be ready in ten minutes, and they're draping the other dress." As she leaves, the sound of a saxophone playing "On Broadway" drifts up from the street through the open window.

"That guy is back," says Connie.

"He's so awful," say Arnold. "He only knows, like, four songs. I'll tell Jerry to go down and give him ten dollars to move.

"The major problem this season is the lengths," says Arnold. "Dresses just don't look good to me short."

"I thought he was going to say that the biggest problem with this collection was this saxophone player," says Timothy, laughing.

"Timothy, call Mr. Solovei," says Arnold.

"Yes?" says Jerry, as he comes into the room.

"What are we going to do about this man?" says Arnold, referring to the street musician. "Tell him somebody's terribly sick up here."

"That's what I told him last week," says Jerry.

"Tell him to go to Rockefeller Center, where there are a lot of people."

Jerry goes to the window in the next room and the music ceases. "He stopped!" says Arnold.

"He's taking a soda break," says Jerry, coming back in. In a few minutes the music starts again.

Arnold is fitting a jumpsuit that has a sequined, sleeveless top and very wide-leg double-layer chiffon pants. "I like the look of evening pajamas very much," he says. But he certainly doesn't like this particular style, since he pulls the top shoulder seams apart. "Get the sketches for this and call Margaret in," he says to Timothy. "It's to be completely open on the side."

Margaret comes in and Arnold tells her to tell someone to "stop working on the red jacket." She goes to do his bidding, but thirty seconds later Arnold looks up and says, "Where did Margaret go?"

"To tell her to stop working on the red jacket," says Connie.

"Well, I'd rather have her here," says Arnold. "Timothy, go call her." I don't say anything but I smile at Timothy, thinking, Either this man is crazy for working here or he has the patience of a saint.

Margaret comes into the room, and, hearing the saxophone player, says, "You know, he's played so long that you'd think there would be an improvement. He's there in the morning at the subway when you go to work, playing the same three or four songs."

"Margaret," says Arnold, "you have to explain this because this is really a mess. I want the pants narrowed so you can tell they're pants. Right now it looks like a dress.

"Timothy, we need a note here," says Arnold, meaning that Timothy should write down what Arnold is about to say. "It's a very important note. We're going to do four-inch hems. The underhem will be done by machine and the overhem by hand." Saint Timothy writes.

Arnold's receptionist comes in and asks Arnold what he wants for dinner. "Grilled cheese," says Arnold.

"Me too," says Connie. "With tomato."

"That's our favorite," says Arnold. "But don't write that down. It'll ruin my reputation."

At 6 P.M. the saxophone music stops and another model arrives. Arnold goes out to give her a dress to try on. He comes back saying, "So far we only have six girls for the show. Her hips are too big, but if we put her in loose clothes she'll be OK."

The model comes to show him how she looks in the dress. She turns around, and he says, "We can't close the dress in the back?"

"No" says the model.

"I'm sorry," Arnold says, meaning he can't hire her.

"God, she's enormous," he says to Connie as the model leaves. By normal standards the girl is quite slim, but normal standards don't apply to fashion. Everyone and everything that goes out on the runway must look perfect.

Connie tries on a jumpsuit with a white chiffon top and blue sequined pants. "Ellin Saltzman will love this," says Arnold of the Saks executive. "Do we want it ankle-length or long?" Then, answering himself, he says, "Ankle."

"Long," says Connie. "It's so beautiful long. It's like a long drink of water."

"What do you think?" Arnold says to me.

"Long," I say. He makes it long and tells Connie to walk. She strolls back and forth. "OK," he says. "Stop."

"Sorry. I'm just having so much fun wearing this outfit. I can't believe you got me excited at this time on Saturday night."

Next she tries on a floral print dress that is much too tight at the waist. "What did they do?" she says. "This fit me perfectly yesterday."

Arnold rips the seams, discovers that the facing is too tight, and cuts it. Outside, the saxophone player is playing the "Pink Panther" theme song.

"There he goes," says Arnold. "That guy could really put a designer off, and then people will look at my collection and wonder what's the matter."

Show Week
Bill Blass *October 31*

The first morning of show week dawned cold but clear, a good omen for the editors, retailers, and models who will spend this workweek shuttling around Manhattan—from lofts to showrooms to grand hotels—to view, or participate in, as many as eight shows a day.

Bill will be holding two shows today in the Cotillion Room of the Pierre Hotel, shows which will cost him a combined total of $200,000. The first, at noon, is for the heavy-hitting members of the press and the retail, and social communities. The three o'clock show is for the less prominent members of the same three groups.

A runway cuts the Cotillion Room in half, and chairs are set up on either side of it. On each chair is a little brown Bill Blass notepad, a pencil, and a tiny bottle of Bill Blass perfume. I walk past the workmen who are hanging the Bill Blass logo up on the rear stage wall and head backstage, where a long row of fresh-faced models are sitting in front of an extremely long vanity table that stretches the entire length of the room. Most of them are putting on their own makeup, while two others are having their hair blown dry.

Except for two models who are appearing at Rebecca Moses's 9 A.M. show, the girls are all here, and Bill is pacing the length of the room, watching them get ready. "It's hotter than Kelsey's nuts in here," he says. "Craig, have them turn down the heat." As Craig leaves, Bill continues stalking. Like a large, powerful, uneasy lion, he walks from one end of the room—where the dressers are all assembled, sitting at round tables, eating danishes and drinking coffee, and where two women are ironing dresses—to the other, which is the exit to the stage.

Most of the clothes are hanging on wheeled racks pushed against the wall behind the models. Each outfit has been assigned to a model and every group of outfits is labeled with the name of the girl who will be wearing these particular clothes. Plastic bags underneath each outfit hold its coordinating shoes and accessories.

As Bill stalks, Tom takes two models out onto the runway and explains the show's procedure to them. "We try to keep three girls on the runway at once," he says, as he walks with them out into the Cotillion Room and to the end of the runway. "You exit here," he says, walking left and leading the girls through a narrow hallway full of electrical wires, and then through a kitchen filled with large stainless-steel refrigerators and stoves. The models look at each other and giggle. "Then you go through here," Tom says, walking into an empty room, "And then back again." He passes through a door that takes them backstage again, by the breakfasting dressers.

"Got it?" he says.

The models nod.

"Of course you'll have to move quickly," he says, and he takes two more models out front.

Bill, still stalking, is smoking. Pointing to a full cup of coffee standing at the edge of the models' vanity table, he says to Craig, "Whose is this?"

"Tom's," says Craig.

Bill stubs out his cigarette on Tom's saucer and Craig laughs. Bill sprays breath freshener into his mouth and continues to pace. There is nothing left for him to do but wait.

"We're very organized this time," he says. "Last time we didn't have enough assistants."

Gail Levenstein, Bill's director of licensing, arrives, and Bill, who obviously has a great deal of affection for her, visibly brightens as he says, "Look who's here." Gail looks at the models and mumbles something, and Bill says to me, "She hates models but then most plain women do."

"Nice," Gail says. "Very nice."

Grinning, obviously pleased with himself, Bill says, "Mrs. Bailey said to me, 'I must say, I'm tired of all your smartass remarks.'" As Gail laughs I realize how much Bill loves to tell stories and to be admired for his humor. He stands with Gail and Tom, who has abandoned his coffee without comment, and Gail asks Bill what he did last night. "I went to something for the gastric whatever, stayed twenty minutes, and then I went to the Plaza," he says. A black-tie evening being billed as "The Night of the Stars" was held last night at the Plaza under the auspices of the Fashion Group.

"How was it?" says Tom.

"Awful," says Bill. "I mean, it was all right. Etta was involved [Etta Froio, editor of *Women's Wear Daily*]. But those awards dinners are always boring. Ivana wore a pink dress with a brown sweep down here [he gestures toward the floor] and she added her own touch—pink flowers in her hair."

"Good taste knows no bounds," says Gail. She goes to get a cup of coffee, and when she returns and starts to sit down, she almost misses her chair. Bill, who is inspecting a tray of jewelry at the end of the vanity table by the stage exit, doesn't notice.

"I did it again," Gail says.

"Did what?" he says.

"I almost missed the chair. I'm missing my center of gravity."

"No," says Blass, pointedly looking at her ass. "Your center of gravity is very apparent."

"He must pay you a lot," says a model sitting nearby.

"Yes," says Gail. "I get paid a lot to be abused."

"So are you all jittery and excited?" she says to Bill.

"No," he says. "I took a sleeping pill last night so I slept."

At 10 A.M. the two models who had been in the Rebecca Moses show arrive and sit down to have their hair done.

Bill walks out onto the runway and sees Elsa Klensch from Cable News Network, who comes over and gives him a big hug. They sit on the edge of the runway and talk, and Tom takes one of the just-arrived models out front to show Bill her outfit. She has put on a white lace jacket and navy blue pants that Bill had thought might be too long on her. The pants are fine.

After a few minutes, Bill, Elsa, and a cameraman come backstage. "What's this?" Elsa says, looking at the box of jewelry on the vanity table.

"Jewelry we're not using," Bill says. "Help yourself."

She does, placing some of the jewelry in her pocket and putting on a pair of earrings. Then, at 10:05, the cameraman turns his camera on Bill, and Elsa interviews him. "My collection is a lot more American than last season," says Bill. "Take the tennis sweaters as an example. They are typically American. They personify the collection."

As Bill is being interviewed, Tom calls out the models' names in the order in which they will appear. Carrying their first outfits on hangers, the girls follow Tom onto the runway.

"Were you influenced by Europe?" Elsa asks.

"I think it's important to trust your instincts," Bill replies. "If American designers are going to make it on our own, we're going to have to do it on our own."

After the interview Bill shows Elsa the clothes, while her cameraman films the models, who have returned from the runway and are finishing their makeup applications.

As Elsa heads for the back of the room to get a cup of coffee, Bill says, "I like your earrings."

"They're yours," she says. "I just stole them from you."

Bill leaves Elsa and paces back to the front of the room where Tom is sitting, reading today's *Women's Wear Daily*. "I hate the cover," Bill says to Tom, who closes the newspaper and looks at its front page. There he sees a terrible picture of Bill standing, with his mouth open, next to a model wearing one of his beaded tennis sweaters and a pair of wool flannel pants. Bill really does look awful.

Tom says, "Hmmmm," and Bill, ever the storyteller, changes the subject and says, "I said to Elsa, 'I love your earrings,' and she said, 'They're yours. I just stole them from you.'" Tom laughs obligingly and then goes back to reading the paper. "This is the longest morning," says Bill. "We're too organized."

At 10:20 Bill gives an interview to a reporter from the *Cleveland Dispatch*, who tells him, "I really admire you. Sunday school Nativity pageants are more hectic than this."

As Bill impatiently paces to the front of the room, Craig pulls a scarf off the back of a model's chair and shows it to Bill. It has a bullfight scene on it.

"Nice," says Bill. "It's definitely time for animal prints again." He is already thinking about the kinds of fabrics he will purchase for fall.

Helen O'Hagen, publicity director for Saks Fifth Avenue, arrives. After everyone says their hellos, conversation turns to last night's Fashion Group event. "Could you believe those chickens last night were served ass side up?" says Helen. "I didn't eat them. That's the one thing Mrs. Trump should have paid attention to."

"The place looked good but the food was terrible," says Bill.

At 11:05 Bill says, "Here comes Patricia," as the hat designer Patricia Underwood walks toward him carrying a shopping bag full of hats.

"I love that picture of you in *WWD*," she says.

"Yes," says Bill. "That's really Halloween."

Gail is reading Tom's copy of *Women's Wear Daily*, and Bill looks at it over her shoulder. "How do you like that crack about a sumo wrestler?" he says. In its cover story, the newspaper reported the goings-on at various design houses last Friday and pointed out that, unlike other designers who were scurrying to meet their deadlines, Bill took the time to go out to lunch. Commenting on that fact, Oscar de la Renta said, "Bill has to keep his weight up, like a sumo wrestler."

Jumping to another subject, Bill says, "Craig and I were in a bookstore and he asked what autoerotic meant and I said, 'Screwing in a car.'"

Gail gives a halfhearted laugh.

"Do you like that?" he says. "Are you going to use it?"

"It's very quick and funny, Bill," she says.

At 11:10 Bill asks if it's time for the models to get dressed.

"It's too soon," says Craig. "They shouldn't be walking around in these clothes."

"It would have been better if we'd had the show at eleven," says Bill. He goes back to pacing.

"It's so calm," says Laura.

"We can fix that if you like," says one of the models.

Bill walks back to the front of the room and tells Gail to go out front and spray his Bill Blass fragrance into the air. Gail walks to the full-length three-way mirror to put on eyeliner. "Oh, look at this," says Bill. "She's putting on eyeliner."

"Yes," says Gail. "Because this is my day. When that applause happens it's for me."

Bill rolls his eyes and walks by the models, inspecting their hairdos.

"What time is Marc Jacobs's show?" Bill says.

"Eleven," says Tom.

"And then they're coming right here?"

He paces some more. At 11:30 he says, "If Marc Jacobs starts on time, what time will everyone get here? It's eleven-thirty and there's not a single person in their seats. It's going to back up the whole day. That was dumb, to have so many shows so close together."

"There's no way we're going to start on time," says Craig. "I think it's because of Paris. All the shows got crammed into this week, and no one wants Friday."

At 11:45 Bill shouts, "Now is everybody's hair done?" It is, and the models are by the clothes racks, inspecting their outfits.

Bill walks to the video monitor at the stage entrance and, peering at it, says, "Not a soul is here yet." He stares at the monitor as if he could somehow make his audience appear, and then goes back to pacing but at an increased speed.

"Tom," Bill says, pausing for a minute, "who decides this, who decides who shows when?"

"Well," says Tom, "there's Ruth Findley at the Fashion Calendar but she doesn't really decide it. She records it. But you know what did this? Paris showing so late. It pushed everyone back. I don't know if it will be the same next season."

At 11:55 Bill looks at his watch. Tom is glued to the video. "Do you think we could get the girls in their first outfit?" Bill asks.

At noon Tom says, "*Harper's Bazaar* is taking their seats." He pauses and inspects the screen. "*Women's Wear Daily* is here. Etta is here. Those girls can start getting dressed."

"OK," Bill yells. "Everybody in their first outfit."

"Why are her pants so short?" says Tom, looking at one of the models.

"They're supposed to be like that," says Bill.

At 12:05 Bill says, "Craig, can I have the girls in lineup as nearly as possible?"

The sound of voices from out front carries backstage and the flash of photographers' strobes is visible. "OK," Bill says, standing by the entrance, watching as the models line up very calmly, single file, in their first outfits. The show starts, and Bill, who is very tense and smokes throughout the whole thing, inspects the models as they walk out, making final adjustments to their necklines, jewelry, and gloves. "Hurry up," he yells frequently at the girls, as, after changing into their next outfit, they inspect themselves in the full-length mirror near Bill. "Hurry up!"

One by one the girls pass, and in what seems like no time at all the show is over, and Bill, extinguishing his cigarette, squares his shoulders and walks onto the runway to acknowledge the applause.

Then he's back, and at his heels is Ira Neimark, chief executive officer of Bergdorf Goodman, followed closely by a large Saks Fifth Avenue contingent, and then by a crowd of magazine editors. Bill calmly accepts their congratulations.

The models, many of whom are appearing in the 1 P.M. Carolina Herrera show across the street at the Plaza Hotel, have already changed into their street clothes and are scurrying out, running as fast as they can across Fifth Avenue. At a much slower pace, the retailers and editors follow, and Bill, even though he still has one more, less important, show to do, can relax and start thinking about the fabrics he'd like to purchase for fall.

Arnold Scaasi *November 1*

Despite the cold rain falling outside, and despite the fact that this 4:30 P.M. Scaasi Boutique show is the last in a day jam-packed with other presentations, most of the seats in Arnold's Seventh Avenue showroom are jammed with retailers, magazine editors, and fashion reporters who have come to see what he has wrought for this season. If you remember, Arnold didn't preview his collection to anyone.

I get seated in the front row, along the side of the runway. On my left is Ed Villiotti, vice-president at Martha's specialty store, and on my right are two young buyers from Bergdorf Goodman. Executives from Saks are across the runway. Behind me, the seats reserved for Bloomingdale's are empty.

As the show starts, Ed says to the woman seated on his left, whom he later identifies as a friend, that "some of these models should retire."

Another man across the aisle mouths to Bernadine Morris of *The New York Times*, "I like your hair. Very nice." Bernadine nods her thanks.

Throughout the entire show, Ed and his friend converse as though they were in an airport lounge and not at a fashion show. "Those clothes," he says, referring to a woman only the two of them know the identity of. "That dress with gray velvet shoulders. For day?"

"She's pretty," says his friend.

"You've been hanging around uptown too long," he says. "I'm worried about you. And that jewelry."

"She's Trump. Those are Trump jewels."

"She's gross."

There is a smattering of applause for one of Arnold's chiffon dresses, but Ed ignores it. As a pink dress with quilted fabric on top and chiffon on the bottom comes out, Ed shouts, "Ellin!" Ellin Saltzman, who is sitting across the aisle, either doesn't hear him or pretends not to.

"Ellin," he calls again. She looks at him. "Wasn't that your own?" he says, referring to the pink dress.

She nods and says, "Well, it's a retrospective. It's twenty-five years." Quite publicly, they are insinuating that Arnold is repeating his designs.

The next dress is a long navy blue one with large white polka dots, accessorized with a red-and-white polka-dot scarf wrapped around her shoulders. "Oh, Jesus," says Ed. "Would you look at this."

A slinky red dress gets a smattering of applause, but Ed ignores it and says to his friend, "I think Kitty Dukakis is the worst-dressed woman I've ever seen. Imagine if he wins the election. That's all we need."

When the show ends, I ask this awfully rude man why Arnold is treated so disrespectfully at his shows.

"We're all here, aren't we?" says Ed. "It's five-thirty and it's the sixth show today. It's the last one, and we're all here."

A reporter from *Women's Wear Daily* asks Ed what he thought of the collection. She was sitting too far away to hear his snide remarks, and now he rhapsodizes: "It's pure Scaasi. Very glamorous. The chiffons were beautiful, and some of the short cocktail was nice."

Ed turns back to me and says, "We sell the clothes very well. Arnold knows what his customers want and like. He's very valid. We sell both the made-to-order and the Boutique line." Why, I wonder, if Arnold's clothes sell so well, is everyone so disrespectful of his work during his shows? I've never seen behavior like this at any other designer's show.

I later ask Arnold why so many people talk during his shows and he says, "Well, they're talking about the clothes, aren't they? At least that's what the models tell me." I let the subject drop.

Donna Karan *November 4*

Preparations for this show were the closest thing Donna has ever experienced to her nightmares. Fabrics and accessories were delivered up until the last minute, and now, at 11:15, as the press and retailers begin to arrive for the noon show, some of the clothes are still being pressed.

Donna and the designers worked through the night, coordinating looks. They all went home at 7 A.M. to take showers, and now, looking rather green, they are backstage helping the models get dressed.

"I'm about to have a heart attack, I want you to know," Donna says to me by way of greeting. Dressed in the black sweater-wrap pants she showed to the *Bazaar* editors during their preview, and a black sweater, she is reviewing the jewelry that has been laid out on a large table standing next to a full-length mirror. This mirror will be the models' final checkpoint before they head out to face the heavy-hitting audience composed of representatives from all the top fashion magazines and the city's largest newspapers as well as the most prestigious stores from across the country.

At 11:30 the show's free-lance coordinator takes the models out into the show-room to show them where, and how, they have to walk. Looking at these models, who are still wearing their own clothes, and many of whom have rollers in their hair, it is hard to believe that a fashion show is scheduled to begin in less than an hour. The models look down the length of the runway, where three low, wide pedestals break up its smooth expanse. The models are to step onto these pedestals and pose for the photographers. "There should be four people out at once," says the stylist. Then, looking at the runway, she says, "Wait a minute. There are only three platforms."

"It should be three at a time," says Patti. "Four is too many pedestals for the girls to get on and off of."

While the girls walk the length of the runway, Donna reviews the show lineup. Composed of colored sketches of each of the show's sixty-nine outfits, the lineup identifies the order in which the clothes will be presented, and who will be wearing them in the show. The first group to be presented is the black and bamboo that was inspired by the chairs Donna saw in the Italian gas station. The rest of the colors are rose, celadon, taupe, white, and navy.

"Oh, shit," says Donna, as she finds some mistakes in the lineup. She changes the order of some of the sketches and, calling Edward over, says, "Gail Elliott is not wearing that. She's wearing pink chiffon pants with a white chiffon shirt. I am pissed as hell because I said how I wanted this. I can't believe the changes I had to make."

As the stylist returns backstage with the models, Donna calls her over and shows her what she has rearranged.

"Have all the models tried on their shoes?" Donna yells, but no one answers her. Elsa Klensch from CNN, wearing the earrings she got at the Bill Blass show, sticks her head around the partition separating the makeshift backstage area from the runway and says, "How are you?"

"Whenever you're ready, I'm ready," says Donna.

Elsa walks backstage with her cameraman and begins interviewing Donna. "How would you describe your collection?" says Elsa.

Although Donna is as tense as I have ever seen her, she lets her body go limp and says, "Relaxed. Sublimely, beautifully relaxed, but tailored. It's the contrast between the tailoring and the ease of the fabric. The ease of Garbo, Hepburn.

There's a wrap in it but it's not a wrap to constrict. It's a wrap of relaxation."

"What would you have a woman buy to update her wardrobe?" says Elsa.

"The scarf pant is a definite must, and I would say one of the new jackets in blush [this is how Donna refers to the pink color]. And the new white body shirt, which is absolutely divine. I'm wearing the pants right now. I couldn't wait to get them on."

"Are prints important?" says Elsa.

"I only have one print. It's my first introduction to print: a black-and-white paisley."

"What about skirt lengths?"

"I love them long and I love them short, but the key is relaxed."

And then Donna says, "This collection was inspired by an old photograph of my mom and dad. I echoed what my heritage is about. I hadn't seen it when I started to work, but then I was looking through an old photo album, and when I saw this picture I said, 'My God, that's where it's coming from.' I remembered what my parents looked like even though I was only a baby.

"This is probably the hardest collection I've ever had to design," she continues. "When I started I thought, How am I going to do it? How am I going to bring that relaxed feeling that I've fallen in love with because of DKNY into my collection? Today, I feel I've done it."

The interview ends, and an assistant snips a label out of the back of Donna's pants. The label had been visible through the thin fabric. Donna kisses jewelry designer Robert Lee Morris hello and, looking at her watch, calls out, "OK. It's time to get ready. I can't believe it's ten of twelve and I'm just saying it's time to get ready. We are showing in ten minutes."

Another woman from a cable TV show comes backstage to say hello. Donna nods at her and says to the stylist, "Audrey, get them dressed. We are five minutes away."

As the models get dressed Donna, sounding truly terrified, says, "Right now I'm crossing my heart and praying to God because when you've got something and you might lose it . . ." Her voice trails off and then she yells, "Dressers, I beg of you to get the girls dressed. It is twelve o'clock."

One by one the models, wearing their first outfits, walk toward Donna. "I have to tie her," Donna says, and she ties a scarf around the model's head. Another model complains that her shoes are too small. "I was given an eight-and-a-half," the model says. "I need a nine."

"I am so glad that the first thing I asked people to do was to try the shoes on," says Donna as she hunts underneath the accessories table for another pair of shoes.

"I am nervous because everything was so last-minute," she says to me as she hands the model the shoes. "It was just dreadful. This dress changed last night," she says, pointing to one of the dresses.

I see Doreen, the fitting model, and note the amazingly dark circles under her eyes. "She's in the wrong pants," Donna says, pointing to a model, just as Dawn Mello, then the president of Bergdorf Goodman, comes backstage to give Donna a kiss.

The video man says to Donna, "When you come out at the end of the show . . ."

"I don't want to talk about this right now, OK?" Donna snaps. He retreats.

"Edward," Donna calls out, "I need my Polaroids because I can't tell what my accessories are without my pictures." She is going to put the jewelry on the girls just before they walk out, and she needs these pictures as a reference.

"I'm not opening the jacket, no?" says the model Dalma.

"No," says Donna.

Edward carries out a bulletin board covered with the Polaroids Donna requested. Looking at the pictures, Donna calls out for the jewelry that she needs, and, standing behind the accessories table, Robert hands it to her piece by piece.

The models are all on line now but the hairdresser is still braiding Iman's hair.

At 12:07 Patti, who has been seating the audience, comes backstage, and Donna says, "I need five more minutes."

At 12:13 Donna says, "OK. We're ready. Congratulations, everybody, and good luck. This isn't going to be easy." The show starts, and, from the very first group, Donna's work is loudly applauded.

Throughout the show, Donna places jewelry on the models and makes last-minute adjustments on their outfits—tying and untying—while Peter Arnell, crammed into a small corner by the partition, takes picture after picture. When not accessorizing and dressing the girls, Donna dances to the music and snaps her fingers, while two hairdressers spray the models with last-minute spritzes of hair spray.

Looking at one of the models, Donna notices that her dress is too big. "This wasn't fixed," says Donna. "I can't believe they didn't fix this. I need a pin," she yells. I hand her a box of straight pins lying on the accessories table, and she pins the two sides of the model's dress.

Looking at Dalma, Donna says, "I don't believe it. Iman, I mean Dalma, was given the wrong shirt." She says this to Istvan, who is standing at the other end of the accessories table. He laughs.

"Why are you laughing?" Donna says. Realizing he did not respond properly, he cups his hand over his ear and shouts, "I can't hear you."

Ignoring him, Donna looks at two models wearing white jackets and navy pants and says, "You look beautiful." The two girls walk out together and are applauded. The evening-wear section is greeted with applause and wolf whistles from the photographers. "Oh, I love the way this looks," says Donna as models wearing the pink chiffon group walk past her and out onto the runway.

"I need a pink jacket for myself," says Donna, as the show draws to an end. An assistant brings her a pink jacket and Donna checks herself in the full-length mirror. "She is so heavy," says Peter, as he points his camera at Donna. "Really heavy." He means important, not fat.

It is time for the finale, and Donna yells, "I want all the blacks and pinks together." The girls wearing black and pink cluster in a group, and Donna walks out with them. She is met with thunderous applause and is mobbed by people offering congratulations. Some of them, including Dawn Mello, have tears in their eyes.

Since *Women's Wear Daily* is not published over the weekend, Donna has to wait until Monday to see how her collection will be reviewed. This review was worth waiting for. It ran on the front page with the headline: *Donna Karan: An Empress in the Making*.

"If things go as they have been going for Karan," the newspaper said, "she . . . will have a fashion empire." If she doesn't have a nervous breakdown first.

Adrienne Vittadini *November 10*

As I sit in the audience jam-packed into the RCA Building, watching Adrienne's show, I am surprised not so much by what she is showing as by how much of both her high-priced collection and the Active line are not shown. Only ninety outfits (utilizing about a hundred and twenty pieces out of close to six hundred) appear in the show, and therefore Adrienne has included only, as she puts it, "the things I love most," and that are the most directional, like the sheer pieces.

The first outfit out on the runway is the Scottie print, followed by various navy-and-white outfits. Then comes a safari group in solid tan and white. After a few print groups from Active come the carnation print and red stripe group. Included in this group is the wide red-and-white striped circle skirt that, in Hong Kong, Adrienne had wanted to change. If you remember, this skirt requires five yards of silk broadcloth priced at $12.50 a yard, and Adrienne decided it would be much too expensive and that she would make a straight skirt instead. Before leaving Hong Kong, however, she decided the straight skirt didn't look right, and she missed the flowing feeling of the wide skirt. Therefore, despite its expense, that skirt was reinstated in the line. Also in this group are the now correctly made four-pleat pants that in Hong Kong had mistakenly been made with two pleats.

One of the groups not shown was the gold-buttoned double-knit group that we watched Adrienne edit at the factory. Later Adrienne will say that, although she knew that group would be "essential for a career woman," she decided not to show it because it was "not important enough for the show." In other words, it was not new enough to stimulate excitement among the press.

Conclusion

This last show of the Spring 1989 season brings us to the end of the fashion cycle, the cyclical pattern of creation that is repeated season after season in design studios across the country and around the world. As we've seen, personality and the type and volume of apparel designed make for some differences in the design process, but the steps that need to be executed by all of the designers are the same. Each has to choose fabrics or yarns, create groups of clothes that make a coherent presentation on the sales floor, oversee their production, and then supervise their presentation and subsequent sales.

After the fashion shows, the clothing is placed in the hands of the sales and production departments at the different companies. With their sales departments in high gear, and with their manufacturing contractors working at full speed, the designers relax for a few weeks and then turn to conceptualizing their fall collections, which will open for most of them at the end of March and at the beginning of April. (Liz Claiborne fits in a Spring II and Summer line before starting Fall and Donna Karan squeezes in a summer line. The other designers do not offer separate summer collections.) Come January, the designers then begin logging frequent-flier points making personal appearances promoting their spring lines, which begin to be delivered to stores that month.

Here's a roundup of how the various collections sold and what transpired at the various companies since we last saw them up through November 1990.

Liz Claiborne

At the beginning of December 1988, Jay called Dennis into his office and said, "We're going to make some changes here," and Dennis, not thinking for a moment that these changes had anything to do with him, said, "Yes?" and Jay said, "We think you're a square peg in a round hole," and Dennis said, "What do you mean?" and Jay said, "We think that the clothes you design naturally are too sophisticated for our customer." With those words, Dennis was fired.

"I was shocked out of my mind," Dennis told me later. "It was really horrible. I think they didn't like me. I tried really hard. I mean, you saw it. I was a corporate senior vice-president. They never put anything in writing anywhere saying that they were unhappy with my performance, the way a normal company would do. But you know as well as I do, the garment center is not normal."

Dennis landed on his feet, however, and became president of the Andrea Jovine sportswear company. In retrospect he was able to say that being fired was a good thing. "I was miserable while I was at Liz Claiborne, but I made a really good salary. When you make a good salary you start to compromise yourself and what makes you happy, personally and creatively. You tell yourself, 'I have this great New York City apartment and I've got this great car and a house in East Hampton,' and you think to yourself that it doesn't matter if you hate your job, because you don't work every day, and your job lets you afford things—but of course it matters. You bring your job home with you."

No one would agree with Dennis more than Liz herself. The month before their retirement took effect, she and Art invited me to have dinner with them at Le Bernardin, a four-star restaurant, where they were given the best table in the house. Always the consummate professional and role model while she was active in the company, Liz finally felt free enough to admit that she'd been miserable at work, that she felt she'd "prostituted" her talent by overseeing the design of what she calls "tonnage."

"When it comes to appealing to the masses there is a point where compromise becomes distasteful," she said over dinner. "We reached that point years ago." Finally, she said, three years ago she told Art that she simply didn't want to continue working at the company, no matter how successful it was. They then began restructuring the firm to prepare for their retirement, resulting in some of the floundering that we watched them trying to correct.

With their retirement now actually happening, they restructured the company even further. At the same time that Dennis was fired, Bob Abajian was named senior vice-president of women's sportswear design, and he will oversee product development at all three sportswear divisions. Ellen Daniel, formerly senior vice-president of corporate design, relinquished those duties and took Dennis's place as division head of Liz Claiborne Collection. She continues as a senior vice-president.

Then, on February 26, the same day it released its strong fourth quarter results (earnings for the quarter were $26,601,000, or 30 cents a share, up from $22,458,000, or 26 cents; net sales for the quarter rose 21.7 percent to $290,241,000 from $238,416,000 for the year-ago period), Liz Claiborne, Inc., announced to the public that Liz and Art would be retiring from active management in June, but that they would remain on the board of directors.

In June, Jerry, who was vice-chairman, became chairman of the board. Harvey Falk, executive vice-president of operations and corporate planning, became vice-chairman and president. Jay Margolis, executive vice-president, and president of the women's sportswear group, became vice-chairman, but retained his sportswear-group post.

Although they are retired, Liz and Art visit the company once a month to attend board meetings. Since their retirement, says Jay, "the company has pulled together. Everyone picked up their level of work to cover losing [Liz and Art]. The company will never be exactly the same, but always we will keep them in our minds as role models. When we do things, especially in design, we think about what Liz would say or do about something."

The clothing that we watched the sportswear designers create helped turn the Liz Claiborne business around, putting it back on a growth track. The company continues to grow, expanding both its product categories and its retail presence. In 1989 it opened three prototype stores: Liz World, featuring a wide variety of the same Liz Claiborne merchandise that is sold to retail chains and specialty stores; Liz Career, which is smaller and stocks dresses and career-oriented sportswear; and Claiborne for menswear.

This year there are seven Liz World stores, and eventually there will be sixteen. "They are prototypical," says Jay, "in the sense that they show different ways of presenting and selling the goods. In our store we combine all the different Liz Claiborne products and put them together in a cohesive manner. In department stores the different product categories are in different areas."

There are currently two each of both Liz Career and Claiborne stores. The company plans to open four to six more Liz Career branches, while the Claiborne number will remain as it is for the moment.

First Issue, the company's first retail venture, continues to open new branches. It currently has twenty-five stores and plans a total of fifty.

Besides expanding its retail presence, the company is also expanding its product categories. In 1989 it launched Liz & Co., a new division of casual knit sportswear, which is seeing very strong business, as is the large-sized line, Elisabeth. There is also a new jewelry line which the company began shipping to stores in July.

In accepting Liz and Art's dinner invitation in 1989, I told them I had many follow-up questions to ask them, but at the table, they told me to ask these questions of other executives at the company. They preferred, instead, to talk about the new work they were undertaking—helping to preserve the environment.

But as dinner wound to a close, conversation turned back to their enormous success, and each credited the other for it. Liz said, "Art pushed me to accomplish. I would have never done this if he hadn't pushed me."

"And without Liz," Art said, "all I would have been is a successful businessman. We wouldn't be having dinner at Le Bernardin."

But indeed we were. As we walked out of the restaurant and into the black stretch limo they had retained for the evening, I asked Liz how she felt about retiring. "I always worked," she said. "I used to envy all those women at Fire Island who didn't work and could stay at the beach all week, all summer. Now it's my turn."

Arnold Scaasi

On January 12, 1989, Arnold went to Washington to fit some dresses on Barbara Bush, and over, as Arnold puts it, "a wonderful, cozy lunch at the White House" she told him she would be wearing his dresses to both the Salute to the First Lady and the Inaugural Ball. When he got home, a contract for his latest licensing venture—a perfume—was waiting for him. "What more could happen to you in a day?" Arnold said gleefully.

The next morning he called various newspapers, including *The New York Times*, *The Washington Post*, and *Women's Wear Daily*, to tell them that Barbara Bush had chosen his dress for the Inaugural Ball. The First Lady's office wouldn't confirm this, saying that the American public would have to wait until the night of the ball to find out what she would be wearing. According to *WWD*, Arnold denied calling the newspapers, although *The New York Times* and *The Washington Post* quoted him as their source.

Barbara Bush didn't seem to care that this news had been leaked, since she has continued ordering more clothes from him. At any rate, Arnold later claimed that Mrs. Bush gave him permission to call the papers and name her choice of designer. She, like all of Arnold's regular customers, even has her own headless mannequin, padded to her size and labeled "Bee Be" in Arnold's design studio.

As the Bush Administration entered its infancy and it became clear that Arnold was Barbara Bush's favorite designer, the press besieged Arnold for interviews, and he complied, doing as many as seven in one day.

As for the inauguration, he says that week was "the most exciting week of my life. Mrs. Bush wore something of mine every day, and I saw her every day and she saw me. She waved at me at each of the events and sometimes the President would wave to me, too. What could be more exciting?"

Today Arnold has a photo of George and Barbara Bush at the inauguration prominently displayed in the public waiting area of his salon. The President signed the photo, "With warm best wishes and appreciation for your talent," while the more reticent First Lady simply signed her name.

Dressing the First Lady has "certainly been favorable publicity-wise," says Arnold. "When I first began dressing her I was asked to do interviews daily. I got hoarse and tired, but it was so exciting, being a part of history."

As for his resolution to cut down on socializing, Arnold did just that. He no longer chairs the New York City Opera benefit but is active in work to promote literacy. "Did you know that there are a million adults in New York City alone who cannot read?" he says. I say, yes, I do, and I also know that reducing illiteracy is Barbara Bush's prime cause.

"Yes," says Arnold who has made no secret that he gets involved in the causes of his important clients. "It is."

On February 27, Arnold, who has since signed a licensing agreement for intimate apparel and sleepwear and is looking into one for large sizes, presented the last couture show of the spring 1989 season. This time everyone paid significantly more attention to his show, and what conversation took place centered around guessing which styles the First Lady might pick for herself. So that's what it took to earn a little respect, huh, Arnold? It's amazing what dressing the First Lady can do for a guy.

Bill Blass

While Bill shopped for fall fabrics, Harold Leigh Davis began selling Bill's collection on November 4, the day Donna Karan was showing hers. Harold works personally with Bill's five major accounts: Saks Fifth Avenue, I. Magnin, Neiman-Marcus, Martha's, and Bergdorf Goodman.

During the three weeks that the collection was being sold, the company, as always, retained three models on a full-time basis to model the clothes for the stores. The retailers then placed their orders, and, based on the required delivery dates, the goods were then put into production. Martha's and Bergdorf Goodman tied for wanting the clothes the earliest. Both stores were doing Christmas windows with Bill's merchandise, and therefore the merchandise they requested— an exclusive group of black-and-white dresses for Martha's, and some beaded tennis sweaters and a chiffon gown for Bergdorf's—went into production first.

From the overall collection, the best-sellers included suits, a black lace cocktail group, and the chiffon gowns—and, according to Harold, the tennis sweaters "did nicely for their price range."

Sample cuts of fall fabric started arriving at the beginning of January, and

Bill began designing his fall collection, starting as he always does, with the most commercial, simple wool jersey day dresses and short cocktail dresses. As with spring, and as with all his other collections, he saved the more elaborate, fashionable pieces until the end.

In January he announced that for "personal reasons" he would end his licensing agreement for furs once his fall 1989 fur collection was completed. "I don't want to be a part of anything that involves putting an animal on your back," he told me.

He showed his fall collection in April, again, as always, at the Pierre's Cotillion Room. Afterward, as this line was being sold, he turned his thoughts to spring, beginning, once again, with fabric. "This is, after all, the medium I work in," he said. "That is where I start." And that is where, with Bill, we end.

Adrienne Vittadini

Even though this was not one of Adrienne's favorite collections, it turned out to be one of her best-selling. "Spring is like nothing I've seen before," said Richard Catalano, the company's president. "Everything is sold. There is not one bad group."

The company continues to grow, and, as for all apparel companies, this growth is coming mainly from the addition of new product categories. "You can't grow by selling fifty thousand more pieces," said Richard. "The outfit should only be the beginning of the sale. Then you add belts, hats, shoes, handbags, and coats. That can add up being a bigger business than apparel."

To that end, the company has signed new licensing agreements for shower curtains, children's clothing, sleepwear, footwear—which debuted in fall 1990— as well as for a fragrance which will be launched by Revlon in 1992.

To meet the increased design time these new licenses require, Adrienne continued to restructure her design department: Odile was named vice-president of design, and oversees all the licensing as well as the design of Collection. "Odile will take each license to a point where I will be ready to see it," said Adrienne. "In the past I had to sit in on every licensing design meeting, from beginning to end. If I scheduled an hour into my day for a licensing meeting and liked what they did, that would be fine. If I didn't, it would go on for hours and I would lose too much time. I picked Odile to do licensing for me because we have the exact same taste. We can walk into a room and look at five things and she will always, without fail, pick the one that I love best. She can complete my sentences for me."

David, meanwhile, quit the company to go to Anne Taylor as a designer. Adrienne moved Kristina into Active to take his place and hired new people to work with Odile on Collection. Ornella was named executive vice-president of the company and moved out of production to become head of sales for Collection. The woman who had held that position was moved to oversee all the freestanding Adrienne Vittadini stores. In 1989 eleven such stores opened, in 1990 three more were launched and five more are planned for the near future.

As she does each year, Adrienne was already working on fall when her spring line opened. Her cutoff date for fall sketches was December 5, and she traveled to Hong Kong in February to see how those sketches translated into reality. After Hong Kong she went to Europe to pick holiday and spring fabrics and then took a few weeks off to "recharge and cleanse myself." Back in New York, as her staff prepared her fall ad campaign and show, she went to work designing Holiday. She showed fall in April and, four days after the show, was in Hong Kong again working on Holiday. After Hong Kong she again took a few weeks off, then plunged into spring, having approximately ten weeks to design one thousand pieces. Holiday opened in the showroom in June, and like clockwork Adrienne was back in Hong Kong in August to edit and fit the spring and summer lines. Then it was back to New York to work on fall. And that's how, season after season, the design cycle repeats itself.

"I never had the idea of building a company like this," says Adrienne. "I would have been happy with a small, well-controlled company. The bigger a company, the more problems you have. There's so much pressure. I'm bored with designing, but I can't take a break. As a designer you have to be on top all the time, performing all the time. Actresses can take a break; they choose their movies. But designers are on all the time, and we always have to do better than we did in the past. It's a very hard business."

Donna Karan

Donna's spring collection ended up being extraordinarily successful. For instance, at the February trunk show at Bergdorf Goodman, sales hit a record $498,000. "The collection was sold out before I got there, and I was getting myself in trouble," she says. "I had to walk off the floor. I started saying to customers, 'You can find it in Saks,' or 'You can find it in Bloomingdale's,' and that's not exactly why I was at Bergdorf's."

During that same month she launched DKNY. With her company spending $9 million and retailers nationwide spending $4.5 million on catalogs, boutiques, and print and television advertising, the launch was hard to miss.

The line was launched in 320 doors in 30 different cities, and DKNY shops within shops debuted in 65 stores, including units of Macy's Northeast, Lord & Taylor, Bloomingdale's, Barneys New York, Saks Fifth Avenue, Bonwit Teller, and Bergdorf Goodman.

Saks was the New York launch store for DKNY, and Donna, looking happy and healthy, made a personal appearance from noon to 1 P.M. Wearing a navy blazer, white shirt, and jeans, she sat behind what looked like a drafting table set up for the day in front of the department. "This is the happiest day of my life," she said when she saw me.

At first I thought she was referring to the launch, to her happiness at seeing a collection she'd worked on for so long finally hit the sales floor and be so well received. But she wasn't referring to either the strong sales or the adoring fans surrounding her. She was referring, as she frequently does, to her joy in one of her creations. "My jeans came in this morning and they fit perfectly," she said. "I can't believe they really fit. They are sheer perfection." (Donna had stopped production on the jeans five times until they fit her absolutely perfectly. She even had the jeans sent out to her in Vail while she was on vacation.)

Donna turned back to the customers lined up in front of her desk waiting for her to autograph the ad campaign brochures the company was handing out. Every time someone new stepped up to the table, Donna said, "Hello, what is your name? Have you tried on any clothes yet? You should. They fit great."

While Donna signed autographs, models wearing her clothes circulated throughout the department, and her granddaughter toddled about in an oversized

DKNY T-shirt. According to *Women's Wear Daily*, Saks sold close to $285,000 worth of merchandise in the first four days that it was available, roughly twice the chain's initial order. Saks reportedly had twelve hundred pieces of DKNY when selling began on Friday, then reordered another thousand pieces on Saturday.

The line met with that kind of phenomenal success across the country, and, by the end of the spring selling season, most bridge departments were calling DKNY its best-selling line.

The company continues to prosper, but Donna continues to physically deteriorate. When I interviewed her in February, the month articles singing her praises were appearing nationwide—thanks to the DKNY launch—stress had affected her back injury to such a degree that she could barely walk, and she had to put a ball behind her back for support whenever she sat down.

All she could talk about was how much she had done and still had to do: "We opened Collection in November. December was summer DKNY. January was summer Collection. March is fall DKNY. April is fall Collection. June is resort DKNY. August is resort Collection. September is spring DKNY. November is spring Collection again." Thereby she summarized her yearly design cycle.

"Then," she said, "there's shoes, bags, belts, jewelry, hosiery, scarves, furs. I have a due date every day."

"How do you do it?" I said.

"I don't," she said, holding on to her chair as she stood up. "Do I look like I'm doing it?"

You sure do, Donna.